FINDING MY FEET

MY STORY

HANNY ALLSTON

Find Your Feet Australia Pty Ltd

107 Elizabeth Street, Hobart, Tasmania, 7000, Australia

hannyallston.com.au

Published May 2020.

Copyright © Hanny Allston 2020.

ISBN:

Paperback: 978-0-6483929-3-4

Mobi: 978-0-6483929-5-8

Epub: 978-0-6483929-4-1

This book is copyright. Apart from fair dealing for the purposes of private study, research, criticism and review as permitted under the Copyright Act, no part of this book may be reproduced by any process without the express permission of the publisher.

Quote from *The Body Keeps the Score: Brain, Mind, and Body in the Healing of Trauma* is copyright © Bessel van der Kolk, and used by permission.

Front cover photograph © Kirill Talanine

Back cover photograph © Graham Hammond

Managing editor: Belinda Pollard

Proofreader: Alix Kwan

Cover design: Belinda Pollard

 Created with Vellum

This book is dedicated to all those who walked before and alongside me.

AUTHOR'S NOTE

This is my story, a tale of the events, experiences, people and inner dialogues which have shaped my life and led me on the journey to finding my feet. Yet memory is an unreliable narrator and other individuals whose stories are interwoven with mine may recall these events differently. If so, that is their story to tell, while this is mine. I have changed some names and the occasional detail to protect the privacy of some people. However, at its heart, these pages contain a true story, a story I openly share if it can assist others to find their feet too.

CONTENTS

Prologue   1

PART I
GUMBOOTS

Photo   8
Chapter 1   9
Chapter 2   26
Chapter 3   38
Chapter 4   53
Chapter 5   62
Chapter 6   74
Chapter 7   91

PART II
NAVIGATING

Photo   102
Chapter 8   103
Chapter 9   111
Chapter 10   130
Chapter 11   137

PART III
LOSING MY FEET

Photo   148
Chapter 12   149
Chapter 13   155
Chapter 14   172
Chapter 15   187
Chapter 16   194
Chapter 17   200

PART IV
BAREFOOT

Photo   208

Chapter 18	209
Chapter 19	212
Chapter 20	231
Chapter 21	242
Chapter 22	248
Chapter 23	255
Chapter 24	270
Chapter 25	274
Chapter 26	288
Chapter 27	299

PART V
FINDING MY FEET

Photo	312
Chapter 28	313
Epilogue	318
An invitation from Hanny	325
Acknowledgments	327
About the Author	329
Coaching Ethos	331
Also by Hanny Allston	335
Find Your Feet Trail Running Tours	337

PROLOGUE

2005: The Perfect Storm

I hesitate, propped somewhere between innocence and maturity. My foot, clad in a white plastic bag, seems glued to the sterilised floor. The other hangs painfully, wrapped in a cast. My head is spinning and I want to sit down. But the Intensive Care Unit does not offer chairs to bystanders.

I don't want to be back in another hospital. Only three weeks ago, I myself lay bedridden in a white room, surrounded by a white curtain. My ankle painfully swollen from an ankle reconstruction. A serious sprain during the World Orienteering Championships in Japan meant my coach, Max, had told me in his gruff, grandfatherly voice, 'Surgery? If you do, you will likely never run again.' The surgeon had a different opinion. 'Surgery? If you *don't* you will likely never run at this level again.' He said my ankle was the worst he had ever operated on. 'And for someone of your age!' I had lain uncomfortably in the hospital bed, wondering how to overcome these lose-lose odds and find my feet again.

Now, as I await the opportunity to visit my father here in intensive care, I feel so, so far from the agile aspiring athlete that I long to be. I am nineteen. Little do I realise that there is a perfect storm unfolding beneath my one weight-bearing foot. The door to my father's isolation cubicle swings open and the scent of honey, which they use as a burn ointment, wafts out. My safety barrier is penetrated by the rich smell.

Instantly, I am taken back to the laundry at Mole End—my family's farm and my childhood home.

On a hot summer's day, the heat inside that laundry would be stifling, producing beads of sweat on foreheads. Gas burners added to the hot, thick air as they warmed the large carving knives that sat in rusted tomato tins atop stainless steel benches. Here, Dad would stand, carefully scraping wax from each wooden frame to reveal oozing honey, its rich golden liquid bleeding from deep within the hexagonal cells. One by one, he would carve the wax and wipe the knife, carve and wipe, until all the wax had been removed. Then he would gently lower the frames deep into the extractor, a simple action releasing a fleeting shimmer of pride across his strongly-defined facial features. As if drawn to a losing battle, bees would bump and jostle outside the windows we had closed to keep them out.

Mum would lean over the metal extractor, spinning the wooden handle with an air of intense purpose. An old plastic-lined apron tied around her waist, her swimming muscles flexing and relaxing, flexing and relaxing with each spin of the extractor. I loved this mother. Her strength both physical and internally complex. A mother who had mastered the art of giving and who always said, 'You can do anything.' A mum who taught me how to swim, then to strive. A mother who showered me with so much generosity and belief, even during the times when I couldn't believe in myself.

With each whoosh of the honey extractor, small droplets of warm honey would flick against the metal sides before sliding into the cavernous depths. Standing back, pressed against shelves laden with preserved fruits, jams, wines—and honey jars waiting to be filled—would be my brother James and me, waiting for the moment when our parents turned a blind eye. Then we would scrape sticky fingers around the rim of the extractor. Ashling and Ciara, my neighbours and best friends, would love to be there too, helping extract 'Hanny's Honey'. Their family would delicately and sparingly spread the golden nectar across their toast. But us Allstons? We would lather it thickly across our buttery, homemade bread.

THAT HONEY MEMORY RECEDES, to be replaced by a less sweet one from only twenty-four hours ago.

I HOBBLED through the same laundry towards the back door, barely noting the shelves still laden with evidence of a rich childhood and the most perfect youth … wide-open spaces, friendships, family, hand-built cubbies, cheekiness and opportunities. Little did I realise as I reached the back door and patted Flossy-dog—her border collie muzzle resting on well-worn paws—I was closing the door on my childhood as I had known it.

Mum's roses, majestic at the beginning of summer, grew proudly from the rich alluvial soils. Molly, our other dog, an excitable tan and white puppy, ran circles around the garden bed. I wobbled past our cubbyhouse buried beneath more garden vegetation. My foot was throbbing, pulsing, in this unfamiliar ankle. I reached the swing and flopped down into it, partially shaded by the birch tree, a favourite climbing apparatus for this wilder child. I could faintly hear Dad's Jersey cows—Tosca, Carmen and Pavarotti—moving through the lush paddocks behind the nearby hedgerow, accompanied by squabbling chickens and ducks, innocently free to roam. I could not hear any humanness. The adults were deep within the walls of my family home, once an old homestead and now converted into our three-bedroom farmhouse.

I sat on the swing for a long time, trying to ignore my ankle. Flicking sticks to Molly. Fetch and return. Fetch and return. I thought about my university exams now just days away and the piles of medical textbooks still lying open on the kitchen table from yesterday. Then about my brother travelling in Asia. My mind whirled from one random thought to another, like someone licking the last sticky residues from the jar. Empty thoughts filling thoughtlessness.

Faint movement of shoes on mown lawn. Perfume that was not my mother's. A hand on my shoulder. A shaky breath. The words, 'Your father is alive. He attempted suicide. He is on his way to hospital.'

I HOBBLE towards my father's bedside. Tubes protrude from all angles. He looks so small, fragile, papery. We look at one another. I shuffle closer, now near enough that I could reach out and touch him. I love this father so much. A wonderful father, a patient father, a father curious and kind to the living world. Who has taught me how to give and to seek. A father who has imparted a love for the art of stillness, reflection and writing. He is here. He is alive. Safe. I am so sure of that. Silence passes like unspoken sentences until his hoarse, childlike whisper breaks across the void: 'I am so sorry ...'

His honest words send a sharp pain into the core of my being. It has seeped through the cracks in my internal walls and reached somewhere far within. My soul whispers to me, *I'm not very good at this.*

IN MY FAMILY, we rarely voiced our emotions. Cold, tired or hungry— that was all okay. But during sadness or madness, we quickly left via the laundry door. Our emotions required fresh air and wide-open spaces. A pair of gumboots, a garden, a load of washing, a cubby or tree. I would scale the oak's branches, each ridged limb acting as a rung and allowing me to climb further and further from confusing internal discomforts. From this vantage point I could act like a spy, the watchman of the valley, finding reassurance in the nobility of the position. Time would pass in a swaying oak in a quiet valley.

Surprisingly, it seemed there might be rare occasions when muddy walks across the fields or hands buried in the garden's fertile soils couldn't cure the emotions. On these occasions, I would stand at the end of our long hallway and stare at my parents' closed bedroom door. It became the chamber of secrets, where adult emotions were kept. I would look at their closed door, wondering what adults did when they were upset, and then I would be out the laundry door, tugging on those gumboots and off to climb my tree.

I LEAN MORE HEAVILY against my crutches. I am hit by a whoosh of truth. From the pastures of the family farm at Sandfly outside Hobart to the reality of hospitals; from the dais of the recent World Championships to the fearful reality that at nineteen I may never be able to run freely again.

I am walloped by the sensation that I am in one almighty, steep-sided hole. I drag my eyes up to meet Dad's and our gazes lock. In this moment of father-daughter intimacy I feel a warmth. A strength beginning to infiltrate the chill of fear and sadness. I feel myself standing taller, the crutches no longer the prop holding me upright. I find myself pulling back my shoulders and lifting my head just a few millimetres higher.

'I am so sorry…' Dad's four barely-audible words of honesty herald the end of the adult secrets. It is over. We have found ourselves collapsed into an unwelcome ankle reconstruction and now an unexpected suicide attempt by a bipolar depressive father. In nothingness there are only the heartbeats of hope.

In that moment, standing at the bedside of my father, I verbalise my own four words of honesty, representing the end of innocence and my transition to adulthood. 'It is okay, Dad.'

As I turn towards the door, I vow to myself, then and there, that I will clamber out of this hole. Mud, twigs, embankments. Fear, sadness, disappointment. No matter what obstacles stand in my way, with honesty and openness underpinned by the determination and discipline I learnt in youth, I will find my feet and flourish.

PART I
GUMBOOTS

1990–2005

First overnight wanders, Central Plateau, Tasmania (Photograph: Julia Hutchinson)

1

Crouched low, knees pressed into gravelly sand, young hands clawing into the shimmering grains of granite. Each granule a unique colour. Sunburnt-pink feldspar. Luminescent quartz, white like the flesh of the squid being gutted on the jetty this morning by local children, their BMX bikes propped against wooden railings nearby.

The tide had been lower earlier in the day, exposing barnacles and sagging green sea lettuce clinging to the wooden pier. Now, shadows were shortening as the sun crested overhead. The tide had inched towards us while the wind whipped at hair and hat toggles. Flinders Island, a forgotten paradise off the north-east tip of Tasmania, spreading around us and extending into the horizon.

We dug together. Dad to my left. Mum to my right. My brother opposite. One unit, one family, one hole, digging for rocks.

My family's digging forays on Flinders Island triggered an early interest in rock collecting. A large nugget of Killiecrankie diamond—a colourless topaz—became the first precious jewel to be tucked safely into the old boarding school chest my brother and I inherited from my father.

Most of the treasures in that chest were collected through the labour of our dirt-etched fingers and scanning eyes. From the Freycinet National Park on Tasmania's east coast came tiny pink feldspar nuggets and clear chunks of quartz. A little further south on Maria Island we delighted in fossils from the peaks where we sourced dolerite and sandstone. From holidays in mainland Australia in Crumbly—our orange kombivan with a habit for incidental failures—we returned home with pockets full. Year by year, adventure by adventure, our little rock collection grew at a similar pace to us, until we reached a point where we no longer needed to measure our growth against the pencil marks on the doorjamb.

My childhood home sat poised on pillars of stone once collected from the valley's flanks, perched on a gentle slope leading down towards the confluence of the creeks. Our old weatherboard cottage nestled into the slopes of Sandfly—a small rural valley around thirty minutes south of Hobart—surrounded by fertile soils that once hosted berry plantations. This was a childhood paradise, a place of inspiration for my brother, me, and our three lifelong friends—Ashling, Ciara and Andy. Little Andy received my hand-me-downs until he finally overtook me when his growing legs reached college. We were the Famous Five—children of the wild with an extensive playground. Private property laws didn't apply to us.

When the winter rains seeped into even our grandest plans, we sought shelter and adventures in the barn or amongst the dusty cobwebs of the world beneath our home. Torches at the ready, we tiptoed over Mum's flower gardens, sidled between roses, then crawled beneath the stone columns to commando into the gloom. Our explorations revealed that our home was formerly inhabited by a bootmaker. His discarded creations, crinkled with age, were evidence of a story now buried while our own was just beginning.

Emerging from the gloom at the sound of a large bell heralding dinnertime, we blinked in the bright evening light and dusted off our knees. Mum's cooking wafted towards us through a doorway opening onto the deck that we had helped Dad build.

Mum was a phenomenal cook. Her creations, crafted from the plethora of organic produce from my father's vegetable garden, fuelled our childhood adventures and later, athletic endeavours. In these early years, dinner could include the occasional portion of meat buried deep into vegetable matter to obscure it from my brother's tastebuds. However, as frustration mounted and the scars of taking our pigs to market etched deeper into my father's soul, we evolved into a family of vegetarians. From homemade pasta to oven-fresh bread and soups—another desperate attempt to utilise Dad's bountiful zucchinis. My mother became a master at her craft and inspired my love affair with fruit crumbles.

Raspberries. Strawberries. Apples. Pears. Quinces. Gooseberries. Cherries. With nicknames my parents gave me such as 'Possum' and 'Fruit Bat', growing up in Sandfly was more than an idyllic childhood. It was a sublime, fruit-smeared-mouth, full-tummy haven. At dawn, Ciara and I wandered up the home-cut bush tracks that terminated on the nearby berry farm. Avoiding barbed wire, electric fences, and moody bulls, we sneaked across the open paddocks before finally reaching the dripping raspberry bushes. Under their drooping limbs we hid, one hand holding the cane, the other grabbing at the rosy-ripe berries. When the smartly dressed city-folk in sunhats and clean, crisp shirts, began to arrive, we sneaked back down the paddocks and trails, two possums united in friendship with groaning stomachs and ruddy-stained mouths.

Summer brought the fear of bushfires. On the hottest days we drew all the curtains to stop the warm air gaining access to our home. Restlessness would inevitably set-in, so James and I would slip outside to locate my father as he paced the farm, his shirt gaping open, suntan lines etched deep into his arms, his eyes scanning the sky for the subtle brown wisps heralding fire. On more than one occasion, we began to prepare the farm for the potential approach. James assisted Dad to empty the gutters, while Mum and I filled buckets to the brim. The radio on, the bath full, we listened with nervous anticipation. Thankfully, the bushfires never arrived.

My childhood adventure ground, while no longer 'mine', still lies in the depths of a lush valley, the creeks still bubbling through its soul, our home still standing proudly at its heart.

AUTUMN, golden autumn highlighted the beauty of Hobart's tree-lined avenues and the European tree species planted by Tasmania's early settlers. Autumn, when lashing winds swept from the wild, jagged coastline of Tasmania's remote west coast. Autumn, when the beech designated *Nothofagus gunii*—Australia's only native deciduous species—turned on a brilliant display of colour as it clung to the slopes of dolerite peaks. Autumn, with its unmatched tranquillity.

Autumn: this was always the Allston family's time to play.

Autumn 1990 was wildly wet and unusually cold. It was Dad's fortieth birthday and an excuse to embark on our first overnight family bushwalk. I shadowed him, my oversized raincoat hanging low over my face and hands, gumboots clomping alongside his on the uneven rocky terrain, my pack filled with four packets of two-minute noodles, a sleeping bag, and a large toy rabbit. My eyes prickled with emotions as the bold winds swept across this exposed central plateau of Tasmania. We walked together, a family leaning into the landscape. Dad striding in Dad-length paces. Mum strong beneath her load. James proudly trotting alongside. And tiny me, four-years old and not sure she wanted to be there.

After searching for Dad's perfect campsite—a routine that would drive my mother nearly to tears in the coming years—the tents were slowly pitched. A green pyramid-shaped shelter for the boys, and a newer blue tent for my mother and me. I waited beneath a vast log, evidence that a forest once existed on these now-exposed plains scattered with alpine tarns and lakes. As the tents went up and our cocoons were prepared, I watched the rain sheet down, dripping from my wrinkled timber shelter, the log's etchings marking the lifetime it had lived prior to the early settlers and their ambitious farming dreams.

The rain beat down on our tents long into the night before giving way to an empty silence. I lay awake listening to the noiseless sounds. A foreign sensation for a four-year-old who had only known the hushed farm of her childhood. When darkness finally gave way to a subtle dawn, we unzipped our tents and stepped into dense fog.

As my parents packed down the camp, their backs turned to their mischievous son, my brother ran into the low, scratchy scoparia bushes with a tin of lemon fizz, a treat kept for camping trips. A small spoonful of this delicious lemon powder was meant to be added to a mug of water. When the fizzing and frothing subsided we could sip a tangy, refreshing drink. On this occasion, with a spoon in one hand and the tin in the other, my brother had levered off the lid and began shovelling the innocent white powder into his wide-open mouth. The substance began to fizz and froth, setting off a sneezing fit so intense that white foam began to escape through his nose, spraying out into the grey undergrowth. White graffiti in a grey landscape from a now-humbled artist.

Both James and I expected our normally reserved parents to show dismay. Instead their laughter burst into the still morning, filling the day with a chorus of chortles and joviality. I loved that I felt so loved as I watched my parents wipe tears of joy from the corners of their eyes.

Over the years to follow, rain would soak our striped thermals as Dad searched for his perfect campsite while the days lengthened into teary pleas for a reprieve, and I would vow never to inflict this torture on my own children. However, with a salty packet of two-minute noodles inside contented bellies and Mum reading to us by the light of a small candle poised carefully in the gateway to the tent, all would be forgiven and forgotten.

BACK IN THE VALLEY, Crumbly the kombivan once again tucked into the entrance to the woodshed, hiking packs replaced by school bags, we would all slip back into the routines of a united family living a rural lifestyle.

Mum would rise early and begin stoking the fire, her swimmer's body-clock chiming the time for slicing dense homemade bread and preparing lunchboxes. Dad always woke early too, rising with the dawn in summer or under the intense darkness of winter. Each morning I would hear him rise and tiptoe down the hallway past my bedroom. I would snuggle deeper beneath Mum's handcrafted quilts, waiting for the glow of Dad's kerosene lantern to intensify and reflect onto the walls of my bedroom. The perfume of roses and damp earth flowed in through the always-open window. Mum's roses. A small, beautiful part of my parents' immense, labour-intensive organic garden. Soon I would hear Dad pull on his gumboots and flop-flap-slap down the concrete walkway outside the bedrooms, his lantern and milking bucket creating a disco of shadows and brightness wrestling together as he made his way deeper into the night. When darkness returned to my room as he headed towards the stable, I would be left with the essence of kerosene and love for a childhood still evolving.

In June, when the days were at their shortest and the sun's rays were still to creep over valley walls, we scraped ice from the van's windscreen. We breathed a plume of steam into the depths of Dad's kombi and pulled quilts over scratched knees while we trundled as a family over the foothills of Mt Wellington towards the city of Hobart. Mum left the vehicle first, her employment as a general practitioner beckoning. Then Dad battled through traffic lights and the Bridgewater Jerry—a fog which crept from the mountains to the Derwent River's mouth where it gaped into the ocean. It brought a damp, freezing air that enveloped our school atop an exposed hill in the northern region of Hobart. As we approached the school I would sink deeper in my seat, hoping no-one saw my brother or me as we emerged from the bright orange van, and that no-one heard the loud, joyful Simon & Garfunkel music which blared from the van's speakers as Dad's hands drummed on the oversized steering wheel. If then was now, I would be sitting in the front seat, proudly tall and cranking up the tunes thinking, *How cool are we!*

HOME AGAIN AND UP to the barn I would head, the food-scrap bucket in one hand and an empty pail in the other. Nestled on my belly on top of the hay bales, I could scoop up handfuls of grain from the large forty-gallon drums that stood beside them. We purchased the grain as chicken food from the Cascade Brewery in Hobart, where it was used in the beer-making process. I would then slowly let the individual granules slip through my fingers, savouring the texture and smell of roasted barley. Even now, on a cold winter's morning when I run past the Cascade Brewery, with its nutty smell of roasting barley and an aroma of fermenting apples, I am flicked back to this childhood task. Pail filled with grain, I would head back down the hill, ducking beneath the birch trees before placing my buckets on the ground to open the wire gate into the chicken pen. Squawks. Feathers. Probing beaks. The chickens' delight at seeing me was chaotic and welcome. Filling a childhood need to be noticed … valued.

Mum claimed that our frenzied fowls were the most educated members of our family, because the lunches that accompanied us to school each day often returned to end up in the chickens' food trough. The most famous uneaten sandwich came from the fateful day Dad's lunchbox accidentally ended up in my school bag—cream cheese parched by dry bread, watercress from the creek leaking into soggy raisins. I don't know if even the chickens enjoyed their education that evening.

I would leave the chickens and head in search of my father, normally to be found seated on a small wooden stool, gently milking his beloved Jersey cows, each named according to an operatic theme. Tosca's golden hide would quiver as I entered the stable. Carmen and her son Pavarotti gaily munched hay in the stable next door. I'd lean over the opposite gate, discussing the school day while soaking up the smell of the damp hay and sawdust lining the earthen floors of the stable. Old Humphry Horse jostled for my attention while Naughty Nina used the distraction to bury her head in his dinner trough.

Nina was a jet-black Shetland-Welsh pony, four feet off the ground with a girth as wide as she was long—the perfect gift for a four-year-old. When saddled up and bridled, she earned herself the nickname 'Naughty Nina'. She would stomp on our feet, head-butt us in our bellies, and drag me under the scraggly plum tree as it stood proud and alone in the centre of the paddock. She adopted the habit of bolting to the nearest gate, stopping abruptly and sending me—her blonde companion—catapulting over the reins.

JAMES. MY 'BIG BROTHER' in age and physical presence. Two years older with a blond mop of loosely cut hair, broad shoulders, deep chest and feet large like a swimmer. He definitely could have been a swimmer, and for some years we shared this passion. But James' free spirit and poor eyesight made the coaches' whiteboard an unwelcome sight. Even at this early age I felt his discomfort. While he had the body that could pull him effortlessly over the top of the chlorinated waters, he was a wilder child at heart. In hindsight, I probably was too. In James' wake was always Little Andy, his best mate, white-blond hair also cut loosely, narrow shoulders and a shallower chest. Feet small enough to borrow my gumboots. An inquisitively sharp mind. A sense of humour preparing him to be the stand-up comedian that he is today.

The two boys would trek across the paddocks towards the Top Land, a patch of semi-scrubby woodland that looked down upon our home nestled into the fertile soils below. Huckleberry Finn and co. Akubra hat on, spade in one hand and a handful of Dad's tooth-breaking Tararua biscuits in the other. And little me, usually trailing behind, wishing to be seen and hoping to be heard.

On this occasion the boys were on a mission to build a bunker, an underground cubby. Amongst a patch of open grassland with a view over the valley they began to dig, enthusiastically flicking patches of shredded grass, spots of heavy clay, and the occasional rock. Millimetre by millimetre, sweat beaded on foreheads, jumpers were discarded, and the hole grew slightly deeper.

Watching two boys dig to China eventually became tedious. I wandered back down the hill into the vegetable garden with its linear rows of perfect seedlings—beetroot, French Touchon carrots, silverbeet, spinach, and miner's lettuce—an odd green that looked like a lily pad and tasted like very little. Trellises dripped with peas, runner beans and sweet peas. The tunnel house was always a warm haven of thick, heavy air infused with basil, tomatoes and cucumber. Dad would stand amongst it all, an icon of concentration, an individual so at home with his hands in the soil, happy just being himself.

Up through the flower garden I would then weave, skipping over the large blue-tongue lizard on the rock stairs. Usually, Mum could be found leaning over a flowerbed, a pile of weeds strewn behind her on freshly-mown lawn.

'Can we go for a horse ride?' She needed little temptation. We would walk side-by-side towards the stable, a mother and daughter bonded by a love of activity. Friends.

When the rains wobbled into Sandfly, drifting in on an extensive south-east low, they toyed with our little valley, blanketing it like one of Mum's quilts—a cobbled monotone of grey and white. The two small creeks running through our property would swell with pride, bursting their banks. James and I would stand beside them, two raincoat-clad figures bouncing from foot-to-foot as we poked sticks into the foam.

When inspiration struck, James ran back up towards the farmhouse, returning minutes later dressed like a seal. A black wetsuit clinging to gangly arms and legs, a bodyboard clasped under one arm. I looked on in awe and amazement as my big brother sprinted in his bare feet across the wet paddocks before launching himself onto the ground and skimming across the thin sheet of water that had spread far from the banks of the creek. He whizzed and darted, leaning to the left, skimming to the right, until his momentum slowed and he stood back up, a drowned seal with a swollen grin. He let out a whoop, and I a giggle, and together we played in the soggy paddocks until our screaming fingers couldn't stand another minute of the damp cold.

Back towards the house we trundled—the seal and I—passing close to the Jersey cows who hung their heads in despair, water sheeting down their shivering backs. As I passed Humphry the Horse and Naughty Nina, I trailed my hand along their flanks in a gesture of apology. Then slosh, slosh, slosh we ran, the seal struggling, ungainly against the friction of his heavy skin, and me? I was dancing along in front. We were united, the seal and I, a sister and a brother, dancing through the rain in search of our family and the fireplace.

But we weren't always so collegial. A snipe here, an argument over the front seat of the van there. A blind eye to James' advice on my homework, soap on his toothbrush one evening. Then came the day he climbed a tree and refused to return to the ground until I left. With streaky tears of frustration, I grabbed a book and leant back against the trunk to play out the game, leaving him stranded high above until penance was paid. Yes, I knew how to push his buttons, and he mine. We bickered without fighting, taunted without arguing.

Finally, Mum and Dad stepped in with a challenge: 'If you two can last three whole months without bickering, we will take you to Cradle Mountain.'

Cradle Mountain, a pristine alpine valley and rocky escarpment in the north-west of Tasmania, was our absolute favourite holiday destination. The challenge was set. James and I barely spoke to one another for three months. If he went to open his mouth, I would shush him. Suddenly, I was allowed to quietly tag along behind the boys. And as days turned to weeks, weeks to months, and finally the months added to three, we found ourselves bundled under sleeping bags in the back of the kombi, heading along narrow weaving laneways through slumbering towns. Fertile grasslands gave way to the winding hills and valleys heralding the beginning of the Tasmanian mountains. The temperature plummeted and our excitement grew.

On this landmark trip heralding the end of our youthful taunts, we pulled up outside our cabin in the dark, a light flurry of snow crystals shimmering down onto the windscreen of the vehicle. After a light dinner, we crawled into the loft and watched as the snowflakes fell quietly into the silent world around us. When our eyes grew heavy and we couldn't watch any more, James and I fell into a deep sleep, side-by-side, a history of bickering long behind us, dreaming of the wonderland that would greet us in the morning.

SNOW DIDN'T ONLY FALL in the highest mountains. At forty-two degrees south, closer than most landforms to the Antarctic, Tasmania is a strong attraction for the cold southerly fronts that sweep in from the southern oceans. Three hundred metres above sea level and nestled into the foothills of Mt Wellington, the Sandfly valley could occasionally catch these blasts of winter snowfall. We longed for those days. We yearned for them! On days with even a remote crispness, Ciara and I would stand in the living room, the fire not yet lit. We danced, jigging around the room in the hope that our snow dance would create white crystals to flurry from the heavens. Next, we were out the back door, running towards our birch tree to sit in her tops and stare at the sky, willing the dark storm clouds with a hint of the 'duck-egg' blue that Dad said heralded snow. Even better if these rare skies eventuated on a school night so that we might be snowed-in and prevented from attending school. After seeing the first flurries fall to the ground the night before, we would wake before dawn to lie perfectly still, listening for the silence that evidenced a blanket of snow on the ground. Silence? Yes! Bedclothes on the ground, tugging on track pants and woollen socks. Bedroom door open. Back door open. Out onto the landing and …

On some occasions the silence indeed heralded snow, a thin, white, perfectly smooth layer covering the lawn and gardens. It would usually be spring, the clumps of daffodils just distinguishable as they drooped under the weight of the snow. As Dad's lantern roared into life, it created sparkles across the white landscape. Our world would be transformed. As the sky began to lighten we would pull James' homemade sled from the shed and drag, slide and tug it kilometres to the neighbours' hilltop.

Towering over the valley, we needed to prepare our braveness. The steep slope plummeted downwards towards barbed wire and blackberry bushes. Perfectly white, with all the cow pats obscured, the slope looked so innocent.

We would rocket downwards. Sled tracks would leave vivid parallel lines in our wake. Cow pats were exposed, small flicks of grime ricocheting onto the white perfection. Squeals. Whoops of joy. Veering left. Fence approaching. Tumbling off and sliding downwards until we naturally came to a stop. Pulling the sled out of the blackberries. Giggling. Intoxicated by adrenalin. Then the long plod back to the top.

After breakfast, we would clamp the old metal ski bindings onto the tips of our gumboots. Flap, slop, slide, wobble. We 'skied' our way out across the paddocks, commando-crawling beneath each electric fence we encountered, legs splayed, skis digging stubbornly into the ground. Then teetering back to our feet and sliding off again. We were definitely not naturals and I can now only giggle at the fact that I married an elite skier!

Tasmania was blessed with long summer evenings, where the glow of dusk lingered into the night-time. This was the perfect inspiration for 'tent time'. Standing on a chair, then the desk, and finally reaching up into the heights of Mum's sewing cupboard, I was able to pull down the old green tent from our bushwalking shelf. Scrabbling deeper, I could drag out the old Trangia stove, a bottle of methylated spirits, a hefty blue sleeping bag and a foam mat. Then off down the gravel road I would tramp to Ashling and Ciara's house.

On arrival I would be greeted by their frenzied mother. 'You're doing what? I don't think tonight is the night.' However, children can be very manipulative. With gentle coaxing, highlighting the fact that we were already packed and ready, we would slink out the door to find our own perfect campsite. Neighbours' fences meant nothing to us. We saw ourselves as the custodians of the valley, a privileged position that lent itself to crossing borders. Clambering through the barbed-wire strands, helping each other to loosen caught hair or clothing, we would finally reach the perfect spot in the centre of a neighbour's cow paddock, right next to the bubbling creek.

We took pride in setting up our camp, ensuring that each sleeping bag was perfectly placed. We would crawl in and test the sleeping arrangement to make sure that we would not be resting on hardened mud made lumpy by the cows' hooves. Next, we would boil the billy, proud of our independence as we produced steaming mugs of black tea laden with sugar. Hilarity, daring games or lying in the grass watching the light in the trees ensued. But as the light began to fade and we began tugging on our jumpers again, our bravado always began to dim. Lights could now be seen in the houses perched higher up on the hills, and we knew that our mums and dads would be beginning to head to bed. It always felt a little lonely as we clambered into the depths of the down parlour, flicking on our torches and lying face up, feeling damp air from the cooling valley traverse our faces. We would whisper then, the shield of darkness allowing us to share secrets, desires and ambitions for a future unknown. In the quiet of these nights we could sense a world bigger than just us.

A SCHOOL FRENCH teacher once said to me, 'Johanna, it is the naughty ones that we remember the most.' Johanna. My formal name, used only when I was in trouble, preparing for airline travel, or lining up on a start line. Johanna. My alias for all things naughty.

There was no greater recipient of my cheekiness than our neighbours, a couple with grand plans for their idyllic hobby farm. Little did I know that twenty-two years later I would end up on a prominent government board with her, sitting beside one another as equals, with me apologising for the youthful jokes that left them close to despair.

The humour began from their love of moving around their property with minimal clothing. A gaping long anorak and a pair of gumboots. A platter quickly placed across their private areas when we entered their garden asking for milk. A lawnmower left running on the road verge when I rounded the corner on a bike.

Their openness irked the parents of the valley. Their noisy Labradors added to the kerfuffle.

When they began depositing their discarded grass clippings on Ashling and Ciara's side of the road, we decided that we would take matters into our own hands—literally. Handful by handful, we shuttled two acres' worth of lawn clippings back to their property, piling them in front of their carport in the most enormous pile, which nearly obscured the lower half of their small brown hatchback. This left them no option but to reverse through the mess when they headed off to work. Terrible!

On the day the local labourer came to bale the valley's hay, we were allowed to stay at home and help. We sat on the back of the tractor with Dad, jumping down to hoist the heavy bales into a neat pile on the trailer. Once finished, we ran down to Tim and Chloe's, firstly checking that their vehicle was missing from the garage—indicating their absence from the valley. Then we began to create huge towers from their hay, dragging bales from all corners of the paddock to pile them up and up and up. They would be impossible to reach!

It was a very sad hour when, from the heights of our kitchen window, we watched as Tim and Chloe drove their vehicle and trailer right alongside our leaning towers of Sandfly, plucked the bales easily from the top, and within minutes had disappeared back to their hay shed.

By Christmas time, we had honed our skills. Each year one family hosted a Christmas party in the valley, and this year the honour went to Tim and Chloe. Everyone brought a plate of their favourite festive food, and stood around talking about the weather, gardens and children. Inevitably, youthful boredom kicked in and we began those games: 'Dare you to …'

By the end of the party, we had somehow managed to change the time of every single watch, radio, wall clock, wristwatch, car, microwave and oven display. We wound the clocks back thirty precise minutes, conscious that it would be better that our neighbours would be early rather than late to future appointments.

Proud of our impressive feat, we then quietly mentioned this to 'The Parents'. We expected to be in trouble, but the adults simply burst into laughter. All of them. So we joined in too.

The neighbours eventually found out. But not till two days later when they went to watch the news on television and found a gardening show. It was our parents who copped an earful on our behalf, and we were warned to steer a very long way away from their property's boundary, which we did … for a while.

Following in the creative footsteps of her own mother, Mum was a wizard in the kitchen. Baking days. Scraping fingers along the sides of the mixing bowls, pleading to be able to lick the spatula before it was plunged into the soapy suds in the sink. Mum's spatulas …

While my father was a practical man, he was also a philosophical and sensitive one. His 'love language' was the written word, while my mother loved the art of giving. And she loved Christmas!

As a mother-daughter-brother team, we prepared gingerbread houses, Christmas puddings and festive biscuits. We made gifts too: pyjama pants, embroidered jumpers and pots of jam, all mounded beneath the Christmas tree that we hauled in from the front porch—where it lived throughout the year. Then we smothered the poor sapling in tinsel, lights, homemade decorations and a few extra baubles. Its feet buried in wrapped parcels awaiting their recipients. Stockings were hung by the wood fire and the hearth was cleaned for the arrival of Santa Claus.

When only flecks of chocolate remained in our empty advent calendars, Christmas morning would arrive. The contents of our Santa stockings would be strewn across the homemade quilt on my parents' bed. Then we rushed out to tend to the animals, soaking up the smell of roses that I now associate with this time of year. After breakfast and more presents, we would pile towels and bathers into the van and race towards the beach, arriving in a flurry of goosebumps for our traditional mid-morning Christmas swim with all the families of our valley.

One fateful Christmas, we were down to the last present. Piles of tissue paper sprawled across the living room. Cards read, goofy smiles, a family Christmas photo. Dad handed Mum a carefully wrapped gift. She read the card, smiled warmly and stood to give him a kiss. Then she returned to her place in front of the fire, leveraged off the sticky tape, pulled the paper back to reveal … a spatula. A red, rubber one with a beautiful wooden handle. A spatula.

Mortified, she looked up at my father, searching in his face for the hint of a joke. But Dad never did 'Dad jokes'.

Our family collected a plethora of spatulas after this day. Dad's birthday—a spatula. Mum's birthday—another spatula. Next Christmas —yet another. The spatula became revered, a red, blue or pink token of humorous love, a gift that said, 'Thanks for all that you do for our family even if I hate bloody spatulas!'

CHILDHOOD. A flurry of scuffed black school shoes kicked off on the porch. School bags dumped inside the front door with a thud. The red-blue chequered school dress discarded in the laundry basket, replaced with baggy shorts, t-shirts, friendship and hearty appetites.

Childhood evenings, a time for running wildly amok before dusk became night. Down the gravel road I would fly, bike wheels spinning below and hair billowing behind, eagerly anticipating the adventures that could be squeezed in between the 'now' and 'night'. I would provide a polite knock with a hint of impatience. A hasty push of the glass door and an entry into the familiarity of Ashling and Ciara's living room, my second home. Emanating from the kitchen were always the familiar smells of freshly fried potatoes, marinated meat and sautéed greens. I would greet their mum and dad before turning to my friends in dismay, seeing their plates still piled with food. I would sit beside them and talk but my glance would flick to the clock by the back door, counting down the remaining minutes until my own mother would be dishing up dinner. Unable to bear the slow movement of food around their plates, like a puppy I would quietly accept the food offerings they passed to me across the table when their parents were not watching. Yes, I would literally do anything, including eating my best friends' dinners, to be back outside, flying around the hills on our bikes, making the most of a precious evening.

Even at this age, I was well aware that each day, each moment, each second, is sacred.

As I grew bonnie and strong, my best friends accepted my hand-me-downs and played along with my wild ideas. We played hard, worked hard and, at times, fought hard. We were children of the wild.

Ciara put it beautifully the other day as we walked side by side up the Hobart Rivulet marvelling at the complexities of adulthood. 'When I turned thirteen, I actually cried. I just didn't want to grow up. I didn't want to become an adult.'

I recall a flashback: my mother gently carries me along the gravel road behind our home. She whispers in my toddler ears, 'Don't grow up Han, please don't grow up.' At heart, I don't think I have.

SANDFLY WAS the rock underneath our family. Wild adventures with my brother, close ties to my parents, the development of my wild spirit. Base camp for adventures in Crumbly Van.

I could return from a brain-searing day at school then, later, university, kick off my shoes and wander out through the garden, grass on skin—'earthing', as Dad would say. I could close the bedroom door, lie on the floor and listen to the farm life outside. I had trees to clamber up when I needed even more 'me' time, pathways to roam when my love affair with running began, and neighbours with similar hobbies to encourage me along.

Every element of my youth at Sandfly was complete. The cosiness of our nineteenth-century farmhouse with its central fireplace and Huon pine dinner table crafted by Grandfather. Family memories formed within the uninsulated walls of our home. Wild adventures with enduring friends—or our four-legged friends. Sandfly played host to each important milestone that together sculpted my childhood.

During this childhood, our home in this steep-sided valley was the pillar that held me steady as I found my growing feet. It would soon come to anchor me when the winds of life whipped around me, my father gravely ill and my mother's heart aching for a gentler breeze to return. Little did I know the sense of loss that would then come when the 'For Sale' sign would feature on the property's front fence. No, in my youth I lived buried in the moment of every day, filled with child-like wonder at the sprouting world around me. I was my childhood and Sandfly was my soul.

I recently returned to the valley, rolling my adult-sized bike along the familiar roads and trails. As I whizzed down the hill, wattles budding and waiting for their moment to shine, I couldn't help but marvel that the valley had not aged, with not even one tiny wrinkle line to be seen. Our old family home still sits so proudly at its core, aloof and untouchable. It had outlived my childhood.

2

My feet were cold as I stood on the damp concrete beneath the mouldy, dripping canvas ceiling of the Clarence Swimming Pool. Ten minutes from the CBD of Hobart across the expansive Derwent River, the pool's curved dome gave rise to its nickname, 'The Bubble'. I shifted from foot-to-foot, alleviating the searing chill in my seven-year-old feet, but also shaking off the discomfort of waiting for the starter's whistle. I glanced to my right, straight across the bathing-capped heads of my competitors, towering above their shorter frames. I was used to being placed in the back row of school photos and people looking taken-aback when they realised I was only seven years old.

I looked to my right. There were no more competitors for I was standing in lane eight. I was the last qualifier, the lucky one. I saw my mum's excited face reassuringly watching on. I desperately wanted to be like her. Strong, dolphin-like in her love of water, and disciplined in her willingness to swim laps like the squad swimmers—although she usually swam alone in the empty middle lanes where the fastest grown-ups swam.

The whistle sounded and I hoisted myself up onto the blocks. Two feet together. Bent at the middle. Arms hanging limply. I was ready.

'Take your marks …'

I grasped the cold metal of the block's underbelly, listening intently for the sound of the hooter being squeezed like a lemon in the starter's hand. When the start sound resonated above the sloshing of water, I launched myself into the chlorinated blueness. Silence. I frog-kicked hard and 'wiped the bowl' with my arms to form a breaststroke, just like we had been taught. Popping to the surface I began to frog-kick and wipe the bowl, frog-kick and wipe the bowl. I was breathing hard, oblivious to where the other girls were. All I wanted was to frog-kick and wipe the bowl so cleanly that I made my mum proud.

I touched the wall and stared straight up through foggy goggles into the official's face above. Immediately the whistle sounded, and the official waved us to the side of the pool. I levered myself out, bathers sagging under the weight of moisture. *Dad would laugh*, I thought. He always waved me off to the pool with a, 'Don't get wet!' Wet I was. Shivering too, from the adrenalin of the moment.

Mum greeted me with a towel and wrapped me in a hug. 'How did I do, Mum?' She pressed me forwards and we began to wander back along the cold concrete to the shallow end.

'Great, Han. Just great. You were eighth.'

I ONLY EVER HAD THREE goals. They materialised from the glossy pages of the *Australian Swimming and Fitness* magazine and dinner table conversations with parents and their adult friends. Three written statements in the front of every dog-eared journal I owned.

1. Be an Olympian.
2. Live at the AIS.
3. Become a doctor.

These journals became the outpouring of ambition, eventually telling the story of nine chlorinated years through which I strived to find my feet.

In many ways, I lived in parallel worlds. I had an aspirational dream to become a swimming champion, but I was also a wild child with a heart embedded in the valleys of Sandfly.

I was a daughter, bonded strongly to her family who lived by the rolling foothills of Mt Wellington, slightly removed from the world of private schools and sleepovers. While my school friends walked the pavements home after a day in the classroom, James and I helped tuck the animals into bed. When parties and boys became cool, I opted for pony camp and—with Ashling and Ciara—established a cleaning service for residents of our valley, 'The Busy Bee Gang'. Five dollars to clean a rusted car that had never been washed. One dollar per house window. I tucked each penny into a porcelain piggy bank that would eventually fund my sporting endeavours.

I was a dreamer who lived the night-time hours through the world of books and stories, a love I shared with my father, mother and brother. After reading of the exploits of Dawn Fraser and other champions, each inspiring book was returned to my bedside table and I would lie and watch through my open bedroom window as three faint lights across the valley randomly flicked on and off. They were far up on the hill, the left one a little higher than the right one, the middle one the highest of all. Deep down, I knew these lights only represented the lives of a family of neighbours living within the walls of their hilltop home, but to me they represented the positions on a sporting dais. I especially loved the way the middle light shone the brightest of all.

I loved the idea of becoming something, of turning my life into a journey towards a meaningful outcome. And thanks to the glossy *Australian Swimming* magazines—which were tucked carefully in piles beneath my bed—I was heavily swayed by the glitz and the glory of those shiny pages. I wanted to be an Olympic swimmer.

As night rolled into day, and weekdays into weekends, homework gave way to cubbies and competitions. Mini-Olympics with apple-shot-put, gravel road cycling, backyard tennis, and long-distance running to the creek and back. I thrived on the opportunity to practise being an athlete. And I loved to win! We filled rain-soaked hours, clustered around the wood fire with board games. But when the sun shone once again we were back outside and straight into fierce cubby-building competitions against the boys.

We were crowded around the dinner table one evening when my brother said, 'So, Dad, I was wondering if I can kill and skin one of your cows? I'd love to cover my new teepee with a real animal hide.' Needless to say, the teepee was never completed. Dad's precious Jersey cows continued to contribute to Mum's ongoing headache of how to utilise the buckets of milk and cream that filled the laundry.

Time passed, and James' affinity with wild cubby building was slowly replaced with homework, computers and a knack for the saxophone. On the evenings when he practised with his teacher who lived high up on Mt Wellington, I would jump on my mother's bike and race along the quiet road that traversed the mountain's slopes. On this natural backdrop to the city of Hobart, I pretended I was in training for the Olympics. I envisaged my red, blue and white school uniform as the tracksuit of the Australian Institute of Sport. On the rare occasion that a car whipped past, I pretended the driver was a talent scout, and willed my legs to pedal even faster. But when I reached the crest in the road where Hobart was laid out far below, I would pause to look down on the shimmering lights of the city beginning to settle in for the night. In this moment of tranquillity, beads of sweat clinging to my forehead, Mum's old steel bike propped against the white road marker, I would make a wish. 'I wish to be an Olympian!' I was ready to start my racing career.

I WAS NEVER PUSHED into sport or competition. I felt drawn to the excitement and adrenalin of it, the brightly coloured tracksuits and the shining gold medallions that hung like marks of perseverance from the necks of the champions. I loved the sensation of becoming something, and even at a young age I knew just how special living with purpose and intention was.

I was also surprisingly quiet and private with my aspirations. I wrapped ribbons around my journals to hide them from any potential prying eyes. I carried them in the depths of my school bag, pages dog-eared and worn, filled with notes of my training successes, weaknesses, and teachings from my mentors.

I was a bag of bones and muscle, a large sponge absorbing inspiration from the chlorinated squad environment. I almost embarrassingly admired my elder swimming peers, and endlessly flipped through the pages of the latest glossy swimming magazines. I launched at any biographical book telling the tales of champions, thriving on those which described the overcoming of adversity. And slowly, each page that I read, each lesson that I learnt, and each lap that I swam fuelled a burning bonfire of aspiration deep within me.

But not a soul could know. I was happy to stand at the back of the pool deck, a tall girl awkward amongst her more confident peers, hands fiddling with goggle straps while her heart burned with Olympic flames.

I KNEW champions trained in the mornings. I was also inspired by my mother, who for years had made the dawn pilgrimage to the pool, alone, carefully manoeuvring along the smaller laneways around Sandfly before turning right onto the broad highway that cut through the foothills of Mt Wellington and eventually terminated in the ghost-town streets of Hobart.

The day of my first morning training session, I awoke before Mum, and lay twitching with excitement to get up, listening to the sounds of a sleeping farm through my open window. After a mug of sweetened tea and a teddy bear biscuit, I proudly sat beside my mother on my maiden pre-dawn journey to the Clarence Pool. We crossed the Derwent Bridge to the first rays of the new day, swept off the highway, down, around, and under the vast Derwent Bridge's long spans. As my mother turned into the pool's car park, I knew I was diving into the next phase of my athletic career.

The novelty continued for a while. Each day beginning with an awakening shake from Mum and a mug of tea left to steam beside my bed. I would tug on my togs in the semi-darkness of the living room, trying to pretend I was wide-eyed awake.

Each morning, we shared the road with tradies and the occasional log truck carting vast stumps of Tasmania's ancient rainforest and eucalypts from the belly of the giant southern forests to the woodchip mill, where they would be chewed into tiny morsels by enormous machines, loaded onto trawlers, and carted over the oceans to be turned into paper, or cardboard boxes, or toilet tissue. Each truck cast a shadow across my mother's face. So, to cut through the double darkness, Mum would turn on ABC morning radio while I turned my face towards the window, watching a dark landscape sleepily pass by.

Over time, the routine became just that, a routine. A series of packing bags, trying to remember underwear and school ribbons, squeezing in dinner and hurriedly finishing school homework before fatigue overwhelmed. I have strong memories of being perpetually tired, and as I grew into my shrinking school shoes, this fatigue translated into a slow falling out of love with swimming and a growing cheekiness in the classroom: 'You know, Johanna, it is the naughty ones we remember the most ...'

I WAS SURPRISINGLY quiet for a child with an impish spirit. Through my primary years I was shy, avoided the boys, and was eager to impress the teachers. After all, I wanted to be a doctor and an Olympian. Even at four years of age, when I was given 'neat scissor' challenges and a pair of scissors by my kindergarten teacher, I was desperate to impress. Not knowing if she wanted speed or accuracy, I would aim for somewhere in the middle, rapidly cutting around her outline of a teddy bear with rough hacks of the scissors. Hack, chop, stop. Only to be disappointed in her comment: 'Hanny needs to try harder.' How hard did I need to try?

These comments were to follow me through primary school and my early high school years. In Year 8, at thirteen years of age, my body was still adapting to puberty and my swimmer's physique. I was the uncoordinated, long-armed Great Dane puppy of the class. Anything that required a ball, bat or moving object was a stretch for my limited coordination. I would desperately hurl the ball in an overarm throw, only to watch it bounce, bounce, bounce, then finally roll to a stop well short of the teacher's ambition for us. In cricket, I watched the arc of the ball, wide-eyed, and lurched forwards with the bat, only to be bowled out before wood could collide with rubber. In basketball I darted, bobbed and dashed my way down the court, gaily yelling at my teammates to make a pass, only to fail to get my long fingers onto the round surface.

Eventually, the school's sports coaches decided to take it into their own hands to teach me the athletics throwing sports. They were eager to make use of my broad swimming shoulders, and willing to devote personal time to my development. However, time and time again they would watch my javelin skim like a lawn mower across the grass, put their face in their hands, and release a quiet sigh.

No, I was not cut out for coordination sports, and despite my swimming and running records, my school physical education report had me barely passing—'Hanny doesn't try hard enough.' Combining my lack of coordination with a maverick attitude to learning, I became labelled as a troublemaker who had potential … 'if only she tried harder'.

I thought I knew what I wanted. Deep down, I was disciplined and willing to work as hard as it took to realise my three childhood dreams. My arms would be aching, and I might have mid-afternoon cat-napped on my French books, but I would dive into that cold water for the second time in a day and give training my all. Later, wrapped in a towel, the car bouncing and lurching for home, I would practise my French with my father. Around the dinner table, I would pull out my books and ask the questions I needed to finish my studies. And then I would pack my swimming, school and gym bags again for the next day to eat, sleep, swim, study and repeat.

DESPITE MY PURSUITS OF EXCELLENCE, I remained a child at heart, and at my growing feet there was still a whole childhood filled with family adventures. Kombivan packed with potato and leek soup in a can and tea bags, sleeping bags at the ready for when the heat couldn't reach the back seats, we would bump off into the darkness. Heads lolling to the side, my brother and I would doze and wake, doze and wake, until a bump, shudder, reverse and halt would bring us to a stop in a darkened place at the end of a road far away from home. The kombi roof would be pushed up, bunks untucked, and us two tired children would be huddled inside our down bags, our parents curled up below on the back seat that doubled as a bed.

Dawn would bring the unpacking of hiking boots, backpacks and gaiters. A light drizzle, a slowly warming pot of porridge on the go. Fed and watered, we would then hike off along quiet trails. The Walls of Jerusalem, the Freycinet Circuit, Hartz Peak and eventually the Overland Track—each adventure initially brought fear and trepidation to my growing feet. There was something about these wild landscapes that frightened me, and in some way this uneasiness has never left me. Rather, I have developed resources to lean into the discomfort and thrive.

And then my dad found the sport of rogaining, and I was inducted into this unusual sport at seven years of age. Originating in Scandinavia, rogaining is the long-distance sibling of orienteering. People compete in teams of two or more people, with a set amount of time in which to navigate to as many different control points as possible. Red and white flags mark your arrival at these locations, where points are allocated. Only ten points? The brightly coloured flag was likely hanging on the junction of an obvious track, or somewhere your legs may receive very few scratches. I liked being assigned ten-point flags— they were easy! One-hundred pointers? Ugh, these were the opposite, tucked away on a high hill or a deep, scratchy gully. They often involved tweaked ankles, scanning eyes, and the risk of never finding that damn control at all. When my legs were little, with feet clad in a pair of gumboots to stop them getting soggy and sore, one-hundred pointers were not much fun.

My family were my team. We started with a three-hour romp on Mt Wellington, a mere twenty-minute drive from home. After running, walking and thrashing our way cross-country through steep, rough terrain, we returned gratefully to the 'Hash House', the hub of administration where food was cooked and awaiting your arrival. Sitting around a wood fire, slurping soup and wiping the bowl with lavish slices of fluffy white bread, the fairy lights of Hobart shimmering far below, and a warm tent and sleeping bag awaiting, maybe rogaining was not so bad after all?

Until the arrival of the eight-hour epic near Cradle Mountain.

We drove up in the dark, eyes scanning for wildlife crossing the road. The van's broken headlights made this task even more difficult. Pulling up in the dark, rain on the roof, I had a dark sense of trepidation. I knew how long my father's legs were, and how hard they were to keep up with. Crawling into my tent that night, I felt so far from the glistening, calm waters of the swimming pool environment I had come to love.

Morning came, and so did the rain clouds. My brother disappeared up to his neck in a sinkhole. My gumboots became rubber water jugs. By dinnertime we had waded, walked and waddled our way across thirty-six kilometres of alpine grasslands. But the finish felt amazing!

We later sat with friends around the Trangia stove, sipping soup as our head-torch beams bounced into the dark night. Nearby, our hiking packs lay bursting-full, repacked for the very next morning when our family would embark on a quick three-day dash down the Overland Track, Tasmania's eighty-two kilometre alpine hiking trail. Why drive home when you can walk?

TWO YEARS LATER, I again found myself standing on the start line of another rogaine, this time a twenty-four hour event located in the vast wildflower plains five hours north of Perth in Western Australia. At ten years of age, I was proud to be attending these World Rogaining Championships. However, huddled amongst my family, dressed in our matching black leggings and white cotton t-shirts, I couldn't help but notice just how out-of-place we looked in the midst of this international representation. Multiple flagpoles stretched upwards into the pristine spring sky. Beyond them lay an endless sea of yellow everlasting daisies, their golden papery heads dancing and bobbing in the gentle breeze. We had disembarked for the first time into this unfamiliar landscape from a tattered old school bus only twelve hours earlier.

The journey thus far had been an adventure in itself. From my aunt and uncle's familiar home in Perth's leafy inner suburbs, we had driven towards the bus station, past a river that glistened in flat calmness, and disembarked onto a baking stretch of pavement.

Surrounded by our packs and an excited babble of foreign tongues, we had seen an ancient thing pull into the car park, the lettering 'SCHOOL BUS' still vaguely evident along her flanks. We piled aboard, horrified to find each seat supported by a hard metal bar beneath the cushion, right where our sit-bones needed to rest. Competitors sat either bolt upright, poking their bottoms into the rear of the seat, or slouched backwards in humble resignation to their discomfort. Over three hours, suburbia and industry gave way to hobby farms, which in turn gave way to the vistas of rural agriculture.

The bus suddenly jolted, swerved, growled and let out an enormous, explosive BANG! And then another. The brakes screeched as the bus driver pulled to the side in a flare of red dust. He disembarked in a flap. We all slowly piled off too, wincing as the heat of the day grabbed at our bare arms, and looked at the tattered remains of two burst rear tyres now strewn across the highway.

We sat on the side of that single stretch of road for five hours, sheltering in the narrow bands of shade provided by the height of the bus, and played conkers with pebbles from the road verge. Each time a road train—a large truck towing up to three trailers—rocketed past, the bus wobbled and swayed, teetering in the blast of hot air. Dust billowed towards us and we cowered, humans sheltering from the hostility of arid Australia.

Night had fallen by the time the bus moved again. We climbed back aboard after an Akubra hat- and Blundstone boot-clad local rocketed to our salvation in his ute, bringing with him two bus tyres and a hearty farewell wave. In the dimness of the bus, competitors' heads lolled, flopping sideways and forwards while quiet snores emanated into the darkness.

Eventually we pulled into the campground entrance and I leapt gratefully from the bus to unlatch the gate for our driver. As I stepped off the bus, I was blasted by a tidal wave of floral aroma. A smell so intense that it has been etched into my olfactory neurones like a tattoo. Preparing to set up camp, we searched and searched for a place that would not disturb the flowers growing thickly beneath our feet. But eventually we gave up, pitched our tents and crawled in, only to awaken a few hours later to the brilliance of a desert morning and an awe-inspiring sea of everlasting daisies, stretching from horizon to horizon in a golden arc.

Our family hiked and ran through the daylight hours and swathes of native flower gardens. Our legs gave way just before midnight and we began to turn for 'home', the administration headquarters where our hiking tents were pitched. We fell into a quiet march, my mother and her son striding side-by-side, Dad and his daughter plodding just behind. Our torchlight seeped into the rural night and illuminated the red dust billowing from our footfalls. I held Dad's broad hand, feeling the squeeze of purpose in his grasp. As much as I wanted to fill the rivers in this arid landscape, I knew that tears would not help ease my discomfort.

Sleep did.

The next day, under a new sun and with five hours still to our advantage, we crawled from the tents, and pulled on dust-speckled tights and t-shirts, before charging off towards the horizon.

Energised, we ran from control to control, pausing only briefly to look down onto the plains stretching far below us, watching the road trains growl their way onwards, yellow daisies and bitumen roads the carpet upon which they played.

Then we ran. Ran and ran towards the finish with a sense of urgency. The sport imposes penalties if you are late. Dad was out the front, straining, his hands turned inwards and palms pushing the air out behind him in his distinctive lope. James bobbed next to him, broad chest pressing forwards, chin tilted slightly upwards and his arms driving him home. Mum came next, short strides turning under her swimmer's physique, strength emanating from every step. She held back one hand towards her little chick, me, trotting along at the back, shorter legs taking shorter strides. An invisible rope tied us all together.

I bounced and rolled along at the back in my own little bubble of purpose, a bubble that would become my athletic trademark as the years matured.

TODAY I SIT in the kitchen of my father's home on Bruny Island—a humble weatherboard farmhouse on an enormous acreage of former sheep pasture that rolls down into the Tasman ocean. I shake my head and giggle with him, as we look back on these days with a mixture of fondness and amazement. We hold steaming mugs of tea, a day of labouring and exploring on his farm behind us, and it is easy to fall into gentle reminiscing about these early years.

With the calmness of Bruny Island basking before us, and an opportunity to pause time and reflect on this atypical childhood, it is easy to realise just how lucky I was to have this upbringing. We were exposed to the extraordinary beauty and opportunities that lay within the natural world. We were presented with a childhood so rich in vitamins and playfulness that it crafted a uniqueness in our ability to pursue individual pathways.

I cannot help but tease my father a little now. 'You are lucky, Pa. You nearly broke me in the heart of the wildflower country.' Only now can I laugh at the fact that my ten-year-old legs carried me sixty-eight kilometres at those world championships, for the simple reason that Dad had 'always wanted to see the wildflowers'. What I remember most now is the aroma of those flowers the moment I first stepped off the bus. A year later, in the Flinders Ranges of South Australia, we covered more than seventy kilometres in a twenty-four hour period, because Dad 'always loved this part of the world'.

When you are taking two steps for every one of your father's, feeding off the strength of your mother, who are you to know that this childhood is unusual?

However, before long it was not my father's wild ideas nor my mother's desire to arise early with the dawn for training that set the challenges. No, quickly the tides turned. It was me inflicting the discipline and adventures on myself—and anyone silly enough to join me.

3

I wandered down the long corridor, feeling my way through the hazy darkness until I reached the shaft of blue light emanating from the television. I quietly sidled past my brother, James, his long legs extended like a trip-wire in front of him, his eyes glued to the screen.

Into the study I moved, and as I reached the computer bench I spun, placed both palms onto the smooth wooden surface, and began my exercise routine. Dips first, then push-ups, abdominals, crab crawls, and then repeat. My mind was quiet, eyes closed again, aware of the sensation of rising and falling while going through the motions.

'Hanny …? Hanny!'

My eyes flicked open at the sound of my name. My brother loomed in the doorway, his six-foot presence towering over my small frame clad in pyjamas and held in the middle of a push-up, hovering halfway between up and down.

'Hanny, what are you doing?'

It was only then that I fully awoke from that sleepwalk. Embarrassment coursed through me and I dropped to my knees. 'I was doing my exercises …'

I WAS FULLY SUBMERGED in my ambitions, always quick to dive into the pool, jostling with myself to get further and faster. I loved the purpose of the pool, and found relief here from the prepubescent taunts of the boys at my school. When I donned my bathers, latex cap and goggles, I felt free of the pressure to fit into my school dress and peer groups, and able to just be the determined, playful me that I had come to identify with.

Our earliest sessions were a mixture of harder swimming and duck-diving. We spent a lot of time hanging from the end of the pool, long, keen arms draped over lane ropes. James joined me, but over time his heart drifted back to the farm and the friendships formed there. The rigidity of the training environment highlighted the differences in our personalities—he a bundle of gentility and spontaneity, me a more energised kid who would later be given the nickname 'Tassie Devil' by her overseas orienteering peers.

Right from the beginning, the joy of training and preparing outswam the joy I found in the competition environment. While I loved packing pyjamas and a bunch of books into the trunk of my mother's new Toyota Camry and turning onto the open roads, I had a sinking feeling in my gut as Launceston and the dripping, low-slung ceiling of the Invermay Indoor Pool approached.

In these early, formative years in the pool, I couldn't understand the juxtaposition of my feelings. I couldn't understand why I felt motivated to strive harder and yet began to dread the competitions. Instead, I would try to pull on my brave face as I hoisted my bathers over my growing hips. I assumed that fearing the competitions was just part of the process to becoming a champion. I could never escape the nerves of State Swimming Championships, lining up alongside two doll-like sisters coached by their father, or the tall prowess of another girl.

The highlight of each day was bundling back into the car, wet hair dripping down the 'new' second-hand seats, and curving our way through the one-way streets towards Kilmarnock House B&B with its heritage good looks, towering ceilings and curving wooden stairwell. Mum would let the two of us into our twin room with beds draped in floral bedspreads, and I would dart towards the toffee bowl sitting proudly on a lace doily atop the antique wooden table. Why this place felt so like home I have no idea. But to lie peacefully under the bedspreads, soaking in the tranquillity of the bedroom with the slight orange glow from street lights outside, knowing that dawn was still a solid ten hours beyond this quiet moment shared with my sleeping mother ... this was the moment I swam for.

There is not one recollection remaining for results achieved or times swum during these formative years. Just car trips and special nights in the company of my mother. Rewards for the hard work.

By the age of eleven, I had outswum my current squad and my gentle, nurturing coach who stood patiently at the end of the pool, her curling hair reaching even further upwards in the steamy chlorinated environment and her laugh quietly emanating into the deafening, sloshing frivolities of the pool. She knew she was no match for the antics of the naughtier pupils who duck-dived and loitered at the end of the lane—who did anything to avoid the actual process of swimming.

While I, too, was a rebellious wild child at heart, I loved my swimming training, and challenging myself to improve. I was becoming frustrated by the lack of structure in the sessions, and so it was a glad-but-sad day when I pulled on my latex swimming cap, plumes of talcum powder spouting from its depths, and turned away from lane three for the stricter squad environments of lanes six through eight.

I was initially terrified of everything to do with this new environment, although I was damned if I would show it. In these boisterous squad lanes there was a strong undertone of discipline, strict time management and routines. This was a cocktail so strong that when added to my vice-like Type A-achiever brain, it created an almost frightening willpower that could make me crawl out of bed and complete strength training in my sleep.

The resulting fatigue ran so deep it left me a ratty rebel at school, a nana every evening, and yawning through kicking sets in the pool.

To my French teacher—who handed me my leaver's certificate at the end of high school, clasped my hand and leant forward to whisper, 'Johanna, it is the naughty ones we remember the most'—I apologise. I apologise for the water fights, for sitting in the willow trees wagging class, and for hiding alarm clocks in our pencil cases to frighten you. I apologise for coming to class after filling my clothes with autumn leaves, and for leaning out the window in a daydream, wishing I was outside. I am sorry I was the naughty one to you, while everywhere else I was a conscientious pupil or daughter. So, it is important for me to say now, I remember you too!

In the swimming squad environment, I held my dreams close to my growing chest. I was terrified and in awe of my two larger-than-life coaches whom the squad fondly nicknamed 'Mini-Mac' and 'Big-Mac'—to reflect the relative sizes of their waistlines. When they crossed their arms across the bulge of tracksuit-wrapped stomachs, I would know to swallow my brave pills. I was nervous of their whiteboard pens that poked from the depths of their tracksuit pockets, always fearful of the enormity of the training sessions they could release onto the whiteboards that stood as a symbol of disciplined structure at the end of a concrete pool.

Unlike my experiences up to this point, every moment of every session was filled with a purpose. In those earliest few months buried in the white wash of this squad's lanes, my arms flailed and struggled to recover from the lurch in training volume and intensity. It wasn't uncommon to be churning out kilometres of butterfly, only to be punished if you broke your stroke when your arms or lungs failed you. And Saturdays unleashed the greatest pain, with sets up to six kilometres in length followed by a run.

During the toughest sets, I sprinted towards the wall, slammed my hand in gratitude onto the slippery tiled surface, and looked expectantly up at our coaches, lungs hurting and chest heaving. I searched in their eyes for a glimmer of recognition for my effort, only to hear a time, read off the stopwatches that hung from their necks, hurled out into the noisy, sloshing, echoey environment. Occasionally, as time passed and strength increased in my growing body, I observed a surprised raise of an eyebrow. Maybe this meant, 'You did good, kiddo'?

While slowly adjusting to the new coaching style and larger squad with its own internal hierarchy, I often felt like an awkward duckling. After I tugged on my swimming costume, I learnt to put my head beneath the surface and block out the noise. I became more skilled at ducking for safety from the bully who chose to swim over the top of me each session. I gained resilience as I shrugged off his 'Bush Pig' name for me.

I found it easiest to just do, blocking out the social pressures and embracing the work. I turned my arms, sucked in the deep breaths, and later willed myself through the hundreds of repetitions of land-based body-weight exercises before each pool session. When age allowed me to sign away my life on the Terms and Conditions of the Aquatic Centre's new gymnasium, I leant into the challenge. Lifting heavier and heavier weights until I gained a new nickname: 'Thomas the Tank Engine'. Over six days of the week, I completed three gym sessions, nine water sessions and four additional running sessions. Stroke by stroke, session by session, day by day, week by week and then year by year, I slowly closed the gap until one day, skin bruised and scratched from a morning of clambering through blackberry bushes and exploring the valley's ambling creeks, I cruised into the finish of a low-key, 100-metre freestyle event in a new personal best and Australian Open qualifier of 1 min 01 sec 76. I had just turned thirteen years old.

The more I delved into the underwater world of sprint freestyling, the more I knew I wanted to be a champion. But I also became aware of a groundswell of internal pressure. The process of becoming a champion gave me a thrill and inspired me to become one of those athletes highlighted in the glossy pages of my swimming magazines. This dream helped me to rise in the darkness, to tug on my bathers, and to nestle into the cocoon of the car. On those dark mornings, the news would play through the radio as I sipped my tea and watched the electronic display of the vehicle's clock, counting down the minutes until diving into the water … willing the minutes to drag longer.

Despite being motivated to reach the top, I began to suffocate from the reality of the swimming squad environment. I felt uncomfortable around my confident swimming peers, with their loud giggles and confident banter. I began to almost feel afraid of my coach's whiteboard marker, feeling slightly nauseous at the thought of the main set still to begin, and what their stopwatches might record. I had a deep desire to improve, but I also feared the searing discomfort of the increasingly harder sessions, of the lactic acid and the torturous creations of Saturday's inevitable epics, such as the four-kilometre continuous individual medley: 1000-metre butterfly, 1000-metre backstroke, 1000-metre breaststroke and a joyous 1000-metre freestyle sprint to the finish. And I continued to wrestle with a fear of race days.

Looking back, there was always going to be a disparity between my inner wild child and the glitzy environment of competitive swimming. From gumboots to racing bathers, waterholes to swimming pools, I was living in two worlds. However, despite the internal tug-of-war, the hard work and dedication was paying off, with improvements coming in ragged leaps and bounds.

Then puberty hit with vengeance.

I WAS uncomfortable with puberty from the moment it hit me at a young age. I entered this confusing world with naivety. My female friends were not open in their knowledge of the changes about to grasp our growing bodies and emotions, and my family were always private and quiet about this domain too. So, the day when I first tugged down my panties to notice unusual red spots, my heart burst open with fear and embarrassment. I ripped them off, buried them deep in the laundry basket, and clambered under my bedsheets to hide. But Mum found me a few hours later and gently introduced me to the female necessities. I found myself craving to be able to return to youth again, not yet ready for the big adult world of breasts and womanhood.

I clearly remember the first day I snuck down to the creek and sat on a cool, damp rock, hidden by the height of the blackberry bushes. Removing Dad's razor and a bar of soap, I carefully began to strip back the blonde, downy hairs from my lower legs, watching the fine strands whisk their way down the bubbling brook. Next, I raised my arms into the air, carefully removing the darker strands from my armpits. No more torment from the boys.

But as I grappled with a changing physique, and how to manage menstrual cycles as a swimmer, I found it harder and harder to find improvements. Thinking it was to do with my training, I dug deeper and deeper in sessions, until my journal became filled with the jingle, 'Feeling tired'.

In our training squads, recovery was the exception not the norm. It never meant sleep-in and catch up on our dreams. Instead, it meant slow, focused drill sessions to enhance technique, or kick sets, or shorter sprints. Occasionally, on highly memorable mornings, recovery involved an opportunity to jump on the diving boards or play water polo with the squad at the end of a session.

My way of dealing with puberty was to ignore it. While other girls at school explored the world of curving bodies, makeup and fashion, I was still exploring the hills and curving creek lines of the valley and how to continue to lift my swimming to new heights.

The awkwardness followed me to school, as wet hair dripped down school dresses pulled taut across my gym-adapted shoulders. I used humour, cheekiness and dedication to my studies to refract any attention to my body. I became the class clown, with an appetite for sport and dedication to her studies, and somehow slotted into my early teenage years very easily.

However, silently, I still struggled to become friends with my body on any level other than athletically. This was nowhere more apparent than in the swimming squad environment where the Bush Pig and Thomas the Tank Engine name tags continued. When I arrived at the pool, a switch was flicked and I adopted a quiet purposefulness. My body became less about beauty and femininity, and more about function —a tool that I could harness. When I worked out in the gym, I never spent time looking in the mirrors. I rather opted to feel the way in which my body moved—how it stretched, bent, lifted and jumped. This ability to tune inwards would become a strength that served me well when I transitioned into the more injury-prone sport of running.

The National Age Group Swimming Titles were held in Hobart in my first year eligible to swim at this level. Qualifying in the 50 and 100-metre freestyle events, I was excited to represent Tasmania and my club. I lay awake for long stretches of the night prior to the competitions, listening to the crickets singing outside my window and looking at the lights across the valley which still represented my dais dream. I began to wonder, 'What if?' What if this was my time to shine? How would it feel? Mum finally roused me, and I dressed in a quiet stupor before Dad waved us off from the front porch with his usual, 'Good luck and don't get wet!'

Mum was excited as we drove in towards the Hobart Aquatic Centre nestled into the foothill of the Queen's Domain. Swarms of brightly-coloured tracksuits were already there when we arrived. I hung back, trying to control the nervous clouds swirling inside me. Inside, the pool lapped lazily, lane ropes lay calmly, and the dais stood aloof on the far deck.

Then the music started, the loud speakers crackling into a Bon Jovi tune to fill the nervous spaces, and excitement coursed through me. I began to strip off my tracksuit only to hear a snigger forming behind me. The snigger became a chorus which in term became laughter. Glancing around, I realised I was the centre of the joke. I looked down to realise in horror that my bathers were on inside out, the slightly worn, brown lining gaping around my body. Grabbing my towel, I raced towards the girls' bathroom where I wrestled with my togs and humiliation. No matter how hard I tried, I knew I would never fit in. I faded to finish ninth in the girls' thirteen-years-and-under 50-metre freestyle, missing the final by a mere 0.01 of a second.

There was always emotion wrapped in these results, but, deep down, I think I always knew that I just had to stay. To be. To persevere until eventually it would be my day to shine. I had an amazing network of support around me, from encouraging teachers to our swimming team's physiotherapist. I had parents—especially Mum, who was there without fail to drop me off, swim alongside me, encourage me, and help me juggle the responsibilities of school and the pool. And even though I was nervous around them, my coaches were very supportive. They had a strong team of swimmers under their care, two of whom were racing on the national senior team. Big-Mac and Mini-Mac constantly looked for the extra wriggle room for improvement, helping us to form indomitable club relay teams. While I never individually medalled on the national stage, with the girls' powerful breaststrokes and fluid butterfly, we rarely missed standing on the dais. As the famous quote says, 'Insanity is doing the same thing over and over, and expecting a different result'. Our coaches knew that we needed to be different.

However, as the sessions rolled by and more and more was at stake for them and our team's top-level swimmers, we began to swim down a knife edge of preparation. I could feel myself moving further and further away from the carefree Hanny I had once identified with.

Throughout these formative years I had an appetite like a horse, consuming thick slices of homemade fruit toast and a literal fruit basket each day. Bush Pig was my name at squad training, but at home I was fondly nicknamed 'Fruit Bat'. I had a sweet tooth, tamed by homemade biscuits and dried fruit from jars in our expansive pantry. After school, I savoured a muesli bar or bakery treat before the evening's training.

So it was with an element of surprise that I received an offhand comment from my mother at the bakery one afternoon. Munching on one of my favourite iced buns before training, she proudly said, 'You are really growing into a beautiful young woman, Hanny.' In this moment, she was a mother hen watching her young chick growing into an adult. However, it was the first time that I had ever linked food with my body, and my Type-A personality misconstrued her praise. I only heard, *You need to watch what you eat*. So I did, a little, joining Mum more in the kitchen. Together we found joy in preparing muesli slices and wholesome dinners from my new Australian Institute of Sport cookbooks.

But when the coaches bore down on us with their new rules, a smouldering spark of insecurity about my body began to gently ignite.

ONE SATURDAY MORNING, as Friday night revellers were only just finding their pillows, one-by-one our squad members arrived at the aquatic centre, drifting sleepily down the wide concrete stairs to the landing at the entrance to the overly-heated, chlorinated environment. The pool didn't open for another half an hour. Going through the motions, we dragged brightly coloured towels from our bags, laid them down on a patch of concrete and dropped to our hands and knees.

Halfway between down and up, shoulders flexing in the effort of another push-up, I heard my coach order us to stop. We sank gratefully to our knees and curled ourselves onto our towels, waiting in curious expectation of what was to come. They loved doing this to us, surprising us with a torturous stair-running session, or occasionally revealing a soccer ball for a quick, makeshift match on the sloping green lawns of the rose garden behind the pool.

But not today.

Instead, our coaches surprised us by ordering us to stand. 'Right, we want you to sit down if you have eaten chocolate in the last two weeks.' Surprised by the spontaneous nature of this request, we glanced around at each other before many of us sank shamefully back down to the cold pavers.

The orders continued. 'Sit down if you have eaten a biscuit in the last two weeks.' Most of the team joined us on the ground. I had never really thought about the difference between bad food and good food. 'Sit down if you have eaten ice-cream.' Slowly but surely, our coaches rattled off bad food by bad food until only one girl remained standing.

The silence was palpable. As we prepared to get stuck into the remainder of our warmups, their warning hushed the surprised whispers of the team. 'We will be repeating this in two weeks' time. We expect to see each of you left standing.'

I got the message. Not a sliver of biscuit or chocolate passed my lips for two weeks … then three … then four. Many of us left standing during these fortnightly check-ins were girls, and only thirteen or fourteen years of age.

The new discipline around preparedness continued. The next week Big-Mac had a new toy, a pair of skin-fold callipers they used to pinch and measure my thirteen-year-old body.

Every two weeks, the more elite members of our squad lined up in the darkest corner of the pool deck to be measured and documented. As results rose and our team profile developed, further testing procedures entered the pool deck. Before we knew it, we were also being pricked and lactate tested through tougher and tougher swim sets. With nervous fear, I watched the sport scientists of the Tasmanian Institute of Sport cart in their equipment, tug on white latex gloves with a slap and snap, and pinch our ears with a gentle squeeze, while our chests and lungs heaved with the exertion of rigorous sets.

My body has a capacity for hard work, but as the pressure and expectations mounted, combined with the strictness of the newly imposed rules, I found it harder and harder to show results from the hard work. I watched in frustration as my competitors from other squads laughed their way through short, playful sessions on the other side of the pool, only to narrowly out-touch me into a bridesmaid position at each competition.

As better results continued to elude me, I grew quieter and more dedicated to the pursuit, while believing: 'Maybe I am not trying hard enough?' For how else do you interpret diminishing results?

I DRAGGED my body from the still-turbulent waters of the squad lanes. Entering the change rooms, I dropped my bag onto the slightly damp metal bench and wandered into the shower. As the lukewarm water hit my skin, chlorine emanated from me into the already thickly chlorinated air. I had grown used to the permanence of this unusual odour, though my friends always commented as I plopped down beside them in class.

And yet, today when I opened my training bag, I wouldn't dig for my school dress and slightly scuffed brown shoes. Rather, I pulled out a pair of baggy blue and white shorts with a matching long-sleeved, oversized t-shirt. I huddled into myself as I tugged them on, pulling at the drawstrings of the shorts in a bid to keep them from flopping back down around my ankles. They certainly weren't made for athletic fourteen-year-olds! I could feel the other squad members staring a little as I brushed my hair and, in the mirror, observed the bold lettering across my chest and down my right arm—Sydney Olympic Torch Bearer.

Butterflies had already entered my stomach as we passed the gates to my school and continued onwards into the narrow strip of suburbia called Taroona—a place later made famous as the home of our Tasmanian princess-by-marriage, Mary, Crown Princess of Denmark.

It was also the home of my grandmother, for now at least. At ninety-three years of age, she was a woman of the world. Originally from England and a trained physiotherapist, she followed my grandfather across the globe through his role in the British navy. From rainy British streetscapes to Canada. From maple syrup to the great Aussie barbecue.

My grandparents finally came to rest amongst the rolling pastures of Launching Place on the north-eastern outskirts of Melbourne. Here they established a cattle stud, before my grandmother sold her hoofed friends in preference for moody alpacas, instigating Australia's first ever alpaca stud. However, family called, and together they finally relocated to the sleepy coastal stretches of Taroona, overlooking the gaping mouth of Hobart's Derwent River.

My mother and I pulled up in front of my grandparents' sleek blue dwelling. Complete with a swimming pool, it exuded 'Greek coastal retreat' rather than a grandparents' home in Tasmania. Inside, we huddled around the folding breakfast table, lavishing slightly-charred toast with butter and the yeasty, salty, brown stickiness of Bovril, her gloopy British spread. 'Smarty Grandma' we called her, for her little glass jar of multicoloured chocolate buds that always sat slightly out of reach atop her kitchen cupboards. Smarties—a sweet-toothed, comforting weakness that has followed me into adult life. Maybe in my ripe old age I will be called Smarty Grandma too?

Soon it was time to walk up to the end of her road and await the arrival of the official buses as they crawled from marked light pole to marked light pole, each one indicating the short section where famous people would run, proudly bearing the Olympic flame. *What am I doing?* But before long I was waving goodbye to my support crew and taking a seat amongst adults. We were encouraged to stand as the bus ambled through the suburbs, and share the story that had led to our selection as Olympic torch bearers. I listened to the stories of wilderness advocacy, fire rescues, medical breakthroughs and knitting nanas, all the while wondering, 'How do I explain that my brother and I huddled around the kitchen table with Olympic fever and completed our own applications with instructions from the local newspaper? And how do I reconcile that while I sit here, my equally-deserving brother sits in a classroom?'

I slouched lower into my seat as the bus trundled past my school, took a U-turn and then slowly began dropping us at our designated start points. However, once the waving students disappeared behind me, an excitement began to seep into my wintry toes—I was living a small part of my childhood dream to represent Australia at the

Olympics. Whether I had earned this opportunity or not, and feeling decades younger than most of the other Olympic torch bearers, I knew that there was no other place I would rather be and no greater honour than to run watching the billowing flames that had travelled around the globe to my island home.

I was wrapped in Olympic fever, also knowing that in just a few weeks' time I would be able to dive into the silky blue waters of the vast Olympic swimming stadium in Sydney to represent Tasmania at the Pacific School Games—the Olympics for school-aged students from the Pacific nations and Australian states. For a moment in time, I felt one step closer to my Olympic dream.

I LAY face down on the massage table. Tucked deep into the basement of the Sydney Olympic Park swimming pool complex, the noise of the Pacific School Games boiled around us. My right shoulder ached, a lingering discomfort from a recent subluxation of the joint during training. For weeks, I had trailed the squad on a kick board, unable to rotate my shoulder or even lift it above ninety degrees. However, this event was something I could not miss.

It was a mere month from the beginning of the 2000 Sydney Olympic Games. Our youth event hosted a broad range of Pacific Nations as the trial run for each of the state-of-the-art sporting complexes. From Tonga to New Zealand, New Caledonia to Tasmania, athletes from around the Pacific converged on the region, billeted with families during the competition week.

I was entered in many races and yet I felt underprepared. My shoulder was weak, a discomfort that gnawed into my confidence. In the night I had lain awake with a searing discomfort in my shoulder, so I rose early and made my way to the basement of that pool by public transport, to seek out the skills of the event's masseuses.

Initially, there was nothing unusual about the way his hands moved over the muscles of my back, flushing from the lower spine all the way up its length until dissipating out over the shoulders. Long, deep strokes, easing, softening, stretching. I was vaguely aware of other competitors walking past the floor-to-ceiling glass windows that looked into that space, their brightly coloured tracksuits and varying depth of bronzed complexion a hint of their homelands. I felt partially insecure with my bathers pulled down to my waist, but that was normal for us. For years, my squad coaches instigated massage as a vital part of our pre-race preparation. But suddenly the familiar became unfamiliar. I felt hands reaching under the fabric, moving over my buttocks, squeezing, travelling towards my chest. Tightness gripped my fourteen-year-old heart. I tensed. I feared. The hands continued to wander, lower, deeper, to a place where I had never known hands to wander. And then suddenly I pressed up off the table, exposed, grabbed at the towels and yanked my bathers up. I spun around, wet hair slapping across flushed cheeks before I disappeared into the crowds, too afraid to look over my shoulder for fear of what I might see.

I ran into the women's bathrooms, feeling sickened by the sight of happy, laughing faces. All my brain could think was, 'Why me?' I caught a glimpse of my reflection in the mirror, the outline of strong shoulders on a more womanly body. Behind the locked bathroom door, I gathered my wits, knowing only too well that when I left the privacy of this cubicle I must tell someone. My mother was in the crowds, there to support the team as a medical professional. And it was her that I finally chose to tell first.

But I knew that police and psychologists would follow, and my mother would be so concerned. She was quite rightly very upset. Seeing her so upset gave me added resolve. The only weakness in that moment would be not rising above it. I rallied against the helping hands of concerned adults. 'It was a one-off,' I told myself. A time of discomfort and confusion, but one to be shrugged off. My only desire was to be just like the other athletes there at the Sydney Olympic Complex, heartfelt, diving into the quivering competition pool.

Later, I boarded the train back to my billeting family, feeling a sinking nervousness. My eyes darted along the mostly empty rows as the carriage rocked side-to-side, lurching occasionally as we lunged into a corner. A fearful jolt. A deep intake of breath. 'Did I just see him?' A glimpse of tight-cropped hair, greasy and slick. 'Is it him?' I bundled my bags into shaking arms, and darted back through the rolling transitions between carriages until I was standing in front of the guard's station.

I turned to face the front of the train, watched as commuters came and went, all the while feeling a very long way from the sheltered valley of Sandfly.

4

I became more sensitive to my body, poring through the Australian Institute of Sport cookbooks, striving to create healthier options for my lunchbox and begging my mother to replace oil with water when she sautéed onions in heavy cooking pots in our newly renovated kitchen. For two consecutive years, I avoided all chocolate and biscuits, seeking low-fat whenever possible.

Slowly, slowly, the results began to show. Like most of the girls in my squad, I was leaner and meaner than many of my Tasmanian swimming competitors, capable of lifting heavier weights, and beginning to achieve a few small wins. This only confirmed for me that what you dream you can achieve.

The only problem was, I was measuring my self-worth by results and praise from others, and growing further and further from my world as a wild child on the farm. And the sad thing about it all was that I knew I was no longer very happy in this pursuit. I no longer bounced out of bed in the morning. I found it increasingly hard to giggle at my father's playful pre-race taunts because, in many ways, I did not feel like getting wet.

My favourite day of the week became Sunday, when I could lie snuggled beneath the doona as the sun poked its head through the shimmer of clouds above the valley's embrace. I could lie and listen to the morning chorus of exuberant birds beyond my window, before slowly pottering into the kitchen in my pyjamas, flopping onto a stool, and watching the heart of our family home come alive. Avoiding homework studies, Mum, Dad, James and I sat united as a family around the kitchen table and slowly unwound together from the week. We shared thick slabs of toast, turning up our noses at Dad's attempt at stinky, pale, homemade butter, and pulled out the old and tattered green Oxford Dictionary to look up a word or concept that manifested from our conversation. This tradition of sharing meals and stories around the family table is of absolute importance to me today, a symbol of unity and stability in an otherwise busy and occasionally confusing world.

Little did I realise that I had been slowly falling out of love with swimming for a very long while. I could have stepped back at this point, but swimming had become part of my growing identity. I was used to being asked about it by my teachers, friends and extended family. The routine had also become etched into my life. Money had been invested, dreams dreamt.

So, while I withdrew inwards, it was hard not to notice that it was also becoming rarer for each of my family members to smile. My brother began to shy away from his homework, spending more and more time outside or on the old family computer in the study. As Monday morning loomed, he withdrew further into himself. On the journey home from the swimming pool each evening, my father would sit in taut-lipped, forehead-wrinkled contemplation. Where once we had cranked up the speakers with some Simon and Garfunkel tunes or a little deep-throated Cat Stevens, now the darkness of night-time had begun to filter through the glass into the interior of the car. I tried to crack through the chill with bubbles about the school day and my latest prank on some poor teacher, but on the worst days I resorted to pleading: 'Just smile, Dad!' However, my dad was always a farmer at heart, healed by the heavy fertile soils engrained under thickened fingernails. As the urban sprawl gave way to the quieter rolling pastures on the approach into the Sandfly valley, he slowly, ever so slowly, released the internal pressure, wound down the window and began taking in large lungfuls of damp air. Only then did the conversation begin to flow again.

As the male figures in my world disappeared into their man-caves, my mother became an increasing pillar of strength in our family. She pulled back from her full-time role at the general medical practice she had assisted to launch. She spent more time bundling mud-stained clothes and school uniforms into the hungry washing machine; feeding flour, yeast and water into the equally hungry new breadmaker; or doubled over, hoe in hand, in the expanding waistline of our organic garden. However, the call of the man-caves grew louder, until one day the door of my parents' bedroom closed in adult secrecy and I was left standing in the corridor wondering what had happened.

BULLYING IS WHAT HAD HAPPENED. Not to me, that time, but rather to my big brother, with his slouchy Akubra hat and gentle caringness that made him an easy target for the immature. After withdrawing into himself until he could withdraw no further, and his friends could not hold back the wave of injustice being inflicted on him, he chose a new pathway. He trialled a few other schools, then chose the home-schooling option, supported by parents who were willing to ride this new journey alongside him. So, as I tugged on my school dress and stiff black shoes carefully polished by my father in front of our roaring wood fire, James pulled on his ugg boots and turned towards the study.

It was a grateful day for me when my parents sat me down and asked if I wanted an academic sea change too. I was certainly eager to join Ashling and Ciara in the world of public school, so I nodded my head. However, after visiting their school, my parents instead opted for a school I had never heard of. Did someone say 'Farm School'?

Oh gosh! As we pulled into the curving circular car park with its carefully placed visitor parking and towering front steps leading up to a heritage building blanketed in creeping wisteria vines, I began to worry. And when I saw the hideous clashing of egg-coloured school dresses with mud-brown blazers and sand-brown socks in brown-brown shoes, with not one ponytail missing a brown and gold hair ribbon, my heart sank. 'Farm School?'

But I was there, at what was actually called Fahan School. I quietly followed the principal on a tour before returning to the car where my parents enquired, 'What do you think?' Aside from the hideous uniform, I found myself commenting on the beauty of the school grounds, with its private creek flowing through extensive green spaces, its weeping willows dragging dancing fingers through cool waters. Little did I realise that this creek would become the heart of my life at this school.

I hung my head in dismay at my Year 7 Orientation Day. Determined to start on a positive note, I had carefully helped my mum to select a matching corduroy pants and jacket combination for me to wear. Bless my beautiful peers and their ability to withhold judgement, for we soon looked back at this eclectic dress sense in good humour. As we turned the pages in our school books, ran laps around the school grounds, and swung like youthful chimpanzees from the drooping willows, I slowly found my feet and a strong sense of belonging in the school.

So, with every hard punctuation that hits, there comes a silver lining. James' confrontation with school bullies initiated my transition to Fahan School, and the beginning of a wonderful education infiltrated with friendship and the exploration of my potential, not to mention a fostering of my increasingly maverick spirit. Most of my peers at Fahan came from outlying rural properties, and appreciated the wilder imp within me. For James, the silver lining came in the form of days spent on our farm under the careful tuition of my mother and the Distance Education Office, and his introduction to the sport of orienteering.

TASMANIAN SHEEP PADDOCKS IN WINTER. A frosty landscape of frozen water beads hanging from strands of barbed wire. Bracken ferns and thistles stood stiffly in mown-dirt paddocks, the ground frozen into a solid permafrost. Wattles glistened as the sun began to melt their frosted icing, and nearby the partially filled dam breathed steam into the freezing winter air. Into this paddock we would pull up, our orange kombivan a lighthouse amid the car park.

From the four-wheel drives and station wagons emerged orienteers clad in bright, baggy, nylon pants and oversized fleece jumpers, which more closely resembled pyjamas than athletic attire. Steamy breaths accented cheerful greetings as the orienteers sat on folding camping chairs, to strap ankles and tie shoelaces with coloured electrical tape. Thermos flasks lay scattered behind vehicles, a testament to the long, icy drive that had brought them to this random destination in a forgotten backland of Tasmania, the finishing point for that day of the orienteering competition.

James had a natural flair for this sport, a love affair that began at school. His mathematical mind had a knack for processing and retaining vast amounts of information. He could look at a topographical map and quickly calculate the fastest route.

This unique sport originated in Scandinavia. Competitors start at short intervals and navigate from the start to the finish via a series of controls marked by orange and white flags which dance lazily on metal stands at the foot of obscure objects—such as a rock, or a one-metre-high cliff buried in bracken fern. There is no marked route, but rather the athlete uses his map and compass to determine the fastest way for him. For my brother this was often a straighter approach thanks to his physical strength. For me, I felt I had more fitness than wombat-ability, so I would often barge out to the tracks where I could run faster—anything to avoid crawling on hands and knees along tight animal tracks through impenetrable scrub.

The icy hinterland of sheep paddocks and the scrubby Tasmanian landscape that lay beyond was a very different brew of orienteering, and into this my dad launched himself with gusto. For the majority of our visits to Tasmania's local orienteering competitions, we all whizzed around our respective courses and were soon heading for home. However, occasionally my father opted to join the elite ranks despite his limited orienteering experience, and it didn't always turn out as well as he would have liked. On these rarer occasions, a chill would return to my sweaty body while I eagerly loitered around the finish. Then James and Mum would return, and we would consume hunks of homemade fruit cake and chatter to our new friends. Later we would walk aimlessly around the perimeter of the paddocks, stopping to gaze at the view or the results board, eventually returning to the van to lie draped across the back seats, watching our neighbours' cars file slowly back out of the thawing paddock and turn onto the distant highway.

Then he would return, frustration and twigs tangled in his damp hair. After we all bundled back into the van, the silence would finally crack. 'I just didn't see that track ... and then I found a gully ... I thought it was up there ... but then I wasn't sure ...' After a while I would tune out, watching the pastures be replaced with suburbia, which was slowly replaced with pastures again as we closed in on home.

I really wasn't sure about this sport, with the daggy outfits and long Sundays away from the farm and my friends. The running felt awkward, and I was even less keen on the nerdiness of analysing maps. But I had to admit that, like my big brother, I had a knack for the navigation and a base fitness to draw upon.

While I chose to submerge myself in the chlorinated lap lanes of the local pool, James quickly climbed the ladders of competitive orienteering, and soon travelled far and wide to orienteering camps and national events, often accompanied by my father. Together they would return to Sandfly, telling high tails of friendships from other teams and pranks that involved bacon, plastic sandwich wrap, and bus engines.

I began to feel a swell of jealousy. It sounded so carefree, and filled with friendships. I felt torn between wanting to join them in pursuing this carefree sport with its non-judgemental community and the original plan of following the swimming pool's black line in the direction of my dreams. For a little while longer I chose the latter, freshly shaven legs and windmilling arms propelling me towards what I hoped were long-held dreams.

WHEN MY PARENTS opted for the role as managers of the State Schools Orienteering Team bound for Canberra, for the first time ever I joined my brother on a plane as it lifted from the small single strip of the

Hobart runway. I had been competing strongly in orienteering for some time, capable of making the state team—but my swimming aspirations had always taken precedence. Now, however, with Mum and Dad at the helm, I wanted to experience the excitement of competing at the Nationals too.

As the fog-filled valleys of Tasmania disappeared beneath a bank of cloud, I leant back in my seat, my Tasmanian tracksuit adorning my swimmer's body. On previous trips to mainland National Swimming Championships, I had felt nerves. Now I felt a different sensation—a tingling of excitement and anticipation. The team around me came from all walks of life. None of them seemed judgemental. All were just as excited for the experiences.

Over the course of that week we ate as a team, raced as a team and even went as far as dyeing our hair red, green and yellow ... as a team. There were no low-fat, pasta-laden dinners, nor did we need to shave before the races. Rather than returning from the morning of competition needing to have a sleep, I would come back, forget to shower and run around the soccer pitch with the other athletes. More interestingly, I ran well ... really well!

Three weeks later, I ran down into the garden in search of my parents, a letter from the Australian Orienteering Federation flapping in excitement. 'James and I need a passport!' New Zealand and the National Development Orienteering Team were calling.

This rapidly growing enthusiasm for orienteering began to bubble into the pages of my swimming journals. My scrawling handwriting was beginning to reflect an inner rebellion against the artificially chlorinated world and the pressure to perform. It was beginning to feel like an unnatural chore, and I secretly longed to lead a more adventurous lifestyle.

I wanted to travel the world. I wanted the chance to represent my country. Yet, my swimming performances were plateauing. Those three carefully scribed goals that had once kept the fire lit seemed more like pages in one of my childhood storybooks than a chance at reality.

Picking up on my inner turmoil, it was actually Big-Mac who pulled me to the side. 'Han, maybe you could try mixing up the training a little? Would you like to take a night or two a week to enjoy another sport?'

On Tuesday nights, I chose to join my school friends at the athletics track. On Wednesday evenings, I ventured to another patch of Hobart bushland for orienteering training.

During one athletics training session, I strode down the home straight and was greeted by the coach: 'You are a pretty good swimmer for a runner.' That tiny backhanded compliment, coupled with rapid improvements in my two new sporting outlets, changed my outlook on sport forever.

The change was reinforced when the plane touched down in Auckland and I had my first taste of foreign orienteering terrain. I had assumed there would be a time lag between understanding their unique sand dune terrain and feeling competent to perform. And although I initially made some enormous errors in training, by the time the competitions came around I felt very at peace with myself and my capabilities with map and compass. In between, our team all bunked down in a school dormitory and enjoyed the one-dollar ice creams from the local dairy stores. It was summer freedom at its finest. As races flowed to races, I really began to find my foreign feet.

Looking back, I am amazed at the great trust my parents placed in their fourteen and sixteen-year-old children. We had flown together to New Zealand, travelled with carefree athletes up to twice our age, fallen for individuals of the opposite sex, and returned excited by our successes.

At the conclusion of this week, I sat in a contemplative mood on a sandy patch of Kiwi soil. The Australian national orienteering coach, a soft-speaking Tasmanian with a lasting Belgian twang, came up and plonked down his wiry weight beside me. 'Han, you started a bit rusty, but you got there in the end. You are a pretty good orienteer for a swimmer! Have you ever considered trying out for the Junior World Orienteering Championships?'

I looked back at him, wide-eyed and confused. This was my brother's dream. 'Where are they?'

'Estonia,' came his reply. Naively, I just nodded my head.

When I later stepped off the plane into the familiar crispness of a Tasmanian evening, I knew exactly what my pathway forward was.

But first of all, where in the hell was Estonia?

No longer did the sheep paddocks feel so foreign. No longer did I cringe when I pulled long socks up to meet my three-quarter tights, and crashed my way through the thick bracken undergrowth. Where once orienteering had seemed like a hobby shared with family, now it felt like a pathway to travels and opportunities. I had no idea how strong the competition would be on the other side of the world, but when I saw a few other Australian superstars finding their way into the pages of the Australian Orienteer, a World Cup medal dangling around their necks, excited faces looking back at me, I was sure they were encouraging me —'You can do it too!'

I never officially returned to the squad swimming lanes. Worried that I was letting down my parents and coaches, I took a few sessions with a sports psychologist—then took my brave pills and walked onto the familiar Aquatic Centre's decks. Barely able to look my swimming coaches in the eye, I quietly explained, 'I need to quit swimming to pursue my orienteering.'

And just like that, my bathers were replaced with runners, and swimming journals became orienteering-laden. When the green, gold and red of Tasmania was replaced with the green and gold of Australia … When solo pool sessions were slowly engulfed with mornings running through the quiet paddocks of Sandfly … When trips to mainland aquatic centres were replaced with flights to the lush forests of remote European provinces … I knew that I was finding a true love affair with sport. One where the racing excited me as much as the training. A sport rich in friendships and opportunities. The perfect sport for a child of the wild.

5

I tumbled from the aircraft, hair limp, eyes bloodshot, and feeling like I belonged in the Harry Potter book that I carried in my daypack. I somehow followed the signs to the baggage carousel, eager to get outdoors and meet up with Sarah, my orienteering friend and fellow debutant on the Australian Orienteering Team. She was only a year older than me and not yet eighteen. We had travelled domestically together a few times, but never overseas. There in Helsinki Airport, and a long way from our respective homes in Tasmania and Western Australia, our small, blonde friendship would reunite when she greeted me as I emerged from customs.

Except she was not there to greet me. I walked out the door into a throng of blonde Scandinavian women and men, and a plethora of Birkenstock sandals. Amongst the crowd I waited, fearful to move anywhere should Sarah have just popped to the bathroom … or the information bureau … or …

As the minutes ticked past, I tried not to panic. Our plan was rock solid. Sarah was to fly in from visiting family in Germany, and would arrive three hours before me. She knew my arrival details. We were going to set off together into the great wide yonder of Europe.

After two hours, I felt panic starting to settle over me like the blanket of fatigue I was trying to push back. I kept scanning the arrivals board for cities that sounded German. For not only did I not know which airline Sarah was travelling on, I did not even know the name of a German city other than Frankfurt. My basic school geography classes, in which I had spent more time plotting nuisance tricks than studying, had not prepared me for this first overseas experience.

Only months earlier, I had purchased a mobile phone, proud of its epically-small proportions, where the buttons were so insignificant I could barely fit my oversized seventeen-year-old fingers on the keypad. The only technicality then with my phone was that it lacked a sim-card … and Sarah's number … and also was not charged.

Time had passed, and it was bedtime for small children. In a hazy moment of hunger and fatigue, I realised that I was fending for myself.

With the helpfulness of a few strangers and their English-Finnish translation skills, my phone became sorted, although I calmly made the rational decision not to call home. Alerting my parents and raising their fears was not an option. I could imagine them tucked up asleep, a wintry night shrouding our farm. The nickname for our home, 'Mole End', after Moley's home in the *Wind in the Willows* storybook, suddenly felt more significant. In that moment, I was Moley. Alone. In Finland. On my first solo trip overseas, and with oceans between unknown and known.

I pulled out my training journal. Tucked into the back sleeve of it lay a slip of paper handed to me by a member of my local orienteering club in Hobart. After wishing me well at the upcoming Junior World Championships in Estonia, he had passed me the slip of paper with a name and phone number and exclaimed, 'Only call him if it's an emergency!'

Is this an emergency? I thought. Five hours had ticked past since my arrival and my head had begun to feel like a fitball deflating with fatigue. This was definitely an emergency! I began to tap in the numbers.

'Aimo!' I reeled at the bluntness of his greeting, and released a babble of English explanations over why this seventeen-year-old Australian was calling, out of the blue, in 'an emergency'. After a pause, then silence, then another pause, Aimo quietly responded, 'I be there in fifteen minutes. Meet me at the big clock. I am very tall and have BIG feet.' And like that, the phone became silent.

I stood alongside the big, big clock, head turning like the crowd in a tennis tournament. *Tall man, big feet. Tall man, big feet.* The phrase formed a sleepy mantra in my head, a meditative thought process calming my concerns. Then he appeared, striding into the airport with a height dwarfing everyone. And his feet! In gratefulness and naivety, I rushed forwards and found myself wrapping my arms around him in an almighty hug of Aussie gratitude. He stiffened, and then untangled himself. He looked everywhere other than at me, and reached for my large duffel bag, careful to avoid further physical contact.

'Follow me.'

I did not find anything strange about following this quiet man to his car, nor that no-one else knew my whereabouts. What I did find strange was opening what I thought was the passenger door only to find myself looking at the steering wheel. Even once I was in the passenger seat, it still did not occur to me that anything was odd about driving deeper and deeper into the Finnish woodlands on the 'wrong side' of the road, my new friend still mutely leading the way. Nor did I find it strange to follow his exceptionally big feet through the front door of his forest cabin. Rather, I was too baffled and preoccupied by the complete lack of furniture while seven cats ran excitedly around my feet.

I finally entered a state of shock and dread when Aimo's first word since leaving the airport was 'no' after I enquired as to whether he had anything I could eat for dinner. After being shown to my upstairs room hosting a mattress on a wooden floor, and listening to his footsteps disappear back down the stairs, I quietly wandered into the bathroom, peeled off my travelling clothes and gratefully stepped into the shower. As goosebumps began to appear across my naked body, I pushed, pulled, turned, prodded and finally banged in frustration at the shower's unfamiliar lever and button. Despite my silent pleas, the water insisted on pouring out through the bath spout and so I sat naked and hunched on the cool ceramic bathtub, splashing my body, and feeling a very, very long way from home.

I awoke in the hazy semi-darkness that signifies summer nights in the northern hemisphere. Realising that Australia would now be bathed in winter daylight, I scrabbled for my mobile and punched in the digits for Sarah's family home. Her concerned mother answered, and soon I was plunged back into a long, deep sleep, safe in the knowledge that Sarah's flight had been cancelled and she would be due to arrive on Finnish soils in around twelve hours' time. It was a dreamless sleep.

Sunlight poured into the room. Hot and groggy, I shrugged off my sleeping bag, dressed, and headed quietly downstairs. A lone wall-clock ticked in the sparse living room, and I was surprised to see that it was past eight in the morning. 'Aimo?' The house echoed with emptiness and feline purrs. They rubbed and stalked their way around my confusion. So I turned for the front door and tried the handle, only to realise that it was locked. Looking out through the window to where the Finnish trees trickled light onto a sparse forest floor, I suddenly realised that I had no idea which direction the airport or city was, and for the first time it occurred to me that maybe this really wasn't a great idea after all.

I turned back into the house, coming across a phone lying alone on the barren timber benches. I picked up the handset and fished for my scrap of paper. I tapped in the numbers. 'Aimo!' Again, I reeled at the bluntness of his Finnish pleasantries, and once again released a babble of confusion. 'My brother be there in one minute.' I put down the phone. One minute? In less time than it takes to tie my shoelaces, there was the sound of a key turning in the lock. The front door swung open and a burst of cool morning air rushed in to join the cats and me. Standing on the porch was the looming, spitting image of Aimo. I knew not to run, and not to offer an Aussie hug. So instead I offered a little wave. He was as quiet as his brother, and just as tall, with equally oversized feet wrapped in old running shoes. He reached for my duffel, jostled it into the back of his rickety little hatchback, and soon we were weaving our way back out into the sunshine and broad stretches of the airport freeway. I came to know him as Aato. Aimo and Aato. Two brothers sharing semi-detached cabins in a quiet patch of forest on the outskirts of Helsinki. Two forest creatures with a love affair for cats and orienteering.

On the steps of the Helsinki International Airport, I bundled out of the vehicle, offered a little wave, and watched him drive back off into

Never Never Land. The only remnants of my bizarre evening were a growling stomach and a swathe of fine cat hair adorning my clothes. As I turned towards the Arrivals lounge, I could not help but giggle. What would my parents think? Little did I realise that this would not be the last time I leant on the generosity of Aimo and Aato.

A week later, Sarah and I were squashed into the back seat of Aato's same little bubble car, heading north along five hours of endlessly straight freeway towards the largest one-day orienteering event in the world—the famous Jukola Relay. We had heard so much about this event, with its 20,000 competitors racing in 3000 teams from twenty different countries, swathes of tents, supermarkets made from black plastic, makeshift saunas, showers shared with a thousand other naked women, and orienteers running in endless trains through endless forests. This was something we knew we had to see, and if it meant a quiet road trip with Aimo and Aato to get there, it would be worth it.

Quietly reassuring Sarah that the heavy silence in the vehicle was completely normal, I seemed unable to stem her tears of fear as our two silent friends decided to pull off the freeway with a single statement, 'We are off to visit our cousins.' We bounced our way through weaving forestry roads until we pulled into a large clearing, finally slowing to a stop outside a dominant Finnish homestead, its barn-style home surrounded by rusty-red-painted outbuildings. As I opened the door, gentle guttural grunts and the stench of pig faeces joined Sarah as she huddled deeper into the backseat and whispered, 'They're serial killers!'

A jovial, smiling family wandered down the front steps of their home and ushered us into the low-ceilinged space of their living area, where the heads of a deer's family loomed off the walls. But soon the room was wafting with the aroma of cake and coffee, a babble of laughter and Finnish chatter echoing around our confusion. Our fear of a premature end to life began to dissipate with each sip and munch of our morning tea, and yet, and yet, the wall clock loudly acknowledged each second passing, counting down to the race's start.

'Where in the world are we, and why are we munching cake in a stranger's home only hours before our international orienteering debut?'

WHEN I LOOK BACK into the fond memories of my younger, muddier years, trust is a word that readily springs to mind. From a very young age, my brother and I could wave my parents goodbye, turn our backs on the cultivated fields of our farm, climb and commando-crawl like experts through barbed-wire and electric fences, and head for the hills. It is with gratitude that I now thank my neighbours – Uncle Franz, farmer Michael, Mike the berry grower, and Tim and Chloe – and all those beyond their neighbourly borders too. It was our dirty gumboots that strained your tight fences, that left a little campfire in your bushland, or that occasionally played practical jokes on you. Yes, it was us who used the local Christmas party to change all your clocks forward thirty minutes so you were early to work on Monday, or who borrowed the row boat on your lake, or who sneakily ate at least a ton of your berries over the years. I am sorry we sold you lemonade that probably tasted more like floor cleaning liquid, or that we woke you in the middle of the night when we camped in your front paddock. Yes, it was us you saw crawling through your creek lines, hoping you had not seen us, or sneaking through your uncut hay paddocks. And yes, it was definitely us who left tobogganing tracks down your paddocks when our prayers for snow were answered. Through all our wild adventures and silliness, maturing to school parties and first cars, there was an embedded trust from the adults around us that we would always pause at the line between right and wrong. And so, we did.

It was with similar trust that my parents had no qualms about me travelling alone to Finland at the age of seventeen on this first significant overseas trip. Their trust gave me the confidence to trust Aimo and Aato, and to run my young heart out in the sloshy forests of Finland, before jumping on a ferry and crossing the short straight between Helsinki and Estonia. It was in their trust that I tried to make careful, calculated decisions, even if they resulted in spending a night alone in a stranger's home, checking into a brothel before I realised my mistake, or ending up escorted by Estonian border guards after our Australian Junior Orienteering team was suspected of trying to illegally cross the Estonian-Russian border.

But from the depths of their trust came a trust in myself, a deep-seated desire to know in my heart that I had done the best that I could, to prepare and perform with a quiet confidence that whispered, *You deserve to be here.*

I had taken no short cuts in training for my first Junior World Orienteering Championships in Estonia. For months before the trip I had clambered out of bed and instigated my own hard-swimming sessions, diving into the lanes alongside my old squad and pushing myself to a breathless fatigue. Swimming was still the language that I spoke when it came to physical preparedness, and it would be some years before I began to swap my bathers for running shoes in the mornings.

While my friends ate sandwiches or tuckshop lunches, during the school lunch hour I clambered into my running clothes and headed for the parklands, hills and sandy beaches surrounding Hobart, running alone until the clock told me I was out of time and my French teacher would be getting grumpier in my absence. Then I would sit quietly, munching my own sandwiches at the back of the class, hoping that the odour of chlorine emanating from my hot skin would not deter my friends.

Yes, when I embarked on that plane for Finland and then began to run using the training maps for the Junior World Orienteering Championships, I had quiet confidence that I was well prepared. But as I dodged through the dripping, damp undergrowth and pushed my way through neck-high fields of stinging nettles, I suddenly came to an almighty realisation of just how different the nature of orienteering was, overseas.

As a proud representative of the down-under over-there nation, and as a Tasmanian citizen who has to take a plane across water simply to reach the 'mainland', there are challenges everywhere if we are to reach the world championship level ready to match it with the world's best competitors. Coming from Australia, we eagerly board aircraft after aircraft, only to disembark in Europe with fat feet, lie restless at 2 am, eat dinner at midday, train for a short period in relevant terrain, and then come out hoping we are ready to compete against our friendly rivals. With such a vast world between us and the European hub of this complex sport, we are certainly the Down Under underdogs, and one of the least technically prepared nations.

For us, everything is back to front in Europe. Here I am not talking about dinner times or the direction of water spinning down the plughole, but rather the landscape. Our Australian landscape is ancient, harsh and unique. Our baking sun will parch an exposed patch of ground, making it nearly impossible for vegetation to grow. Through these areas we can run fast, dancing over the occasional log, skirting around boulders and through creek beds eroded by the summer storms that hit in drenching deluges. But this fast, open running never lasts. When we come into contact with our Aussie scrub, it is harsh and scratchy, tearing at our scarred knees, pressing thorns into our arms, and whipping us in a way that seems to torment us: 'Toughen up, princess!'

So we begin to resent it. Instead, we look for wider, clearer running options, loping amongst the scattered trees. Often the ground is stony. Barbed wire fences can block our passage. Eroded creeks can be deep, cliffs impassable, bracken neck-high and unrelenting. Yes, when I think of Australian terrain, I think grey, drab and messy. To make matters worse, to remain in sync with the European competition seasons and to avoid the heat of summer—and, with it, snakes—we orienteer during the winter. Frozen fingers clutching the map. Frosty paddocks. Cars belching steam in a soggy car park.

As Australians, when we arrive in the European landscape we are immediately struck by the greenery. Europe seems younger, richer and lusher. Exposure to sunlight and frequent precipitation usually causes plants to explode—especially nettles and young saplings. The sparser trunks, limited undergrowth and deciduous leaves that fall during a vibrant autumn create a soft, runnable carpet. European forests are often well managed, with branches trimmed and woodcutter tracks weaving through their rolling landscapes. Either this, or the forests feel ancient and untouched, as if they are maintained by pixies. Vast trees covered by green mosses while, beneath, the forest floor can be a carpet of wild blueberries, strawberries and raspberries. For us, this can feel like we have arrived in heaven, a landscape so lush and undeniably different. Grey to green. Scratchy to forgiving. Hard to soft.

Therein lies the challenge for us pale, wintered, Aussie orienteers.

When race day rolls around, we are driven from our hotels where pillows are square and dinner is served at lunchtime, out into the depths of a forest, to somewhere secretive and unknown. Here we finally dismount with inquisitive looks and a quiet whisper to our team coaches: 'Where are we?' We lie around on beach towels or cheap picnic rugs, swatting at mosquitoes and feeling the dampness seep out from the rich, moist earth. After warming up by running and crashing through a surrounding forest cordoned off from the rest of the forest by white flagging tape, we peer into the embargoed competition terrain before nervously squatting in rented portaloos while pretending we are not nervous. Then we are ready.

Heading towards the start line a coach inevitably tells us to have fun and, 'Good luck!' I hate that phrase. What does luck have to do with anything?

We literally pick up the race map on the start line, entering the forest at short intervals so that competitors cannot follow one another. Pressing through the timing gates we race off into the forest, spinning and folding the map as quickly as we can in an attempt to locate ourselves and our first control flag. By now, we are interpreting as much information as we can while running at close to full speed through the terrain. Orienteering courses rarely provide opportunities to follow man-made tracks, so instead we crash through the undergrowth, over hills and through creeks and marshes. From the bamboo of Japan to the chestnut forests of Switzerland and Italy; from the open eucalyptus bush of mainland Australia to the harsh, dense vegetation of Tasmania; from the alpine meadows of Bulgaria to the fells of Scotland; from the grounds of Prince Fredrik's summer palace to the intricate detail of an old village in England; we run through it all while spending most of our time glancing down at the map.

Naturally, mistakes happen. It is said that the world's most elite orienteers make the same number of mistakes as recreational athletes, but instead of feeling baffled for long, lonely minutes, the elite's mistakes usually only cost them mere seconds. That is, they quickly work out where they made a technical error in judgement, or lost accuracy while navigating, and within seconds can be back on their chosen pathway.

However, in these early, formative orienteering years, the precision required to be a top athlete eluded me. Like my father, I had a frustrating habit of navigating with near accuracy for most of the course, only to make one large error. Whether I was running the sprint-distance course for fifteen minutes, the middle-distance race for thirty minutes, or the long-distance test of endurance for eighty minutes, I would inevitably make a big, big mistake. In these moments, I ran like a squirrel, searching with no strategy, aimlessly scanning the forest for the red and white flag that marked the elusive control. Despite the best teachings of my coaches and mentors, I was too frightened to stop running, to take the time to carefully review the map and reposition myself. Luck sometimes saved me. And on the frequent occasions when it didn't, I would inevitability end up letting out a sigh and laying down my ego with the humbling realisation that if I didn't finally look at the map with logic, I may end up spending the rest of my days out there.

And therein lay my downfall in the Estonian forests and my first Junior World Orienteering Championships.

With the rain teeming down, our soggy coaches would approach the soggy finish line and enquire with soggy expressions, 'What happened?' I was young, fuelled by ego, and quick to find an excuse such as 'I didn't see the track' or 'the map was a little weird there'. I was not alone in these experiences. It is rare that an orienteer will have a clean, mistake-free run, especially at the international level. Even the competitors racing on home soil were entering the finish with soggy hearts, battered legs and welts from the stinging nettles growing rampant in the forests.

Australia is certainly a starkly different country and I was always quick to point the finger of blame at this. I was unaware of a deeper current that led to misjudgement and error—the pure and simple fact that I was too focused on results. I was too distracted by my own ego as well as the bright colours of the competitors as they streaked past, just too eager to get to the finish line. It would take me four years to master the art of honesty, patience and humility in orienteering, three important human qualities that I have come to believe are essential if you wish to perform at your greatest ability. That is, to perform wilder.

I AM SO glad that orienteering found me. When I tumbled back off the aircraft from Estonia with fifty-six hours of travel behind me, I carried in my piggy bank of experiences a new-found appreciation for the sport, and a modest result of sixty-second place in the long-distance race. Through the jet-lagged fog, I knew that this was simply the beginning. My heartstrings had been pulled so dramatically by this sport. From the rich friendships that I had made with team members from other countries, to the rolling, green landscapes with their ancient cultures; from the moments where it all came together and I thought, *I think I get this sport*, to the humbling moments when I felt so lost I wondered if I would ever make it to the finish, I loved every minute of those three weeks. I returned humbled and more focused for the next year's experiences. As my feet hit the tarmac and I began walking back to the terminal in the chilly winter evening, I was already longing to return to Europe. And, deep down, I knew I was capable of so much more.

When I had set off on my journey to Estonia, I had been a young woman insecure about her transition into the orienteering world. I still saw myself as a swimmer, and carried deep within me the insecurities about my growing body. Early on, I felt confused by the informal preparations of the orienteers, with their later nights, lack of stretching, and short warmups. I was perplexed by the small bars of chocolate they ate and the bottles of coke they sipped after training. However, by the time I returned home from Estonia, my insecurities with my body and the confusion I felt about food had quietened.

For the first time since my swimming coaches had insisted on our restrictive dieting, I felt a sense of freedom. I saw my body as a tool that I could playfully, amazingly, joyously train. I saw that it could lead me in the direction of my new-found dreams. I felt curious. Could I become as good as Martina Dockalova of the Czech Republic, who had won the gold medal in Estonia? Did I have that same potential? Finally, I felt freed from my own internal criticism, and open to the opportunities. No-one other than myself expected anything of me, and I finally felt ready to fly.

When the new day dawned, I felt heavy with jet lag. And yet I was eager to begin my preparations for Poland the following year. While the European athletes were preparing to tug on their beanies and delve into autumn as it heralded winter, I was shedding the thermals and reaching for my running singlet. For many of my competitors and new-found friends, their stomping grounds would soon become hard-packed with ice and deep snow, causing running shoes to be tucked into the back of the gear cupboard and skis to be dragged out of hiding. Here lay my opportunity for a head start. While they would come to crave the sunshine and running shoes, I would crave big glasses of water after another tough training session. It was this single fact that helped me rise each morning from the cocoon of my warm bed. I was a girl on a new mission, an athlete humbled by experience and knowledge, and driven by curiosity. Just how far could I go?

When the new year rolled around, and with further domestic results to confirm my personal ambitions, I entered the local news agency and bought myself a new diary. Turning to the front page, I carefully wrote, 'LONG TERM GOAL: To WIN the Junior World Orienteering Championships in my last year (2006)'. The pathway was set.

I had three years, the perfect training environment, and only improvements to make. What could possibly go wrong?

6

I was sitting in the back of a Volvo station wagon, surrounded by a sea of Volvos. Sweden. Home to cinnamon scrolls, Volvos and orienteering. I tilted my head back onto the headrest, closed my eyes, and wondered for the umpteenth time, *What am I doing here?*

Beyond the car, I heard the *'hoola hoola oola uulla'* of the singsong Swedish tongue, knowing only too well that the individuals behind it would be stripped down to their bikinis and soaking up the fifteen-degree summer sunshine, their gumboots and plastic flip-flops the only other items remaining on their blonde-haired, blue-eyed, brown-skinned bodies. In the distance, I could hear the speaker excitedly calling in the other runners as they stampeded in from the deep, heavy heather of the Gothenburg conifer forests: *'hoola hoola oola uulla.'* I heard the cheers of the thousands of other runners now spectating from the shade of their club's marquee tents, *'hoola hoola oola uulla … Christian! hoola hoola oola uulla … Sophia!'*

I opened my eyes and looked down at my map, still unable to work out exactly where it had all gone so dramatically wrong. Sitting there in my national orienteering kit, holes in my clothes where the dense undergrowth had grabbed and yanked while I pushed and heaved my way through the thick awfulness, I asked myself for the second time, 'What am I doing here?'

I had arrived on Swedish soils four months ago. Finally free from school, and with a whole year to play, I had decided to learn the art of orienteering from the nation most at home with their maps and compasses. I travelled via northern Poland where the Junior World Orienteering Championships had just been staged, and then Denmark for my debut on the national senior team at the World Cup. In this moment I was based in Gothenburg, Sweden, where I was trying to learn the finest brushstrokes of orienteering. However, I felt like I was drawing stick figures, in a sea of blondness and orienteering frenzy.

Sweden hosts some of the largest orienteering events in the world. O-Ringen, a five-day carnival which hosts up to 25,000 competitors who live in tents and orienteering shoes for the entire period, had been my induction. I recalled jumping on a competitor bus from the sprawling campground and watching in awe through foggy windows as we drove through endless lines of tents, camper vans and waving club flags that formed the sprawling campground. I couldn't help but think how like a refugee camp it looked, with kilometres upon kilometres of tents, hosting orienteers whose hearts were held hostage by this unique sport —displaced by a desire to navigate through foreign forests.

On arrival at a car park somewhere on the outskirts of the city, we had marched towards the event's assembly area in a stream of eager runners. I had finally popped over a hill only to feel a gasp escape, my knees buckle, and my jaw drop open. Below me had lain a sprawl of colour, a finish chute the size of an airport runway, and a showering facility filled with thousands of naked bodies. In later years, when I thought of orienteering in Scandinavia it would be the showers that came to mind first. Introduced because of a necessity to quickly look for forest ticks that can carry disease, I am sure they are also a cultural tradition, a warm delight after returning damp and muddy from the depths of the forests. I am sure that the organisers of O-Ringen had not considered the placement of this important cultural tradition when they had stoked up piping-hot wood fires to pump water to hundreds of garden hoses that would drench the white-bottomed, sun-tanned bodies beautifully on show.

I had orienteered dismally at this event. And in every training session with my adopted local orienteering club since. My first senior World Orienteering Championships were inching ever closer, and I had spent more time getting lost and walking home with a heavy heart than navigating like a professional.

Each day in Gothenburg, I clambered from my bed, grabbed a map, and ran towards the forest that lay on our doorstep—just like nearly every home in Sweden. There, the forests were open to anyone. Camping, running, hiking, riding … so long as you respected the neighbouring properties you could literally go everywhere. And everywhere I went, although not always as planned! Each day, I returned home for breakfast with soggy shoes and a soggy heart.

I had been excited to arrive at this beautiful, traditional Scandinavian home with its Ikea-style decor. I had been emotionally prepared to take up the reigns as a nanny and serve the needs of an infant (or young, budding orienteer). However, I quickly learnt that there were no small feet, blonde mops of hair or need to make fairy bread. I was the proud au pair to a young couple in their mid-thirties … with no children! Instead of holding sticky hands and playing in sandpits, I spent my days clipping their hedge, trimming their lawn, washing their clothes and filling their fridge with cheese, yoghurt and fresh bread. When there were no more chores to do, I would head for the forests, and lie by another peaceful lake with my new orienteering friends. Until the evening rolled around. Then we would drive the short distance back to the clubhouse, change into our not-so-trendy orienteering attire, and join the throngs of local orienteers on another training session. Or 'exercise in getting lost' as it had become for me. In plain language, I was in big, big trouble!

After one particular evening where I had found myself literally swimming through a marshy pond while my clubmates gaily ran around the edge, my host, Fredrik, pulled me aside. 'Hanny, I think I need to teach you how to orienteer in Sweden.'

So, with mere weeks before the opening ceremony of the World Championships, we roamed the forests together, learning to look, scan, read and interpret the Swedish terrain. Later, as a reward for my rapidly improving skills, we drove to another forest with another lake and slid kayaks into the water, paddling for hours in the never-ending daylight of a summer's day.

However, here I was, bundled despondently into the back of my host's Volvo, wondering how to break the news to Fredrik—'I got lost … again!'

I departed for the World Championships the next day. I knew deep down that I needed to face reality. Orienteering in Sweden was a whole new level of difficulty. If I was to race with any dignity for my country, then I needed to up my A-Game. I tugged my training diary from my kitbag and grabbed a pen. 'Goals for World Championships' I scribed in careful letters. I paused, chewed my pen and watched as an older male dropped his pants next to me, baring his bleached bottom to tug on fresh undies. Nonchalantly, I turned back to my diary. '1. Not make any major errors. Walk if I have to!' By then, my neighbour's wife was tugging off her orienteering top, removing her bra and leaving generously sagging breasts exposed as she pulled on her bikini top. '2. Compass, compass, compass!' My neighbours were now sitting on camping chairs at the foot of their Volvo, the boot open, cinnamon scrolls and a hot thermos emitting steam into the not-so-warm summer morning. '3. Fake it till you make it. Continuously smile!' I am not sure why I felt that this last goal was so important, nor where the inspiration came from. But watching my new Volvo companions pore over their maps with excited *'hoola hoola oola uulas'* and wave cheerily at the bikini bodies gaily walking back to their own Volvos, I knew there must be some secret within the smiles.

In my mind's eye, I flicked my 'Did Not Finish' result from that day into the 'Do Not Care' bucket. I felt repurposed. I felt empowered. *Walk, compass and smile.* Now I had a plan. Little did I know that I had just tapped into a great secret! I now call this: race with discipline and just have fun!

I HAVE COME to believe that when we are faced with no other option than to overcome adversity, we can rise above it to perform at our best. In this moment, our ego has been stripped away to reveal a humility that can now breathe life into patience and deep carefulness. When we remove the ego, and pressure of personal or external expectations, we are only left with opportunity.

This is how I raced in Sweden. Remarkably, I thrived at the Swedish World Orienteering Championships, hosted near Vesterus.

When I reflect back on the photos from this World Championship, I see 'Happy Hanny' with her broad smiles, teenage excitement and athletic prowess. In Sweden, I strode through the finish chute in the eleven-kilometre long-distance race to finish twenty-fourth, the highest ranked non-European female. I also brought my relay team up to fourth place, where we remained in medal contention until the final minutes of the race. I then returned home with a new-found respect for the sport which had captivated me so strongly over the last two years.

And yet, this very same freedom and quiet independence made returning home to the family cocoon a challenge. In many ways, this was the moment when I flew the nest. However, sadly, it also created a momentary, small divide between my mother and me. As she excitedly tried to fold me back into the family, I could feel my inner teenager tugging away, seeking the space to continue to spread my wings. Neither of us knew how to communicate our needs. Neither of us knew how to look each other in the eye and say, 'I love you, but …' So instead, we drifted with some tension, because not speaking had always been the easiest option, and it was the way us Allstons always bumbled through our emotions.

During this period, I often used a pair of shoes and an open road as my emotional and physical outlet. Running became not just something that I loved, but it became the place where I found 'me time'. The rhythmic process of one foot in front of the other, the light sweating, the quiet head, became an almost meditative place, so that on my return to the house I could more calmly express myself, focus on my studies, and mature as a person.

And, thankfully, my mother and I passed through the initial tango, and once again into a healthy space of close friendship which continued to evolve into something beautiful. She began to accompany me on a bike on many of my training runs, rolling around the hills and valleys of Sandfly as I slowly stretched my wings further and further afield. By then, I finally felt like I had shed my fish fins for a runner's feet. I felt bouncier and freer as I ran on the wide gravel roads and through the apple orchards of the Huon Valley. I no longer felt like an outsider. I was thriving, doing activities that I loved and that heightened my sense of being a free spirit.

As friendships continued to grow with new trail running companions, I began to adopt a new set of beliefs that I too could run longer and faster, just like them. I finally felt capable of turning up each Saturday morning to run with others, mostly males, and to explore the plethora of trails on our doorstep at Mt Wellington. Thanks to their boundless enthusiasm and masculine banter, I found myself signing up to the Cradle Mountain Ultra Run, as the youngest competitor ever to complete this eighty-two kilometre trail run through the heart of the Tasmanian mountains.

I WAS MOVING my way down into the valley, following in the footfalls of the male athlete in front of me, our head torches bouncing in the early morning darkness. Amongst the crowd were my trail-running companions, as eager and excitable as ever. Faintly, framed by a glowing starscape, I could see the silhouette of Cradle Mountain, her towering dolerite columns reaching down to join the plateau.

We ran towards her, a snake of dancing torches entering deep gullies beneath ancient pencil pines. I was only too aware of the knot of fear I held inside me. Once I had embarked on that crazy event, there was absolutely no 'out' until I reached the northern shores of Lake St Clair in around sixty-five kilometres. From there, I would still have a further twenty kilometres of rooted, rolling trails to run, beneath ageing rainforests clasped in the protective grasp of Mt Olympus, until I reached the finish line—a literal boot-scrape across the gravel, at the visitor centre which marked the southern-most point of the track. The national park that encompasses Cradle Mountain through to Lake St Clair is wild and relatively remote. The trail runs north-to-south along the length of Tasmania's mountainous spine, framed by a plethora of peaks that protect her from any roads or urban civilisation that might enter her pristine beauty.

As the hills became steeper and the skies lighter, we dropped to a hike to conserve energy, hands pressed down onto thighs, packs swaying with the motion of one foot in front of the other. We hiked around glistening hanging lakes and finally up onto the plateau alongside Cradle Mountain herself. From there, her sheer dolerite columns presented a jagged saw-tooth across the sky. I slipped and caught myself on low shrubs as I traversed the open, rocky plateaus under a brilliant sunrise. Black ice lay on the narrow, train-track boardwalks, and their gently downward slope made this early stage of the trail akin to a giant luge track. We giggled and gibed at those unfortunate individuals who slipped, bumbled and then slid into the surrounding bushes. I loved being amongst these guys. Their home-modified backpacks, floppy hats, well-loved footwear and sloshing bottles all suggested hardcore adventure seekers. There would be no fame and fortune at the end of this long eighty-two kilometres down the Overland Track, here in Tasmania's beating heart. Rather, we were running enchanted by a pure love affair with mountains, wild trails and curiosity. *What am I capable of?*

Ahead of me, Dave was dancing along the trail, his stuffed monkey also dancing a lone jig as it hung from the back of his homemade backpack. That was not the first time his monkey had traversed this famous trail. Rather, Dave and his monkey were old timers, well-known by the locals hosting the event, and well-loved by all of us—a slightly motley group of eager Tasmanians.

As I cruised toward the back of this little pack that had formed, and marvelled at the kilometres ticking past with relative effortlessness, I wondered at what point the wheels might fall off. The sun shimmered onto silent cobwebs, and I danced in my own body.

I swerved as Dave suddenly pulled over to the side, exposing the path now visibly curving off into the distance. 'Right, Hanny, you shouldn't be behind me now. Get a wriggle along and test the waters of your potential out here.'

I was confused, humbled and taken aback. So I tentatively stepped forwards, and soon found myself setting the pace. The trail snaked its way beneath tightly curved, gnarled beech trees, their deciduous leaves long fallen to form a carpet across the black Tasmanian soils. Then we popped out into the open button-grass plains where small pockets of mist hung like a blanket above the grasslands. Breaths rose and fell. Mist lingered with a splash of sunshine. And all the while, the trail flowed downwards, a tumble of roots and rocks, earthen banks on one side and then a drop down to somewhere far below us on the other.

Into Frog Flats I ran. Knee-deep mud and a river crossing greeted me, before I placed my hands on my thighs and began the long grind back up the other side to the halfway point in the track—a lone hikers' hut on the edge of an open plain, with sweeping views to falling mountains that steal your breath away.

It wasn't until I heard the vocal cheers of two volunteers sitting on a flat piece of boardwalk with a bag of jelly snakes, ticking off our numbers one by one as we passed, that I realised I was alone on the trail. As I waved them goodbye, a mouth full of sugar and a heart full of apprehension, I looked around at the looming dolerite columns of Mount Oakleigh, suddenly feeling a very long way from home.

Crossing a stream, I dropped to a walk and then a halt, sinking to my knees to fill my bottles from its fast moving, pristine waters. Despite the fatigue now beginning to show, I had never felt more alive, nor more certain that I was doing exactly what I needed to be doing. I had spent the day running alone down a wild trail, watching the mountains change in hue as the sun travelled perpendicular to my path, transecting the sky from east to west.

Standing beside the rivulet, I took an extra moment to pull another Cherry Ripe from my pack, tearing at the shiny packaging until the slightly squashed and distorted chocolate bar revealed itself. I began to run again, and when I found my rhythm once more, I stuffed the sweet treat into my mouth, curling my nose as the sweetness enveloped me. For a few minutes, I was gasping for breaths and trying to avoid inhaling the fine pieces of cherry-flavoured coconut. Reflecting back, I can't help but wonder, what was I thinking?!

The discomfort finally passed, and I weaved my way through the gentler gradients of the final ten kilometre stretch into Lake St Clair, only too aware that I felt somewhat parched, with sweat crusting into a fine white powder around my face. The track discoed in a shimmer of dappled light and dappled shade. The dry sclerophyll forests had taken the place of the rainforests. The mountains were still present—a blue silhouette on the further horizons—and the valley was widening, an open hug compared to the tight squeeze of the enveloping forests I had left behind. Sixty-five kilometres into the Cradle Mountain Ultra Race, and I was running with instinct and moving in tune with the rhythmic rise and fall of my Nike-clad, mud-caked shoes. I was ultra-running.

Rowdy cheers greeted me as I popped out into the clearing of Narcissus, a small hikers' hut nestled into the low tea-tree bushes surrounding the northern end of Lake St Clair. I could not see the water from here, but I could sense its presence, and was excited by the knowledge that I only had twenty kilometres to go. Volunteers had made the pilgrimage up the lake by a small boat to be there. Bringing with them tubs of homemade Anzac cookies, vast chunks of watermelon, and bottles of coke, which were laid out for us. A few weary hikers loitered in the shade of the huts' eaves. I wasn't sure who had overcome the greatest challenges to be here—they who had carried heavy packs for six days, or me with my mud-caked running shoes and Anzac cookies stuck between my teeth.

From behind, I was suddenly rugby tackled by loving arms. I spun around to find my brother, my father, and my Swedish friend, Frippe. After a quick hug and a high-five, I set off on the final twenty kilometres of trail. I felt exhilarated, knowing that I had already run more than twice the furthest distance I had ever run before, and also knowing that I got to share these remaining stretches with the boys.

As I ran, and occasionally dropped to an uphill plod, Dad told stories of hiking days in these exact mountains with Mum during their early years in Tasmania. Frippe fed me Swedish cinnamon scrolls and whimpered with jet lag. All the while, my brother huffed and puffed like an excited puppy dog. We were an eclectic bunch, united in the moment, and each batting off a level of fatigue appropriate to our levels of preparation. We reminisced about our Christmas holidays swimming in the nearby lakes under unexpected snowfall, and that occasion when Dad dislocated his shoulder climbing out of a waterfall.

As we rounded another bend, lumbered over another hill, ducked beneath another fallen log and looked yet again towards the horizon and the hopeful sight of the southern shores of the lake, we met the familiar gait of my mother. She was jogging ahead of us along a section of smooth gravel. As we closed in on her, the groomed surface provided a welcome relief from the slippery, higgledy-piggledy roots of the trails around the lake. Hearing the chorus of footfalls behind her, my mother spun around and let out an enormous squeal of excitement. She dashed towards me, wrapping me in a sweaty hug. She is my number one fan … and I hers. I allowed myself to absorb her spirit, my head sinking wearily onto her broad shoulders, and in that moment of normality amidst an abnormal day, I had my first experience of the strength of love during challenging times.

Somehow, in the seventy-nine kilometres I had traversed in the prelude to that moment, I had formed a bubble around myself. I had run, shielded by this bubble, finding a capacity to block out the external thoughts and fears to instead focus only on acting in the moment. Within this bubble I was protected from thoughts of results, competitors and pain. It was my protection and, as I would find out in time, a signature feature of my racing style.

However, as I pulled myself from my mother's grasp, I felt my protective walls crumbling. It was like she had taken a pin to a balloon, and my bubble burst, spattering physical and emotional discomfort all over the trail. My walls had burst magnificently around me, and yet I was willed onwards by my family's enthusiasm.

'You are nearly there, Han! The finish is just around that next corner.'

So, on I plodded, eyes brimming with tears, only too aware of the excruciating pain of my pack shifting across the raw, chafed skin of my back, my bruised feet, my wooden muscles. I ached all over, inside and out, and as I rounded the corner ready to tumble to the ground in relief I was confronted by another long, straight stretch of trail bending into the distance.

'Oh, um ... the next corner. Come on, Han! You are nearly there!'

So, I gritted my teeth and stumbled onwards, biting my lower lip and breathing deeply through my nose. This was survival. As I rounded the next corner, I let out a wail of frustration, for ahead stretched another long length of gravel trail.

And so the pattern continued. Mum egging me on, Dad gripping tightly at my hand, my brother's calming presence right behind me. We moved as a family, one unit, united in their search for the elusive finish line ... for three seemingly endless kilometres! I approached the finish line. 'This will make everything after this feel easy!'

Crossing the finish line, I was offered a congratulatory handshake, a bucket of hot chips, and a fifty-cent coin: 'Enjoy the shower on us!' On this one long day out, I became the youngest competitor to complete that event, finishing fourth overall and just missing the women's record set by Helene Diamantides—a British athlete proclaimed to be one of the greatest ever female long-distance runners in the history of the British Fell Running scene.

Mum helped to peel my mud-caked shoes and socks off my shrivelled feet, and placed them directly into the rubbish bin by the wash basins. With each bend and stretch, my body convulsed with cramp. I could not believe I was standing there in the cold campground shower block at Lake St Clair—eighty-two kilometres and ten hours from the beginning of the trail at Cradle Mountain.

I was eighteen years old, and suddenly only too aware of the opportunities I couldn't wait to run towards. The familiar black line of the swimming pool seemed a world ago, and yet I was just so grateful for the leap-start that those disciplined, chlorinated days provided me. While I still had so much to learn about the art of running, I had finally found a world where my strengths could be harnessed, my weaknesses exposed, and my enthusiasm for wilder adventures could blossom.

I had all the willingness in the world to learn from the wise elders of this sport. The trail had shown me both possibility and humility. It highlighted that I was ready to step closer to my dreams, to stand at their feet and marvel at their beauty. Thriving during that long day in the mountains, I became an avid believer that when I set my mind to something that truly makes my toes tingle, even if it is of greater magnitude than I believe possible, anything is achievable.

The following week, as I returned to training at Lower Sandy Bay, I was greeted by the mighty handshake of Max, my coach for the past twelve months. At eighty years of age, he bent the norms and our spirits to create champions. He willed me to lace up my shoes and hop straight back into it. I did not question him. Max did not allow us to rest on our laurels. Successes were fleeting, something we shook hands over and then got on with the 'what next?' This consistent pushing forwards was not foreign to me, thanks to my background in swimming, and my willingness to go onwards and upwards only confirmed that I was willing to do whatever it took to be the best athlete that I could be … perhaps even the best athlete in the world?

However, the following weekend I walked in a daze through the button-grass plains near Cockle Creek in the very far south of Tasmania. Trailing my parents, I tripped more than I danced, catching my toes, and feeling a fatigue greater than any fatigue I had ever experienced before. It weighed me down, making progress along the trail painstakingly slow. As we finally crested the dunes and padded down towards the wild, windswept stretches of South Cape Bay, I dropped to my bottom and then lay back onto the firm white sand. Within minutes, I was asleep, oblivious to the hours and hours that passed by until the beach lost its sun and a deep chill consumed me. Never had I napped so intensely or deeply. My parents clambered to their feet with me and, together, the three of us retraced our steps. A mother, a father, and their daughter bumbling along behind them, dreaming of orienteering in Europe in just five months' time.

IN MY EARLY days in the sports of running and orienteering, I knew so little about the science of training, nutrition and recovery. While I was well aware that there were no short cuts, I became more and more convinced that playing harder and with more purpose, seeking opportunities to feel wild and excitable, and surrounding myself with individuals who inspired me had to be the best way. I appeared to have a body that was capable of coping with these large running loads, and I think my early love of swimming had become a secret weapon for me. I could use my swimming to continue training on the days when my legs needed a reprieve. Furthermore, my early years of gym training, running before swimming sessions, and long hours in the pool had gifted me a very strong, athletic body.

I still rose early each day, no longer lying in bed to watch Dad's lantern-light dance across my bedroom wall. I tugged on my running shoes, made my way up onto the gravel road and crunched gently down the hill, the dawn light only just bright enough to prevent me from falling into the gaping potholes. The world felt sleepy around me, the curtains of Ashling and Ciara's house still drawn tight, only the faintest of puffs of smoke emanating from the house on the corner. Each morning as I rounded the bend onto the slightly larger Halls Track Road, I leant into the effort of the hill, preparing myself to maintain a constant effort until the road breached the shadows of the forest onto the upper plateaus of the dairy farm. From here, often sheathed by a blanket of heavy grey clouds, the flanks of Mt Wellington could be seen.

Careful not to wake the heel-nipping terrier, I tiptoed on the grass beside that house, and then broke back into a run, building and building the effort until I reached the steep uphill climb towards the Herringback lookout—a hill protruding from amongst slightly lower hills, with an electrical tower carefully placed where a more natural summit once lay. Just as I had done all those years ago while riding Mum's bike during my brother's saxophone lessons, each time I crested the steep rise I paused to absorb my surroundings: the vast fertile plains of the Huon Valley spreading below me, and the Mt Wellington and Sleeping Beauty skyline dominant to the north. I made a wish, an inspired vocalisation of my inner dreams, before darting back through sneaky forest short cuts to home. Then, breakfast around the family dining table, commuting and medical studies.

Eat, study, sleep, repeat.

Three evenings a week, I joined Max Cherry's squad. Tempo running along the Hobart foreshores, running long hill repetitions as he drove beside us, or being whipped into action on the track. Somehow, my little legs played the game. On weekends, I mixed this training with orienteering practice, or long runs around the confusion of unmarked hiking trails on Mt Wellington. And when my legs screamed 'enough is enough!' I dug out my bathers, dusted off my bicycle, or asked for a lift to the gym. I became leaner and meaner, running along a knife-edge of physical preparation while living the life of a medical student.

My pockets remained as empty as some students', too. This was not intentional, nor was it due to a love of Wednesday, Friday and Saturday night partying with the other first-year medical students. Quite to the contrary, I was a squirrel, pocketing every penny I earned during my summer, as a bushwalking guide and casual retail assistant at Paddy Pallin—the upmarket outdoor, travel and camping store in Hobart. I loved the anticipation before a tour began, standing in the departure room, maps and beautiful photographs adorning the walls, stuffing emergency equipment and delicious delights for the guests into our huge rucksacks. Every guide was an energetic, like-minded character. We eagerly discussed who our guests might be, and how we hoped that they would want to climb the mountains with us.

For five summers, I guided guests through the length of the Freycinet Peninsula and Maria Island National Park over four days. Early in the mornings, I rose well before the other guides and guests, and tiptoed out along the camp's boardwalks to the beach, where I could break into a gentle stride along the dampness of the low-tide lines. Even when my legs were heavy from carrying huge packs all day, I loved the sensation of floating relatively weightless along the sand before stripping off, jumping into the chilly ocean waters and then racing back to camp to deliver mugs of steaming hot tea and coffee to the guests still tucked up in their glamorous semi-permanent cabins. These are still some of my fondest employment memories. It was always a bit of a let-down to return to the urban environment at the conclusion of each trip.

I also loved my employment at Paddy Pallin. Unable to drive, and unwilling to impose on my parent's needs, after my morning training session I frequently rode the twenty-one kilometres up and over Mt Wellington to work. On some occasions, Graham, a higher lever employee than I, would join me on the ride. Driving from his parents' house in Snug, he would pull up in his white Subaru station wagon at the Sandfly General Store, drag out his mountain bike, and pedal alongside me up the mountain, each of us sharing stories of adventures. His background in elite ski instructing around the world fascinated me, and I loved how he had been able to turn this love affair with snow sports into a career. Between winter seasons, he returned home to Tasmania to also join the guiding and outdoor-retail industry, pocketing his pennies until the time came when the mountains became blanketed in white powder and his toes began to tingle.

When we ran out of stories, we pipe-dreamed about running our own businesses. 'Imagine what we could do if the retail store was ours!' Little did either of us realise that five years later our paths would once again cross, and that another four years beyond this we would be standing in our own little retail store, surrounded by our dreams with a massive gamble on our hands.

By the end of every summer, I was a super-blonde, tanned athlete, hair wilder from the endless swimming, and my bank balance just capable of funding my orienteering and medical endeavours. As long as I could board that plane to Europe, a bag of medical textbooks in tow, then I knew I was heading in the right direction.

BEYOND THE RUNNING, I was also aware that I was taking a different approach to performance in my main sport of orienteering. This was partly due to being isolated from the hubs of my sport, on mainland Australia and Europe further afield. However, it was also due to my intense desire not to waste opportunities. Thanks to living in Gothenburg in Sweden, and being exposed to one of the most technical orienteering locations in Europe, I had learnt how to navigate without my ego. I had also experienced the heaviness that continual orienteering in terrain gives to your physical body, and was excited to be able to return to my home state of Tasmania to enjoy the plethora of athletic and trail running opportunities on offer. I know for certain that this love of running, and ability to train as an athlete all year round, gave me the edge on my European competitors, who had to grapple with skis and snow-running in winter.

I was sure that in the prelude to the 2004 World Orienteering Championships in Sweden, my blond-haired, blue-eyed clubmates wondered who on earth this small, equally blonde Australian girl was, and how on earth she was going to survive competition week.

And yet I did, returning home one-hundred and twenty percent, heart-over-head committed to my dream of becoming a Junior World Champion. Thereafter, at every state and national training camp I finished every session on offer, usually finding myself running alone, or hot on the heels of the men. Whenever I had the opportunity, I pulled aside the coaches that I really respected and asked them to tear apart my performance, looking for any little tidbit that I could use to find improvements. I documented all of this in my training journals, using my weaknesses as goals for the next session or event, writing these on the back of my hand in black pen so that I could hold myself accountable when I entered the grey, scraggly Australian forests.

When I began to feel stale on my local maps, I began to ask Anthony, who I believed to be the greatest technician in the sport of orienteering, if I could come to visit him in Canberra. In return for undertaking babysitting duties and for helping to prepare dinners, he would take me out into his local bushland riddled with spider webs. There he would run behind me for hours—my shadow, my mentor. He was never one to let laziness or fatigue be an excuse for sloppy navigation or compass errors. Under his tuition I rapidly improved, until I finally broke boldly onto the senior stage.

Simultaneously, I began to see results in my running. I had gone from being a participant to being a competitor, finding myself hot on the heels of my training partner, Commonwealth Games steeplechase representative and mother-on-a-comeback, Donna MacFarlane. Whipped into compliance and self-belief by Max Cherry, I gritted my teeth and realised personal best after personal best on the athletics track. I slowly became aware that my running times were now as competitive as my orienteering competitors in the senior leagues of Europe. I was loving life, thriving under the new challenges, and using my physical fitness as a buffer to my slowly improving navigation.

However, deep down, I knew that if I wanted to realise my ultimate dreams, then I needed to become more than just a runner. Even though I had improved, my navigation was still my weakest link. It would take me a number of years and life's harshest lessons to pull me up to the final tier of my sport. Little did I know that this lesson was just around the corner.

The perfect storm was brewing, and it harboured lessons that would ultimately change my life and athletic approach forever.

7

I sat opposite my competitors as we were shipped in army trucks with curved canopy sides, flapping open at the rear of the vehicle. The noise of traffic echoed through the dark tunnel. Through the gap, I watched flashes of vehicle headlights as we tore through this single-lane concrete road construction at top, European-style speeds. The fumes were nauseating as we literally moved beneath the mountains.

Eventually, we popped into daylight again, and through our rear cubbyhole we watched valleys give way to rolling green pastures which in turn transitioned into open forests. Up and up we climbed, the vehicle's diesel engine releasing guttural grunts, stalls and revs as it bounced, bumped, lurched and then groaned its way around the single, snaking gravel road. Up and up. Through the forests we saw glimmers of sunlight marking an open patch in the vegetation, and then the occasional rocky cliff or small boulder. But as we disembarked from the vehicle near the top of the towering mountain, like dazed cattle arriving at auction, we gazed around us in perplexity. 'Where are we?'

I was excited to be there. I was ready to be there.

For hours the night before, I lay on my bed after the excitement of the opening races—in which I had qualified as one of the top three fastest competitors for finals that day. In the quietness of my room, after the socialising and team activities were done, I had pulled my journal from my race bag, and gone through all the what-if scenarios that could occur during the final. What if my shoelace breaks? What if I get caught by a competitor? What if I make a mistake? What if I catch other competitors? What if I hear the commentary? Golly gosh, what happens if I think I am winning?

By the time I was standing on the start line I knew I was ready. I wanted to be there. And I believed I was thoroughly prepared and deserved to be there. All those tough running sessions with Max back home. The endless hill repeats and three-kilometre repetitions on the athletics track. All the extra morning runs I had snuck in before beginning my day at medical college. The tighter focus on nutrition. The early nights. The solo runs from a remote sheep paddock with an orienteering map.

The starter's clock beeped.

Yes, I was ready. And yet, as I reflected one last time on my goals for the day—*compass, carefulness, focus only on me*—and as I picked up my map as one of the last competitors into the forest and a hot favourite in this Junior World Orienteering Championship final, I came face-to-face with a television camera. The cameraman poked his lens at my face and began running backwards, eager to catch any cracks in my race focus. Then he began to run after me, crashing behind me like a baby elephant. I felt trapped. I felt cornered. I felt exposed. So, I ran, and ran, and ran …

Finally, I was alone, running at top speed with the young saplings lashing my arms, legs and face. I hadn't yet looked properly at the map. My alarm bells rang. I knew I must stop. Then I saw the red and white of a control flag and I darted towards it, hoping against hope that it was mine. But when I reached it, I felt my heart sinking into the depths of my tightly laced orienteering shoes. It was not mine … I began to run wildly in circles. *This cannot be happening!* And then I saw her, a flash of red and white, a fellow competitor, and soon we were running wildly together. And then we saw the blue and yellow of someone else, and bit by bit a small pack of girls formed, each running wildly in the hope that the other competitors knew where they were going.

So, finally, I stopped. I took three big breaths and studied the map intensely. I knew that my mentor back home, Anthony, would be disappointed by my lack of discipline. As I settled, things began to slot into place. I focused step by step on navigating cleanly to my next control.

The pack chased me down, and then we were running quicker and quicker, leaping like deer over small cliffs, sliding and scraping down through the dense leaf litter. Thorns from the fallen chestnuts pierced through our clothing and into flesh, and yet that was a pain I could not feel. I was so intensely focused on maintaining contact with the map and these girls that I was unaware of anything happening to or around me.

Thankfully, I had run smoothly through the remaining controls, and soon popped out at the base of the mountain into an open field. From here, I became vaguely aware of the commentary, and the familiar cries of the famous commentator, Per Forsberg. 'And she is so good, she is so good. But no, NO! She is late. She is too late … I think.'

As I began the most relentless dash around the exposed fields, the mountains then behind me, I became aware of my name. 'Haaannny Allstonnnn. I think she is too late! I think she cannot take the bronze medal. This will be SO close!'

I was running with a wild heart and a burning desire that stemmed from a place we rarely access as adults. I was mounting the steep stairs for the wooden bridge that had been purposely built to cross the freeway with its fleeting cars and trucks far below. And then I was entering the final four-hundred-metre-long sprint for the finish. 'For sure! This is the gold medallist and the silver medallist. But the question is, can Haaannyy Allstonnnnn fight for the bronze?'

In one final, desperate surge, I lunged for the finish line, hitting the ground hard and feeling the mown straw scrape across my bare arms. The race was an illogical, messy blur. A run that had played out so differently from my carefully thought-through plan. I had not predicted the distraction of the television camera stampeding behind me at the beginning, and had allowed panic and ego to disrupt my discipline.

However, as I lay there on the ground, straw clinging to my hair and teammates crowding around me, I was a bronze medallist by five seconds.

As I sat in the doping control a short-time later, looking up at the mountains which we had just descended, the paramedics moved from one athlete to another, poking needles at stubborn chestnut thorns lodged into our hands and backsides. One by one, the athletes disappeared into the small portable toilet before returning with brightly coloured urine samples. And once the paperwork was completed, they disappeared with their team chaperones, heading home to prepare for the next races.

Eventually, I was the final one sitting there. My mother and father loitered just outside, waiting to take me back to my accommodation to join my teammates. And yet I could not pee. Whether through the nerves of my first drug test, the stress of the day, or dehydration, I felt bottled up and unable to release the vast volumes of fluids that I had just drunk. But eventually I was able to squeeze just enough into a small beaker, awkward under the observation of watchful eyes, and yet grateful to finally be free. The organisers were already packing up the finish chute.

I grabbed my bunch of sunflowers presented to me at the flower ceremony, and rushed to my parents. We walked gratefully as a family in the direction of their hire car. Only then did the flood of emotion begin. I fought back the tears of confusion and gratitude. I had made the podium, and I had one more year to go two places better! And then there was a second flood forming. I darted for the trees and felt Niagara Falls flood into the soils of the paddock, then serving as an empty car park. As I returned to the vehicle, all I could think was, *I am not proud of the execution of that race, but … I did it!*

TWO WEEKS later I returned home from summery Switzerland to a dark, wintry farm. When I got up for my early morning run, frost held tightly to every surface of the valley. As I ran across paddocks then up gravel roads to the head of the valley, ice sparkled under the torch's beam. Running through dawn, nose dripping, eyes watering, I mentally rehearsed my anatomy. *Femurs provide boney strength, quadriceps provide power on the uphill, innervated by the femoral nerve. Foot dorsiflexes as it lifts off the ground, then plantarflexes as it lands again.*

I returned home to my medical examinations, rolling off the plane one day and into the anatomy room with its cadavers the next. Each evening, after the day's medical exam was complete, I returned to our silent farmhouse tucked into the steep-sided valley.

Fear was my co-pilot in these dark weeks leading up to the 2005 World Championships in Japan. I was a runner by morning, a medical student by day, a farmer by evening … and a hot, sweaty, acclimatising orienteer at night. Mum and Dad were still travelling in Europe, and my brother was now living in close proximity to the university in Hobart. I pulled into the carport, felt my way down the dark sandstone steps to the front door, flicked on the light switch in our vast kitchen and stoked up the fire. Grabbed my gumboots, and traipsed up to the barn, breathing in the smell of hay and the steaming compost heaps destined to fertilise Dad's veggie garden. As I reached the stable—an old, converted pickers' cottage—I opened wide the double doors. First the left-hand stable for the horses, then the right-hand side for the cows. I wandered down through the muddy paddocks, gumboots slapping on the backs of my calves. I found our eager Jersey cows in companionship with Humphry the horse. As I opened the gate, I quickly stood aside as they barged through and then charged up the hill, udders wobbling, hoofs pawing through the soft, fertile soils. I quickly threw a few handfuls of grain to the chickens, and squelched back up to the stable, peeled open a few portions of hay for the crew, and then pulled closed their stable gate. Tucked in, safe, home.

Back inside, the fire was now roaring. I left my thermals on, added a full tracksuit over the top, shut all the doors to the living room, and climbed onto my stationary road bike now carefully positioned directly on the hearth in front of the thriving flames. For one uncomfortable hour I pedalled, sweat streaming down my forehead, trickling down my back and into my underwear. Beads formed down my legs, dripped onto the towels beneath me on the floor, seeped through these and then pooled atop the plastic sheeting protecting the carpet beneath.

This was Hanny's version of heat acclimatisation.

I had ten days. A deep fear of unravelling in Japan's intense summer heat and humidity had instigated this torturous training. Yes, fear was co-piloting me towards Japan and, little did I know, to the beginning of a wilder ride.

I RACED BLINDLY down the tumbling slopes, navigating away from the start location perched on top of the hill. The waist-deep bamboo slapped against my legs, creating the sensation of a bizarre Japanese massage. I was filled with exhilaration, and an adolescent energy stemming from truly loving the challenge in which I now found myself immersed. This was the biggest event in my sport, the World Orienteering Championships.

The eighty-two-kilometre Overland Track race was behind me, and I had returned from Switzerland as a Junior World bronze medallist. I still had the remnants of splinters in my bottom and hands, as evidence of the surreal experience of racing down the Swiss Alps. There, Mum and Dad had stood side-by-side, forming part of the Australian cheer squad. Now, in the heat of the Japanese summer, they were also there, sweltering. This was the first year they had watched me race overseas and I felt a swell of excitement.

CRACK! A splitting, tearing, snapping sound disrupted my flow. Like the pause between lightning and thunder, there was a momentary gap between this and the sudden onset of a searing pain in my right ankle. I then realised that I was rolling, tumbling like a panda cub down the steep slopes, creating a small path of destruction amongst the bamboo as I went. For fear of losing them, I clutched tightly to my map and compass before finally coming to a stop. Carefully I untwisted myself, only too aware of the extreme discomfort emanating from my foot.

I must keep going! I wobbled to my feet. *This is the World Championships. My first race of the week, and it is just the qualifying event. I must keep going!*

With Mum and Dad in tow, I hobbled home to the accommodation of our Australian Team camp, poised on the edges of a vast hydro dam overlooking the textured canopies of the forests. Under hazy horizons blushed with pink, I crawled into the onsen, a traditional Japanese hot spring, then opened the window to the vista to let the hot humid air blow through. Upstairs, I could hear the other athletes debriefing on the day and beginning to prepare for tomorrow. *I should be up there. I am the team's fastest qualifier and I somehow just had the run of my life.* But I felt displaced, torn—both physically and emotionally.

Having not yet observed the damage, I raised my right ankle from the tub and placed it on the edge. The ankle taping had literally split, with the impact of the ankle's twisting as it hit the hole obscured by bamboo. Normally, the lateral ankle cops the brunt of a sprain. This time, the front of my foot was beginning to turn blue, too. I carefully peeled off the shreds of tape. Swelling had already set in. Gingerly, I got straight back out, showered my naked body while sitting on a small wooden stool, Japanese style, and then hobbled back upstairs to find our team physiotherapist. I lay back on her futon bedding, rested my head gratefully on the pillow. I felt tired … and not just physically.

The air-conditioning blasted a chill into the small, tatami-matted room. But there was another chill, too. As my physio lifted my foot carefully from the bed, we both observed the dense swelling and bright bruising that was beginning to appear. Then she lowered it back to the bed. I looked up at her and she looked back at me. 'Nice one, Han!'

We bandaged, iced and then rested. Hours passed as I lay inverted on my bed, my legs resting vertically up paper-thin walls. I was not due to race for a couple of days. I used this time to read endless pages of Harry Potter in the blue glow of my bedroom—a space created by the inventive use of blue plastic sheeting to divide the function room in this small guesthouse that our Australian Team was sharing with our Kiwi companions. I was happy there.

I love Japan. I love the intrinsic beauty of its simplest moments. Such as the way you kick off your footwear at the doorway, slide your feet into a pair of wooden clogs and then line up your shoes neatly beside others where they dwarf your hosts', like a giant's shoes versus a doll's. My heart sings with the simple gift of a small bow when presented with breakfast, or how after a delicate dinner you return to your room to find that your futon and white duvets have been laid out skilfully on the bamboo tatami matting.

I love the quirkiness too. The carrot pieces cut into stars as they float in your miso broth. The way the toilets warm your bottom during the depths of a cold winter training camp. Previously, when we trained during their winter, snow fell like talcum powder on barren ground devoid of vegetation. Winter tucked the once-deep bamboo away for safe keeping until spring returned. But on this trip, it was lush, invigorated by the summer storms as they swept across that narrow, stretched country.

With natural beauty and a gentility to the culture, I find this country breeds compassion from deep within me. It is a place of healing.

In future years this healing would come on a profound spiritual level but, right then, I needed to heal physically, and that was exactly what I hoped to do.

Two days later I was back on the start line. Naïve and a few Panadol heavier, I took off from the start gates. However, this time my mind felt foggier, less sharp, more cautious. Every navigational decision felt slightly cumbersome, every step awkward and disjointed. I was only too aware of the new weakness in my foot, and yet I was determined not to let it affect this opportunity.

I was well-ranked heading into the final, and I could feel the other girls who were starting behind me breathing down my neck. There were big names amongst them, including none other than the Swiss superstar, Simone Niggli-Luder. However, I knew that they too had their own fears.

The heat was sapping. No amount of ice vests or cold water ladled from bamboo buckets had kept us cool during our warm up. I saw the fear in their eyes. Saw the jiggling nerves as they shifted from one foot to the other under the starter's command. At thirty-seven degrees centigrade with a humidity rivalling the onsens, the long-distance final would not just be a test of the best orienteer, but a test of the strongest mindset.

Soon I caught up to a few athletes who had started in front of me. We moved together as a pack. I was climbing the hills strongly and sticking to the race plan I had created with our team coach. Yet every time the pack embarked down a hill, I was dropping ground. Despite the vast layers of strapping tape, I was only too aware of my ankle's instability. As other athletes caught us and we caught others, a large pack began to form. It became a game of the hare and the tortoise. They broke away from me on the downhills, only for me to catch them back up on the next incline.

This was all new to me. I had only been orienteering on the senior stage for two years. In Australia, our sport was a minority one. The competitive fields were smaller, and it was only on rare occasions that I found myself actually head-to-head racing with another athlete. And, in orienteering, athletes start at intervals into the forest to avoid following-tactics. But out there, bamboo obscuring our footfalls, the colours of multiple countries popping distinctly from the neutral colour palettes of the forest, that was a whole new game.

I had lost an understanding of my position, but when the Swiss steam train of Simone Niggli-Luder caught up to us, I knew that I just had to grit my teeth, maintain contact with my map, and ignore the stream of sweat pouring down my forehead, blurring my vision.

As we neared the latter portions of the race, I began to notice that some of the other girls had dropped away. The pace was high, and I could feel my legs beginning to cramp. I knew I might not be able to hold on for much longer myself. I no longer had any awareness of the discomfort in my ankle, but rather focused on the long route-choice leg that was approaching. I could hear my coach's voice resonating in my ears, 'The longest legs between controls will be the game changers. Stay wide, stay wide!'

I saw there was a very wide track option that would get me out of this energy-sapping undergrowth and avoid some of the hills. When the crunch point came, Simone peeled off to the left, taking most of the remaining girls in her wake. I hesitated, then gritted my teeth and raced off to the right. I found the track easily, and executed what would be the defining moment of that race.

Heading into the finish, I realised that there were only six of us remaining, including Simone. We had reunited a few controls back, and raced towards the finish together before crossing the line in a weary mess of muddy, sweaty athletes. I was confused. My legs were cramping, and suddenly my right shoe felt too tight. However, before I had a chance to absorb all this I was surrounded by my teammates, coaches and, best of all, Mum and Dad.

Against the odds and any expectations, I became the first Australian to stand in sixth place on the podium of a Senior World Orienteering Championships. At just nineteen years of age, I had surpassed my own wildest expectations of potential. When fear of foreign terrain, draining heat, and juggling performance around medical school exams could have held me back, I had somehow found a way to navigate through all that to the dais of that competition. Instead of fear holding me back, it had instead highlighted a need to look at things from a different perspective.

I boarded the flight home with so much gratitude. Gratitude for the assistance of my mentors and team coaches. Towards my teammates, some of whom had achieved or surpassed their expectations, some of whom had fallen short this time. Gratitude towards my mother and father, both fresh-faced from a holiday and tied in unity through their common experiences.

Gratitude to be returning to a career away from sport. For even in that moment of elation, I could recognise the void that could be created when returning from such a career-defining high to 'normal' life. The risk of trying to replant your feet without something solid under them, like your studies or a career to anchor you back into the 'real' world.

And finally, gratitude that when I—as the underdog—stood for the first time on the dais of the international senior stage at the World Orienteering Championships in Japan, as heat sweltered and dust blew through the gravel playing field, I knew I was ready to take the final steps.

I had survived my dance on the knife edge, done my dues as a younger athlete, found a love affair with a sport that matched my strengths. I had found the support networks in Tasmania that could help carry me just a few places higher. With my first year's medical examinations now completed, parents returning home alongside me from their overseas adventures, and a heart as happy as any nineteen-year-old's could be, what could possibly go wrong?

PART II
NAVIGATING

2005–2006

World Orienteering Champion, Sprint Distance, Denmark (Photograph: Julia Hutchinson)

8

I eased into a walk and turned towards the ugly brick clubroom buildings forming the barrier between the two ovals. An array of school backpacks and brightly coloured shoe bags adorned the concrete beneath the awnings, and school shoes and blazers were scattered, like testimonies to the swapping of one life for another. Some team members were already stretching, others still alternating between sprinting down the long straights and walking for recovery along the shorter sides of the field.

Max strode into the action, a sheep dog mustering the flock, his tartan beret perched atop wispy, white hair, his green and navy tracksuit identifying him as our coach. I wandered over towards him, standing back until he had finished chatting to some of the crew. When he was ready, he turned to me, caught my eye and then dropped his gaze to my feet. I looked down at my right ankle, bound in strapping tape and still slightly more swollen than my left.

As usual, he was quick with an opinion. 'I don't believe what you are doing is right. If you go ahead with the surgery, you will never run again. Not like now, anyway.'

I brought my eyes back up to meet his gaze. Despite his apparent toughness, I could sense that he was finding it just as hard as I was. His eyes showed a deep level of concern, which he quickly dismissed by thrusting out his hand for the routine handshake. I tried to respond with strength, but I was sure my handshake reflected my fears. He hated a weak handshake: 'It's a sign of a weak character.'

What was I doing? As I walked towards the corner of the playing field—the normal starting point for all Max's deadly sessions—I mentally returned to Kellie's physiotherapy consulting room. She had gently lifted my swollen foot off the bed, grasped it carefully in two hands and tested the mobility. I had heard my mother's quick intake of breath. Kellie had quickly put down my foot in horror. She had pulled gently on my heel but with no restriction, like my whole foot was about to detach from my leg. 'Ligament damage,' she had said. I sat in her consulting room as she discussed my visiting Melbourne to see an expert ankle and joint surgeon, and how she would be willing to help me with my rehabilitation should this plan proceed further.

I floated warily through the training session, tempo running along the stretches of smooth grass playing fields, around the empty bitumen car parks and onto the long stretches of white sand heralding the closest beach to Hobart CBD. From here, you could look back down the Derwent River, see the lights of the city slowly glowing brighter, and the looming, shadowy presence of the mountain to its left.

At any other moment, I would have pinched myself to think that I lived there, able to enjoy that dramatic landscape on the doorstep of the capital city of Tasmania. And yet, on that day, each bump, each shell or divot in the sand, caused a jolt of discomfort that could send my ankle rolling and twisting, with me ultimately crumpling to the ground. My heart and head were there, running shoulder to shoulder with my peers, but on that day, my body was not willing to play the game. As I lagged behind, this was my first real experience of being restricted from my dreams.

I stood in the car park, waiting for Dad to appear. His beloved orange kombivan with its white roof had long been replaced by a sleek silver Citroen, a perk of his new job as the Ombudsman of Tasmania.

I knew that I couldn't live with an ankle like this forever, let alone use it to orienteer through forests and navigate in the direction of my dreams. Next year would be my opportunity for the Junior World

Orienteering Championships. After the results of the past year, I knew I was knocking on the door to that top tier of the podium, and with it, a chance to realise my dream that had started four years before.

Yet, right at this moment, pulling my jacket closer around me to block the breeze which swept in off the Southern Ocean like a frequent guest to those playing fields, I couldn't have felt further from my goal. Just that morning, I had been walking between faculties at university, and in a fraction of a second ended up sprawled across the concrete, textbooks and belongings scattered along the sidewalk. Gingerly standing up, I had looked for the culprit that had tripped me over, only to find the smallest of pebbles staring innocently back.

As Dad pulled into the car park, I knew that I would be boarding my flight to Melbourne the next day, and likely returning home with a whole new hill to climb.

TWO DAYS LATER, I entered the consulting rooms of my prospective surgeon. Mum and I had pottered gleefully around the clothes stores and boutique cafes in the leafy, upper-class Melbourne suburb, to distract me from what was yet to come. While there was nervous anticipation lurking deep within my lean and mean athletic body, I knew that I was making the right decision. That I needed to make this decision to return to the level of performance I was capable of. In a shade-filled waiting room, we flipped through magazines of country homes and fashion, filling in the minutes with mindless material, waiting. Waiting.

Eventually, I was called into a sparse, white consulting room, where Mr Surgeon dismissively waved me into a chair on the opposite side of his wide, wooden desk. Mum quietly entered the room too, and tucked herself into a nearby chair. All eyes were on me.

With a look from head to toe, followed by short verbal statements, he dismissed me as too young. 'We rarely operate on people your age.' And yet he waved me across the room towards a consulting bed resting in the corner. I pushed myself up, shuffling along the bed so that my foot dangled precariously off the end, just as I had done for Kellie just a few short-but-confusing weeks earlier. He, too, cupped his hands around the heel of my foot and began to apply a gentle amount of tension. There was no resistance. The ligaments had packed up and departed my foot. He lowered my foot like it was a hefty chunk of meat. Gratefully, I lay back against the white pillow, feeling the rise and fall of a wave of pain and nausea coursing through me.

I vaguely heard him say, 'So, the way we do the surgery is …'

Just twelve hours later, I lay in an off-pink hospital room, my stomach rumbling uncontrollably as they continued to bump the young one to the back of the surgical queue. My night of fasting, long morning run in tribute to my potentially last ever run, and then a long day lying listless in this hospital room, had left me anxious, hungry and parched.

Eventually, I was poked, prodded and drizzled with anaesthetics until I fell into a heavy, fearful slumber. I woke in the bright lights of recovery, then again on a trolley being wheeled down a long corridor, and then finally in a darkened room with my ankle pulsing so agonisingly that I pressed the emergency bell like my life depended on it.

Despite my desperate pleas, the nurses refused to help relieve the pressure on my ankle, adamant that this extreme discomfort was normal and that they must wait to speak to the surgeon in the morning. So I swallowed more pills and waited for the tide of darkness to return … only it didn't.

By dawn, I was in such discomfort that I was crying into the phone, the morning a blur of tears, anger and frustration before my mother insisted on my dismissal from that god-awful place. Little had I anticipated sitting on my grandfather's couch in Brighton. Once a surgeon and now an avid wood craftsman, he hacked away at the bloodied bandages with a jigsaw to reveal a foot so swollen it had turned blue. The drying, congealed and bloodied bandages had become akin to concrete, cutting off most of the blood supply to my foot as it had continued to swell and swell. Adding to my discomfort, my middle toes on both feet had also required straightening, thanks to a pre-existing hammer toe issue that I had had since childhood.

I was wheelchair-dependent and unable to even get myself to a bathroom. My mother became completely at my beck and call as we lingered in the suburban home of my generous, ever-loving godmother until we could return to see the surgeon.

When I met with him some days later, wheeled into his suite in a wheelchair with both legs protruding awkwardly out in front of me, fearful of the doorjambs and bumps, his grim face said it all. 'Just nineteen years of age and needing a full-ankle reconstruction? Your claim to fame is that *that* is the worst ankle I have ever seen.' He was famous in his industry for establishing new-age practices for ankle reconstructions, so I guess it must have been pretty bad.

DAY AFTER DAY, I lay in bed and on the couch. On the odd occasion that I tried to pick up my textbooks, I hastily put them down again, drifting in and out of a restless, painful sleep. I hated needing to be assisted to the toilet, and that I could not even get out of bed without someone to lean on.

In the darkness of the early mornings, Mum would sneak out of our room, off to the swimming pool for some much-needed fresh air. And yet when she was gone, I lay in an aching loneliness, minutes ticking slowly by as I pined to be out there enjoying the morning with her, all the while afraid that I would need to use the bathroom before she got back.

After a week of bed to couch and back to bed again, and a growing level of stomach distress from the heavy painkillers, we headed home to Hobart. We desperately navigated the Melbourne airport terminal as fast as we could, pain mounting until it threatened to overtake me. I lay gratefully sprawled across three departure gate chairs and, later, the front row seats of the aircraft. I had quickly discovered that whenever my feet had to be below my heart level, it would cause blood to rush into the ankle, pool in the joint, and create an intensity of pain so severe I would become light-headed.

Back home, Dad took over the carer's role from Mum for a while. I lay on a towel in the veggie garden and watched him work, observing the reverence he applied to the gentle tasks of watering, pricking out seedlings and sowing them into the rich alluvial soils.

As the days passed, I began to be aware of a new edginess of discomfort forming in my right foot, where a long pin shaped like a knitting needle was protruding from the end of my middle toe. When they had straightened these hammer toes, they had removed the malformed joint and used this pin to hold the two cut ends of bone together until they healed. Once ready, the pin could easily be removed with 'a few twists and a tug'… apparently.

However, this new discomfort was beginning a percussion accompaniment to the original burning melody from the ankle surgery. After another twenty-four hours it had transformed into a full-blown orchestral blare—a hot, searing discomfort that radiated from my foot and up into my lower leg. Finally, I flagged this with my father. After a quick call to Mum, who was at work as an emergency physician at the private hospital in Hobart, Dad whisked me into the car. He drove five minutes down the road to the home of Hobart's most accomplished plastic surgeon, Craig, who just so happened to be a wonderful friend. A remarkable reconstructive and skin surgeon by day, a farmer and animal welfare advocate by night, he and his wife had created a sanctuary by the rock pools of the North West Bay River.

As we pulled into their driveway, I couldn't help but notice what a far cry this was from our usual visits—the childhood birthday parties and hot afternoons clambering out of Dad's kombivan to launch into the cool river adjacent to their property.

Craig and his wife, Sue, met us on the porch. Their house was truly majestic, painted a brilliant white but softened into the landscape of paddocks and the grey hues of the dry sclerophyll forest by a beautiful English garden. They guided us inside, wary of the border collies dancing around my feet.

I plonked gratefully onto the antique-style couch as Craig gingerly removed the moonboot from my foot. He marvelled at the raw, ten-inch wound wrapping beneath my right ankle, then began to focus his attention onto my toe and the large knitting-needle protruding from its end. He quickly identified the obvious redness beginning to seep up my foot from this toe. The pin needed to be instantly removed for fear of the infection reaching the bone and potentially even the ankle itself.

After discussing in gory detail how simple this procedure was—'just a twist, twist, pull!'—he left the room only to return with a small set of pincers. Fear flooded through me and I rested my head back onto their couch as he gave my hand a reassuring squeeze. I felt him clamp onto the pin only to shriek in agony as he attempted to spin and loosen it from my toe. Dad grabbed at my hands, clasping them in reassurance.

Craig tried again, and still the pin held fast. By now I was sweating profusely, whimpering in agony and fear. 'For what comes next?'

Again, Craig left the room, leaving Sue to calm and reassure. He returned carrying an enormous pair of slightly rusted pliers. 'I normally use these for shoeing the horses.' By now I was completely spent. He grabbed more vigorously on the pin, and I let out another fierce shriek as I felt it slide out of the bone.

Later, as Dad and I reversed out Craig and Sue's driveway, little did we realise that our family would be leaning on them again for strength in the very near future.

THESE EXPERIENCES of being bound to beds, wheelchairs and later crutches were confusing times. The confusion grew when we realised I would be unable to stand or sit for long enough to complete my medical examinations. A letter from Kellie, my physiotherapist, left my examinations lingering in the background, deferred for a few more weeks.

Whenever I had the strength and stamina, I flipped open my textbooks and tried to grasp the complexities of chemistry, anatomy and pharmacology. Quickly, my head would become filled with fog—a miasma that would have me dragging myself back to the couch, or towel laid out on the balcony where I could drape my leg over a bean bag, and feel the blood return to my heart.

I felt like only half of Hanny—stalled between aspiration and setbacks. At nineteen, I was oblivious to the risks associated with defining ourselves by what we do. If I wasn't an athlete nor aspiring doctor, then who was I? I was still focused on gaining my doctor's certification and on realising my dream of standing tall on the international sporting daises but, to be honest, that was as far into the future as I could see. I had little appreciation for what would come after that, of who Hanny was when she wasn't an aspiring athlete, medical student, or daughter.

That moment, with my ankle poised above my heart, perhaps should have been a window into the risk of living in a 'do more to be more' mentality. It could have taught me a few lessons in self-compassion, and helped me reframe a positive self-identity bound not to what we do, but rather, who we are. But instead, I longed to get back into life, my training, and my studies. I tried to hurry this process along with disciplined rehabilitation, nutrition, and attempts to study.

The phrase 'self-compassion' was so foreign to me that later in my adult life I would look into the kind eyes of a psychologist with a perplexed look. 'What do you mean, a sports massage is not self-compassion?' The concept of being gentle on myself was a sign of weakness. From the lessons learnt in the pool, and through the pages of glossy running magazines showing grimacing faces and lean bodies, it was hard for me to comprehend how self-compassion, whatever that entailed, could fit into the development of an aspiring athlete.

And so, as energy permitted, I threw myself into my medical studies. As I barely left the bed or couch, I had no appetite. Muscles began to shrink. Clothes began to feel baggy. I was treated to a few shopping trips to find some new pieces. It felt amazing to pull on a new tank top and jeans and receive unexpected compliments. I didn't strive for this, but having come from the quite masculine world of sport, for a change it was nice to feel more feminine.

Deep down, I sensed my body was not entirely happy with me. I could feel a deep-seated sense of physical stress. My body responded by ceasing my previously infrequent menstrual cycles. I do not believe that anorexia joined me at this stage, although my appetite had definitely disappeared without the exercise I was used to.

When I would finally return to running, I would certainly be leaner and meaner than ever, and desperately eager to hold out my hand and return Max's strong handshake. But I had a few more deep, dark valleys to navigate first.

9

Evening had snuck into the lounge room. Here in Tasmania it does that at this time of year, when spring has crept into summer. The day holds onto the light for longer, before snapping into darkness as the sun dips her head behind the shadows of the hills that lurk on the edges of the valley. I flicked on a lamp to illuminate my father, sitting in an armchair, his face as long as the shadows that had just departed their duties for the day, to be replaced by a continuous blanket of darkness. His eyes stared off into a somewhere that I couldn't access, and, for a moment, his hands were peaceful on his lap. The movie that I had turned on to try and add cheer back into the evening, *Notting Hill* with its quirky characters and catchy music, had failed to work magic. Neither he nor I were focusing on the love story unfolding in front of us.

Frowns and distant stares were not foreign to me; quieter trundles home in the kombivan had been a familiar ingredient in my childhood. What frightened me was the radical transition from Dad—the one who shone with a summer glow as he and my mother explored their way through the Swiss and French Alps, the one who disembarked the aircraft eager to return to his new job as Ombudsman of Tasmania, the one who tucked the chickens into bed each night—to this erratic and unpredictable dad.

I didn't recognise the father who, days ago, had swerved off the highway and tried to clamber in the window of his sister's home in an attempt to patch a long-standing crevasse in his family. I hadn't been able to recognise the father who'd paced backwards and forwards through the kitchen and corridors for many evenings in a row, as I tried to bury my head in textbooks, assignments and teenage messages with boyfriends and friends.

Who was this dad, the father so distant that even a hug couldn't return him to the room? I didn't recognise him, and I no longer knew how to be his daughter. And, so, while we found ourselves together, we were alone, each bound to a chair, with my mother's quilts tucked over our knees. She was at work again, tonight.

He was up again, pacing ferociously through the house. I could hear his footsteps coming and going in varying directions. I was unable to bring any peace to his evening, nor mine. One day I would come to understand the erratic nature of bipolar disorder, the vast swings in mood from excessive energy to the greatest depths of depression. One day I would learn to recognise its onset and flag help earlier. And yet that first time, or the first time I was aware of it, I hobbled to bed in the knowledge that my mother would soon be home from work.

I awoke in the morning, gently kicked off the blanket with one foot, and hobbled on my crutches towards the kitchen. In the lounge room I headed straight for my neat pile of running clothes in the corner where I had left them the night before, a habit I had not been able to shrug off since my early swimming days.

Heading out the door, I was greeted by the exuberance of Mollie, a small brown and white ball of fluff darting around my crutches. She knew we were off on a short excursion together. We wobbled our way along the quiet gravel road, enjoying the sunshine rising beyond the valley, and watched the world slowly come to life.

I stepped back into the kitchen ten minutes later, grateful to return from vertical and ease the pressure on my ankle. I was greeted by my mother's confused face. 'Have you seen your father this morning?' I hadn't, although I had barely touched the breadths of our property on my short morning hobble. Mum continued her morning routines, pulling out breakfast things and preparing for the day ahead.

Ten minutes passed. Then twenty. Then thirty. Mum headed for the back door and I heard the familiar latching as it closed behind her. Ten minutes passed. Then twenty. Then she returned, concern etched into every gentle curve of her beautiful face. Something deep within us, some string that unites mother and daughter, knew then and there that something very, very wrong was at play. She had neither seen nor heard from my father all morning. As ten o'clock approached, we knew that no normal morning routine would ever involve eating breakfast later than this in a household of hungry appetites—my father's especially.

Mum sank into a chair and began wringing her hands in earnest fear. She jumped to her feet and I watched her disappear out the back door again. The latch now sounded louder and more desperate as it closed behind her. Soon, I heard her yelling into the morning, 'Simon? Simon!' I reached for the phone, dialling the numbers of our closest friends and neighbours. As the minutes slipped past, uniting to form an hour, I dialled the police.

Soon, the house was filled with people. Mum had returned, and was quietly weeping as friends rallied around, filling kettles, asking questions, darting in and out the front door. Cars started, cars returned. Steaming mugs of untouched tea. Cooling mugs of slimy tea. More kettles. More questions.

And then the police arrived, their uniforms a stark contrast to the humble presence of our family home. More kettles, more questions. Somewhere in the middle of all this, I was the conductor of an orchestra, emailing my brother who was travelling abroad with his girlfriend, providing suggestions to our friends—Dad's workplace, favourite bushwalks, other friends, corners of the property. I comforted my mother and tried to explain to the police the unusual behaviours I had observed over the previous two weeks.

Each time my heart and head tried to wrestle me to the floor in a confused mess, I would slide out the back door and head for the swings. A brown and white ball of exuberant puppy tailing along behind me.

At some point in that day ... sometime between the breakfast we hadn't eaten and the boiling of another kettle ... the phone rang. I did not hear it. I was alone on the swing, taking a moment to myself, wrestling with a stick and the strong teeth of a growing puppy.

I sat, legs hanging loosely above the recently cropped lawn, trying to ignore the pulsing presence of my ankle. I flicked sticks to Molly to fetch and return. Fetch and return. Fetch and return. It never ceases to amaze me how simple it is to entertain a dog. I thought about the university exams coming up, and the piles of open medical textbooks still lying on the kitchen table amongst police reports and tea mugs. I thought about my brother over in Asia, travelling with his girlfriend, immune to this nightmare unfolding right now. Had he got my email yet? My mind was whirling from one random thought to another, and yet it felt like it was filled with thoughtless thoughts. I was delaying going back inside, my thoughts swinging backwards and forwards with me on this swing: *what is happening* and *what should my next steps be?*

The sound of shoes moving softly across mown lawn disrupted my thoughts. I became aware of movement behind me. Then a smell of perfume that was not my mother's. A hand resting on my shoulder. A shaky breath. The words, 'Your father is alive. He attempted suicide. He is on his way to the hospital.'

Between a slight movement up, and a slight movement down ... a stick in one hand being ferociously chewed and drooled upon by an unknowing pup ... with an adult hand resting gently on a crumpling shoulder ... came the end of childhood innocence.

SOMETIME LATER THAT AFTERNOON, I sat, crutches propped beside me, on the jetty that protrudes into the thick, inky waters of our dam. That large body of water, captured in the few years prior by modifying the flow of a nearby brook, was the brainchild of my father. While I often felt like the custodian of the dam as I launched into the chilly waters after a summer morning training run, this dam was Dad's, built to water his continually evolving garden. Bed to bed, plant to plant, the sprinkler would be moved to help the plants capture the rich nutrients of the soil and the sun when it beat down.

On this day, I was vaguely aware of the warmth of the sunshine as it rested on my face, bare arms, bare legs. While it was warm, I was cold. Chilled so deep into my core that I wrapped my arms around me. My mind full, but empty. My stomach growled, but I was not hungry. My eyes looked, but observed nothing.

And then I heard the sound of a familiar car. Familiar footsteps. An arm wrapped awkwardly around me. I turned to face Josh, my closest friend, my adopted brother. He sat beside me and we stared out across the dam. Our minds full, but hollow. Our stomachs twisted in fear. Then he was guiding me back towards the house, watching as I stuffed a clean t-shirt into my training bag, stripped out of my running shorts—that still clung to my middle—and tugged into a fresh pair. I wrestled awkwardly with my crutches, turned towards the door, and glanced back over my shoulder to where my beautiful but fragile mother was surrounded by a swathe of comforting friends. Right then, she could neither be a doting wife nor a mother. She was simply a person whose walls were caving in, and she was left with the pieces of a breaking heart.

Josh and I flagged our departure with one of the adults, and slipped quietly out the back door. He walked slowly beside me, one hand clutching my snatched possessions as we made our way back up through the rose garden and out towards the long line of cars that flanked our narrow dead-end road.

Thirteen years on, I realise the significance of this moment. Josh had also experienced a splintering of families, the loss of a father and mother as he had come to know them. During his parents' separation he had practically lived at our place, travelling with us to orienteering, hiking with us in the mountains, eating at our family dining table. In many ways, my parents became his parents, and when my brother left home, his room became Josh's. Through this time, I had walked beside Josh, becoming his adventure buddy as we hiked together, ran out of food, slept in a shared tent and talked long into the night. I had walked beside him and carried his bucket in one hand and mine in the other while he navigated his way through the winding trail of life, until he could carry it for himself.

That day, I had to hand my bucket to him. In the manner of the greatest friendships, that day he was stoically carrying my bucket even though he too was feeling the rush of fear and loss as the unknown rose to meet us.

I sank gratefully into the passenger seat of his car and watched the valley slide past, and then behind. We turned onto the open freeway and I leant back into the seat, free for the first time that day of the responsibility of conducting an orchestra, free, too, from the concerned gaze of onlookers. We headed towards the city, barely speaking to one another, for what do you say when your mind is only able to connect to the one thought that is too atrocious to raise—*life or death?*

When we entered his home—a place of only recent significance to Josh—we were greeted by the gentle motherliness of his mother. The fire was lit, the music gentle, the lights bright. I felt as disjointed in this moment as I used to feel when I returned from racing overseas for my country, only to step back into the locker-lined hallways of my private school and be told off by the teacher: 'Where is your hair ribbon?'

Concerned words were exchanged, hugs too, then bowls of steaming soup. Later, we lay by the fire long into the night, for I was too afraid of the dreams that could follow. However, when I finally hit the pillow on the floor of Josh's room, I did not even have time to listen to his breathing as we drifted into slumber.

THE DARKNESS FELT APPROPRIATE. It was hiding my vulnerability. And yet I still had not shed a tear. Somewhere within me was an understanding that vulnerability was a weakness. Vulnerability threatened to shine a streetlight on the breadth and depth of the great, big, awful hole that I had suddenly found myself in.

At some point between sleep and awake, the pain of the day I'd just been through came flooding into me, twisting my stomach and organs into a writhe of confusion, discomfort and fear. Unable to lie still, and for fear of waking the entire house, I slipped out into the night.

My ankle hurt. It was the longest I had been upright since the operation and I could feel the swelling pressing harshly on the red-raw scar beneath my right ankle bone. My crutches pressed into my armpits, rubbing at the soft flesh of my chest. Even my toes ached in sympathy with my heart, still with two healing holes at the distal ends of each swollen digit. Screw pain! Enough, already. I'd rather be numb.

Somewhere beneath my sport-scarred skin I knew that this was as low as I could go. Ankle reconstruction. Looming medical examinations. A father in ICU. A grieving mother isolated from her immediate family, a brother overseas desperately trying to come home, a grandmother mourning the son she once knew. A darkened farm without its caretakers. Out there as I wandered the sleepy suburbs, aware of the tap-tap-tapping echo of my crutches into the hollow streets, I tried to suppress the waves of emotions. The fear. The frustration. The anger. The sadness. The loneliness. My support network was two wooden crutches and a world of pain. I felt trapped.

'Fuck this!' I swore into the night. A foreign word for a girl who replaced the word 'Schweppes' for 'shit' as a kid to avoid uttering dirty words. But, 'Fuck this!' All I wanted to do was tear through the darkened streets and run beyond these emotions.

I was nineteen. *If I was more normal, I would be out with the other medical students now, tipping back the beers and Bacardi Breezers, flirting with the boys or discussing examinations now safely in the past.* Instead, I was alone on a quiet suburban street.

I had to visit my dad. The thought terrified me to my core, bringing on a new wave of nausea so intense that I paused and leant over someone's front gate, only vaguely aware of the beautiful aroma of roses. Roses. Mum's roses. I didn't want to be there when Mum visited. I couldn't hold her pain too.

On I stumbled.

Later that morning, when Josh pulled up outside the Hobart public hospital and handed me my bag, I was aware that I was taking back my bucket from him. I was unsure why exactly I needed to walk this journey alone, but somehow I knew that I had always been walking the journey somewhat alone. I had always been stubbornly independent, and that independence had risen once again to the surface. Aloneness felt like it would give me the strength to climb step by step, day by day, out of that great, big, ugly hole.

To do this meant to be a daughter by day, and an athletic warrior by morning and night. To point my ship in the direction of Lithuania and aim straight to the top of the dais. Winning at the upcoming Junior World Orienteering Championships in my last eligible year would be my way of climbing over those mountains and out of the depths of that vast hole.

I entered the hospital to visit my father for the very first time.

LATER THAT DAY, I was standing in front of the Dean of the Medical Faculty. My mother's best friend, Sue, stood beside me. I felt faint with the pain that had settled into my foot after the long day of being upright, and the long walk from the car to this grey room. I also felt faint with a discomfort in my chest so intense I did not know how to describe it. I felt like I was choking on foreign words, words I never knew I would need to utter, and they came out in jagged sentences. 'Dad …' 'Accident …' 'Uni exams in three days …' 'Ankle …' 'Family …?'

Leaving the room, I felt the adrenalin coursing through me. My armpits which rested atop my crutches were sweating. I needed to sit down. I couldn't interpret the options I had just been presented with. The Dean's voice played over and over through my mind: 'As you have already deferred once, you only have two options remaining. Sit your exams starting in two days or re-sit first-year medicine next year.'

It was only the hours of a dark, disturbed night that distanced me from that moment upon the swing when I had been informed of the event that had thrown me into a new, confusing future. It was only in the hours of this dawning day that I had first hobbled to my father's bedside and felt the enormity of adulthood hitting me like a steam train. And in only hours' time I would be meeting my brother at Hobart Airport as he returned early from his holiday abroad, ready to face the gravity of this awful script.

As I climbed into Sue's car, tears began to roll down my cheeks for the first time, initially a trickle, then soon a stream of anguish and fear. Even though I had a choice, I knew I had no choice.

Words cannot express my gratitude for the friends and family members that rallied around our family through this difficult time. As each of us fell and clambered, fell and clambered as we attempted to climb beyond this gaping hole we all found ourselves in, they remained our rungs and handrails.

There were gifts too, wrapped in layers of selflessness, generosity and at times, simplicity, such as heaving and tugging the temperamental lawnmower around our enormous garden. The cups of tea and lifts to physiotherapy appointments. The consecutive late nights standing in the formaldehyde-filled anatomy room at the university, grilling my muddled mind on the shrivelled anatomical parts of our cadaver, reassuring me that I could pass these exams. The small deliveries of homemade breads, cakes and casseroles that we gratefully divided out amongst those who donated their time to assist Mum and me around the farm. I loved to reserve some of these gifts for Dad, the berries, cherries and fresh peas from a garden, for there were only a few ways you could express your deepest love for someone without using human touch and when confusion created a wall between you.

With words now at my fingertips, I want to express gratitude to everyone who climbed upwards from that hole with us, with a few special thanks ... to my aunt and uncle; my godparents, who identified my lack of independence; and to my godmother who braved her displeasure of boats to bring their gift of a shiny, new, second-hand Peugeot hatchback to Tasmania. I am still humbled by your generosity. Then to the friends who were able to sit alongside our fear and pain, even when others may not have been able while they hurt too. Simply being there with a reassuring hug or to hand over a steaming cup of tea helped us enormously. Each of you has taught me to turn up for others, to sit in that moment of absolute discomfort, and be okay with not having any answers.

I honestly have barely any memory of the weeks that followed my father's suicide attempt. In fact, until I began writing this book, I called it an accident, unable to put accurate words to this event for fear of bringing all the lost memories to life. In some ways, it was an accident—an act of a muddled mind, a neural and chemical cocktail that momentarily stole my father. But in other ways, it was an attempt to end a life, and by putting words to it, naming it, owning it—suicide attempt—I hope to bring it out of the shadows. To allow others to be able to connect with the discomforts of suicide, to stroke it, look it in the eye, and hopefully to begin to heal their own wounds. For we don't talk about these events, and while there are so many difficult memories wrapped up in it all, there are overwhelmingly more moments of hope, love and connection.

Perhaps my strongest memory of this time was being asked over to Craig and Sue's house. This time there were no rusted horse pliers, but rather a cup of tea and an important message of hope for me. I manoeuvred my way into their living room, and rested on their couch with crutches propped beside me. Craig sat beside me. He placed his hand on my shoulder, while Sue hung further back, and turned to face me.

'Hanny, I am so sorry about your father. But I needed you to know that I was the doctor that greeted him in the emergency room when the ambulance brought him in. I thought that he wouldn't survive, that he couldn't survive the strength of the electrical voltages. And yet he did. Maybe it was the rubber of his workboots? However, I believe that the greatness and beauty of your father's soul is what saved him. He has received third-degree burns to over sixty-percent of his body, and yet his face, hands, feet and vital organs have all been spared. Something was certainly looking out for him.'

While I still do not know the details of what happened during the long hours of my father's disappearance, nor do I wish to, all I can say is that I am so grateful for these words from Craig. They have helped me to see the goodness in this horrific incident, and to believe that my father was meant to survive this accident. That all the future events that stemmed from it were all part of a grander plan for our family and for me. It helped me move from black and white thinking to seeing that there is always a shade of grey in the middle. Today, I don't just see the grey, I look for it.

Reaching into the rest of the dark void that surrounded this week is the hand of my best friend, Josh. The slight pressure of it on my shoulder as we prepared to launch into the murky dam, at last releasing a solitary giggle. Holding onto the chewed, slobber-soaked leash of my new puppy, Molly, as I hobbled beside him on long, awkward hikes.

The reassurance of a friend's kinship as we navigated through the darkness.

And my mother. A wilting rose sapped by the intensity of the storms, and yet still pushing her feet deeper into the dark soils, reaching for nutrients, for strength. The quiet moments together, each holding onto one another in a strange cocktail of fear, reassurance and compassion. Celebrating Christmas in the hospital and our friends' homes.

And my big brother. Still big, but sailing his own pathway through the storms, his dinghy bobbing along behind him through summer holidays, university, girlfriends, friendships and beer brewing sessions. There was always space in his boat for me, but I am a weak sailor and instead I chose to walk on the shore, keeping him within reach but also feeling like he was somewhat out of reach. Only time would bring him closer back to shore, and make me a braver passenger in his boat.

And then there was me. A lone duckling, stuck somewhere between adolescent and adult plumage. And oh so many birds of prey circling overhead. Hospitals. Doctors. My own medical examinations with the repercussions of underperforming. Rehabilitation and returning to the gym to sit for seemingly endless periods on the arm and bike trainers in preparation for when the day came that I would run again … because I would! And later, when the moon boot was removed, wobbling across the physiotherapy room with Kellie standing at the ready.

I am so grateful to you, Kellie, for the gentle professionalism you brought to my recovery. How you carefully massaged the swelling in thick gelatinous waves, up my leg, shooing it away from my ankle joint. How you tailored my recovery into an achievable dance that allowed me to take one small step each day in the direction of my dreams. And to my sports doctors too, who noticed as I crawled deeper into myself, finding it harder and harder to return each night to the farm and carry adult responsibility. Who recognised the silent shift in my moods from happiness to confusion, where weight started to disappear from my body and exercise habits intensified. Who saw me desperately trying to clamber back onto my feet, and running boldly towards my big, hairy, audacious goal.

Life eventually had to continue. People drifted away, university started back, and I knew that I, too, should just return to life as normal.

Except what was my normal? Running had been replaced with spinning on the bike in the gym, and rehabilitation exercises. First year was now second year, and our anatomy cadaver lay even more emaciated than before.

And still my father lay amongst white sheets.

Finally, I was able to return to my retail job in an outdoor store in Hobart, and eventually to guiding hikers, squirrelling away pennies for my overseas orienteering ambitions now only months away.

Then, one day, the farm was replaced with the urban Hobart environment, parents separated and became plural, my brother moved to Melbourne, and when Josh asked me to be his girlfriend, I panicked, and instead lost my virginity to an aggressive, dope-smoking hiking guide, only to feel even more alone. Josh left the state, and I can't remember a time when I felt further from normal than then. I felt out of control. A duckling swimming in circles, somehow invisible.

In the middle of some of these hardest times, I boarded an aeroplane to Europe with my previous orienteering and travelling companion, Sarah. The two blondes were reunited! We rolled onto the tarmac in Copenhagen, Denmark to a winter wonderland, a playground of ice, snow, and coniferous snow-monsters which had frozen and bent into icy sculptures in the minus-sixteen-degree temperatures. Taken into the Danish orienteering fold for a few weeks, I navigated through their frozen forests and leant on new friends who adopted me. But I remained silent as to what was unfolding back home. That icy landscape was a salvation, a place where I could hone my skills in anticipation of the World Orienteering Championships that would take place there later that year.

Despite my ankle's fragile state, I was running stronger than ever. I felt light and fast, no doubt somewhat assisted by my lighter body weight, but also freed from the small elements of self-doubt I had once carried. Racing against Denmark's talented athletes—many of whom would go on to become some of the greatest orienteers the world has ever seen—I was running with a new-found purpose and self-belief. I was going to get back from this trauma.

Originally, I had planned to visit Lithuania on this trip, and to prepare for the upcoming Junior World Championships too. But with winter plummeting to minus-thirty-five-degrees, I was unable to travel there. Instead, I travelled up to Sweden to spend more time with my blonde-hair-blue-eyes orienteering family. It was both freedom and entrapment.

I knew that Sarah and my clubmates found it hard to adjust to this different Hanny, the quieter and more driven Hanny, the one who would wake early to clock extra miles alone in the forest and who turned down social engagements. I still needed to adjust to and identify with the woman whose shoes I had been catapulted into, but I also had a deep desire to steer my own course. Eventually, Sarah returned to Australia early. I felt great shame at not being the bundle of fun and joy that we had both hoped I'd be on this journey, and yet coping is never an easy path nor a straight one.

I, too, returned to Australia after three weeks. I shed down jackets for summer singlets, and swapped my map and compass for medical textbooks and a pen.

When the day arrived for the postman to slip a white envelope addressed to 'Miss Johanna Allston' into our farm's handcrafted letter-box, I knew that the fate of my next year would be decided in the couple of moments it would take to open and read it. I glanced at the University of Tasmania emblem in the top corner, and hurriedly read downwards.

Pass.

DAD SPENT NEARLY five months wrapped up in bandages in the hospital. With each few forward steps his body took, further surgery and wound cleaning would send him backwards. He transitioned from operation to recovery, recovery to operation.

One day, just prior to my departure for the European competition season, he was allowed home. When I boarded the aeroplane once again for Europe, I left a mother and father, a wife and her husband, each wondering how to look the other in the eye and return to life as they had once known it.

I didn't know it would be the last time I lived within the four walls of our family home.

After a few more weeks training in the Danish forests in anticipation of the World Championships, I soon boarded my next aircraft to the destination that really mattered to my heart: Lithuania, home to the 2006 Junior World Orienteering Championships.

When I walked the aerobridge and finally took my seat next to the window, I held an absolute belief that I was going to win. This was not my ego shouting at me. Neither fear nor ego were anywhere near my conscious or subconscious thoughts. Rather, I knew that I had prepared so thoroughly and become so bulletproof to pain that all I had to do was stay honest, run with determination, and 'not fuck up!' In other words, 'just get out of the hole, pull yourself over the edge … whatever it takes'.

FOR TWO WEEKS, I darted and dodged, puffed and paused in confusion, through the open coniferous woodlands of Lithuania. I trained alongside my boyfriend, Simas, whom I had kept quietly tucked away in my email inbox since the previous year's competitions in Switzerland. For the first time since my family unit had fractured, I entered a family home and was quickly invited inside by a father, mother, uncle, sister, brother. I learnt about the Lithuanian way of life and, in return, shared some of my own culture with them. From berry cakes and apple crumbles to my brother's famous veggie burger recipe, I prepared some of the meals and then sat around their family dining table to share photos of a life back in Tasmania.

Later, Simas and I would let the evening linger, late sunlight lengthening the shadows as we wandered along uneven, potholed backroads now coming alive with children playing soccer and dogs impatiently walking with their sauntering hand-in-hand owners. If it wasn't for the grey multi-storey apartments, the wire fences and willowy weeds creeping up through the cracks, this could have been a representation of life back home in Australia. I marvelled at how small the world could feel, how intimate moments of normal life could bridge the oceans between cultures.

I felt very at home in the Lithuanian landscape by the time the rest of our National Junior Team arrived, eagerly dragging their duffels and assorted luggage up onto the steps of a grand log home in the heart of a beating forest—our home for the remaining week leading into the competitions. As Simas drove away in his small hatchback car, I waved goodbye with mixed feelings.

From within the building's solid clutches barrelled an over-sized Lithuanian male with a hefty handshake and a sweating forehead. He tugged at the suspenders stoically holding up his drooping trousers, his shirt collar slightly too tight for his rotund neck. Enthusiastically, he waved us inside and began to show us to our rooms with a mighty slap on the back and a deep, growling laugh. We dutifully observed and politely acknowledged every inch of his home, which had been hand-carved by him from the forest beyond. From figurines to representations of the natural woodland species, every square millimetre of his home was carved into a wooden story, even down to the chairs which poked and prodded us as we eagerly awaited dinner.

That training week was perhaps the most hungry that any of us had ever been. From morsels of rice with cabbage broths, to plates of wilted nettles and tough, overcooked chickens that left the boys sweating and frustrated as they tried to carve slivers from the poor birds' chests, the team would go to bed dreaming of food and the pancake parlours that we found adorning the small town of Vesterus in south-eastern Lithuania. So, after each training session, we would tick off another day until the competitions began—and then fill our mouths with wild raspberries, strawberries and blueberries, till mouths turned red and fingers blue. Then we would head back into town and sit beside the Neris River to picnic on baguettes, local salad ingredients and rich cheeses. Or at least, the team did. I was becoming more and more careful of the food that entered my system, and I didn't have the appetite for many of the treats that the others enjoyed. A baguette and an apple and I was done. I sat back and watched the others tuck into Lithuanian delights, wondering which one of us was normal.

I AWOKE FILLED with a sense of purpose. I slipped out of the room I shared with a teammate and entered the quietness of the morning, watching the town awaken as I jogged, stretching and easing my way into an awakened state. Returning to the hotel, I stripped down and stood beneath the beating shower, feeling the water running through my hair, a cascading massage from my head to my back.

Heated to the core, I turned off the water and reached for my towel. It was then that I firmly laid eyes on the three words I had written on the back of my hand last night. Transcribed from lessons in my training journals and the etchings across my training maps, I had summarised the way I wanted to run the race that day in three short words: *Discipline. STOP. Compass.* Act with discipline, avoiding the temptation to focus on the results. Stop when in doubt, to avoid unnecessary risks from rushing critical navigational decisions. Focus exceedingly carefully on my compass lines in the low visibility of the dense young competition forest we were racing in. If I executed the race as planned, the results would take care of themselves.

There are many things that could have distracted me that day. After breakfast, as the minutes slid past, one-by-one I watched my teammates disappear onto crowded buses destined for the race start, the laden vehicles growling out of the hotel's car park with nervous faces peering back.

Thanks to a great seeding, I was due to run later in the morning, wedged into the middle of the starting field. So, I filled time with trusty Harry Potter until it was my turn to leave the comfort of the hotel, too. I swung my bag onto my shoulder, draped my competitor ID tag around my neck, and turned towards the car park, eventually grabbing a seat at the very front of the bus.

While I smiled at my competitors as they too boarded the bus, my mind was quietly on-task, rehearsing my race and imaging each disciplined moment as I paused to read the map, look up and scan the forest, and navigate without rushing.

I have never trained in visualisation, but the concept comes very naturally to me. Before every big race, I find myself turning inwards to rehearse the day ahead, visualising control, discipline, and running strength, as I move through the forest. Whenever I master this, the execution feels second-nature in the race, and the outcome becomes nearly inevitable.

However, on that day, the journey to the starting arena was highly unusual and somewhat disconcerting. As the bus heaved its occupants closer and closer to the forest's edge, dodging oncoming vehicles and swerving around chugging tractors, we observed a four-wheel-drive attempting to overtake us on the muddy verge with one wheel in the ditch. Moments later, impatient about a slower vehicle, the bus driver swerved into oncoming traffic, gamely crossing double white lines and nearly colliding with oncoming vehicles, only to realise there was a policeman trailing in our wake.

Unsurprisingly, we were pulled over to the side of the road. Our driver, meaty hands plonked onto the upper stretches of the steering wheel, gazed nonchalantly back at the prim and proper cop outside the firmly closed doors of the bus. Neither appeared prepared to budge, and so we sat there in an increasingly stifling, nervous swelter watching the cop bang ferociously on the door. Eventually, the driver smacked a large red button and the door creaked and groaned open in a blast of fresh air and angry policeman. The altercation continued for a long time, neither male willing to give in to the other, until a frustrated, twenty-year-old Swede pushed his way to the front and yelled, 'Do you realise this is a World Championship?' Later, when we finally lurched into the forest clearing that heralded the start of the race, the police car pulled in behind us.

As I disembarked from the bus, I had already entered my bubble, my inner sanctuary where external pressures are forgotten, and inner focus is found. I was nearly ready.

Ankles strapped. Spare compass in my back pocket. Long socks pulled up to meet my three-quarter tights. Orienteering is practical but also fashion at its worst. I stood in the queue of athletes ready to enter the starter's chute, neither aware of nor caring about those around me. I had never felt so prepared and focused as I did in that moment.

The starter's clock beeped. The cool feel of the map was in my hand. Tranquillity was disturbed only by the snapping of twigs and undergrowth beneath my feet. Forest slipped past me. I was running, running, running, in complete sync with the challenges of the terrain.

Pausing, scanning, seeing. Steady, calm, collected. Heart beating, lungs searing, legs screaming. Downhill, uphill, under, through. I was completely in control. Heavy quadriceps, crying calves, but a lightness in my steps.

The finish chute was nearing! Speed, agility, the heavy pine needles giving way to deciduous leaf litter and, finally, the grassy finish chute. Gently up, sprinting along, collapsing over the finish line.

Junior World Champion … job done!

I had won Australia's first ever gold medal at a Junior World Orienteering Title.

WE PEDALLED the hotel's novelty billy-carts through the streets of Vesterus, wreaths of birch leaves and wild flowers wrapped around my neck and my head. We were heading to the town square in a blast of hoots and toots, to where a stage was set up to host the medal presentations. I could barely recollect any of the fifty-six minutes I had spent in the forest that day.

The team was whooping and whizzing in an adrenalin-filled show of excitement, legs powering on the pedals and hands loosely grasping the handlebars. As we rushed around another corner, I saw Simas, standing on the sidewalk. He grinned, hands deep in his pockets in quiet humility. I gave him a small wave and pressed my hands together in a gratitude-filled prayer motion. He knew what I was saying.

Thanks … thanks from the bottom of my heart for helping me prepare for today. Thank you for welcoming me into your home and helping me understand Lithuanian culture and your fairytale forests. Thank you for loving me, whole and complete, and making me feel beautiful. Thank you for making me laugh when I feared I had forgotten how, and for holding my hand when I otherwise would have walked alone. Thank you for being you, and allowing me to love you too.

The Australian national anthem resonated out through the town square where we gathered. I looked down on a sea of excited faces:

coaches, managers, teammates, friends in competition, mothers, fathers, and locals.

And then finally I saw her: Mum. I smiled an embarrassed smile then looked down at my feet. I was humbled and awkward in the spotlight. My dream had not involved the gold medal and ceremonial part.

Rather, it had been my war to get back onto my feet, to once again run free, and to punctuate this end to my junior orienteering career in the way I had always hoped for—my best year yet.

Mission accomplished.

10

The red and white of Switzerland and the blue and yellow of Ukraine breezed past me through the green of the Danish deciduous forests. The colours but a blur, an unwanted distraction. I pressed on with purpose. Mindfully, and with heightened imagination, I weaved between the tree trunks, using the changing colours of birch, beech and conifer as pretend checkpoints.

I was far from my island home of Tasmania, and yet I also felt at home here. I loved this place with its reaching fingers of fertile farmland that crept into the heart of the forests. The locals were hospitable and generous. Families had welcomed me into their fold as I prepared for this World Championship. Even Frederik, Crown Prince of Denmark, had provided us access to that forest, his forest, the home of his summer escapes.

I pulled my focus back to the blank paper I carried in my right hand. It was my pretend map. As I ran, I asked my mind to transcribe an imaginary orienteering course onto it. I was running through this forest pretending to race my World Championship final in an active version of visualisation. I looked down at my 'map' whenever my mind wandered or I caught sight of my competitors, pulling my attention into its contours and imaginary detail. Guided by the compass tightly gripped by my right thumb, I weaved and darted through the forest that I no longer saw. I was too in-tune with executing my perfect race.

I was transporting myself forty minutes forward in time to when I would be racing around the intricate gardens of Prince Frederik's summer house. To when I would be racing for the honour of representing Australia at the World Orienteering Championships in the final of the Sprint Distance, there in Denmark. To when I would be racing a perfectly executed orienteering race.

I was running, navigating, orienteering … freely. As I went through the warmup, I allowed this sensation of freedom to lift me up, to assist me over logs, tree roots, and rough ground. Two weeks prior, I had run towards, and then beyond, my goal of winning the Junior World Orienteering Championships, with a massive six minutes' margin, becoming the first non-European to do so.

Today, I was running again, and I felt purposeful. I was navigating towards a brighter future. While my body weaved through the forest, my mind navigated me to the vast finish chute with the commentary and crowds of this pinnacle of orienteering. And as I felt my body loosen more and my feet began to flow over the deep deciduous leaf litter and blueberry ground cover, I knew I was ready.

I turned towards the start line. I was twenty years old. Still filled with turmoil. But chasing positive outcomes. A reconstructed ankle still recuperating. A medical student by day. An athlete by morning and afternoon. A daughter by night. A Junior World Champion as of two weeks prior. Doubters left behind. A girl on a mission … and I was ready.

I WAS RUNNING. Running in a curved arc around a floral garden bed. I barely noticed the plush feel of the grass, nor the manicure and cut of the perfect concentric circles. Instead, I darted behind large conifer trees, registered in the orienteering flags my electronic chip tightly tied to my finger, and then spun around. I sprinted through jumbles of flower beds, each bright with summer and illuminated by the evening glow.

I rolled down a grassy bank with a wide-open sports field before me.

As I looked left, then right, all I saw were fences. Some were just railings that I could duck beneath, others towered into the heavens to stop soccer balls mid-flight. I looked again at the map, trying to interpret which barricades I was allowed to pass over or under, and which of them would disqualify me from this race. But they all seemed impassable, and all I could see was how far around this oval I needed to run in order to play it safe. Could that possibly be right?

Now was not the time to doubt myself, so I arced to my left and ran. I ran for all the energy that I had left inside me. I ran towards my teammates, cheering in the finish arena. To our national coach who had placed his hand on my shoulder and said, 'Have a good run, Han.' For my brother, who loved this sport. For my mother nervously awaiting my arrival at the finish line. And for my father. My father …

I began to hear the commentary as a faint murmuring of 'hoola oolas'. But I was too focused on the execution to listen to this background radio channel. I already had enough internal noise going on. Each time I cleanly located another orienteering flag and began sprinting off towards the next, fear began to chirp, *Han, you are on a perfect race! Can we really keep this up right to the finish?* Simultaneously, the voice of my ego was booming, *Han, you are on a perfect race! Go! Faster!*

Six months ago, when I stood at the bedside of my father and promised him that we would climb from this hole with honesty, always with honesty, I found a new way to cut between my voice of fear and that of my domineering ego. Just like my father in his new role as State Ombudsman, a peacekeeper and gentle negotiator between parties in disagreement, honesty had become my ombudsman and the main voice that I listened to. As long as I leant into the moment, stayed present in the process and attuned to what my body and emotions were telling me, then I would always be able to race with honesty.

I ran downhill, a blur of pinks, whites and stone walls on one side, a sea of waving, cheering spectators on the other. I was looking down at my map, thinking beyond the booming voice of the commentary, and instead entirely focused on the *what next?* However, I sensed that I was gaining too much speed, tipping too close to the edge of my ability to carefully interpret the map. My inner alarm bells rang and honesty, gently implored, *Please slow down, Hanny, you need to slow down.* I applied the brakes and felt myself changing gears, coming back into control.

I was now far enough away from the spectators. I looked up to see more lawns, open and yet interspersed with many dense conifers. Tucked somewhere behind some of these trees would be the final orienteering controls of this World Championship sprint race, their red and white flags dancing a silent waltz in the evening's breeze. The shadows were now longer, and as I ran between the trees I suddenly felt like I was running in a black and white movie. My breath began to catch in my lungs, my legs seared with adrenalin and lactic acid. I found it harder and harder to think clearly, but I had come too far to make an error now, so I let the film clip slow down. By doing so, I navigated with even more precision. I saw the last control flag come into my vision.

This was the last hurdle. I allowed myself to let go of all my discipline. I launched towards it, registered my electronic chip in the control's timing box, and sprinted towards the crowds. One last glance at the map and then I allowed myself to truly believe I was there.

I leant into the challenge, gasping for air with a wide-open mouth, sucking in rasping breaths. My throat was burning, my legs searing, but I just pumped my arms as hard as I could as I sprinted up the long, grassy hill towards the finish. I was vaguely aware of cheers, of commentary, and of the huge film screens projecting this race to the spectators trapped within the arena precinct. Right now, I was focused on only one thing … finishing.

I crossed the line and drooped like a wilting flower, hands on knees, sweat beading on my forehead and running into a neat trickle between the blades of grass at my feet. I felt hands slapping me on the back, ragged hugs and excitable voices. Before I stood up to enter the excitement unfolding around me, I looked down at the two words scribed in blue ink on the back of my hand: 'For Dad'. I felt a more familiar arm, a hug so homely that I was pulled to vertical and leant forward into my mother's embrace.

I had no idea where I was placed in the field, nor how the competitors still out on the course were going. But none of that mattered. No, that day, I ran with absolute honesty and refinement. The lessons of the six months prior had matured me from a junior competitor to an adult, and a fierce competitor at that. I ran with purpose and towards the bright opening from that deep hole in which I saw myself trapped, to where the sunlight would shine brighter, and all troubles would be forgotten. I ran to overcome.

I STOOD BACK from the other girls. Behind me, I felt the stares of the drug testing personnel as I fiddled with my tracksuit, wiped my sweaty hands on my tights, shifted from one foot to the other, and tried to find a quiet moment away from the intensity of what had just unfolded. For a moment, I was hidden behind the large screens. For a moment, I was still somewhat anonymous. But all that was about to change.

We were called forward and I lined up dutifully. The British athlete, Helen, was called for sixth place. I vaguely remembered passing her somewhere along the course. Already the run was but a mere mirage, an experience so foreign that even my muscles hadn't had time to realise they had run to the limits of their sprinting fitness.

Helen bounded up the stage's steps to shake Prince Frederik's hand. Leaning in, she went to peck him in greeting on the cheek, one side then the other. But she turned the wrong way, and their heads collided awkwardly as television cameras caught the drama. With a gasp she recoiled, having fair and square planted a kiss near his lips. The crowd erupted in laughter and applause, and in that instant the tension of the moment was broken. We all began to giggle, allowing our faces to split open in big goofy grins. The mask had been shed and our pride and excitement began to filter out.

One by one, the girls mounted the stage to receive their awards. As they did, cheers broke through the still evening air, until finally I was alone. I watched as my idol, Simone Niggli-Luder of Switzerland, graciously leant forward to receive her award. She had over twenty world titles to her name. She was the goddess, the one who steamed past us in Japan a year earlier, and the one who would no doubt continue to be a force into the future.

But for now, it was me standing back here in the shadows. Alone.

Just me with a drug tester somewhere behind me, watching my every move.

Out there in the crowd, my mother eagerly awaited this moment. She had been an unfailing supporter for this journey from childhood to now. She had seen the injuries, leant into the challenges, and watched me blossom back to full strength. She had ridden her bicycle next to me when I pounded out early, frosty kilometres along silent back roads through the apple orchards of the Huon Valley. She had accompanied me when I drove to remote sheep paddocks, parked the car and then set off into the scratchy Tasmanian undergrowth to practise my navigation. She had dropped me off at airports when I decided to travel abroad for training, and picked up my jet-lagged self on my return. And yet, through all this, she too had faced her own challenges. However, right in that moment, we were celebrating.

IN DENMARK, I became a World Champion by just six seconds. Those six seconds between gold and silver would literally change my life.

Six seconds is how long it takes us to prepare our toothbrush each night. Six seconds is locking the door. Or pausing to think about the next few words I write on this page. Six seconds is the moments we don't know have passed, and yet they can be the difference between taking one path in life and another.

Six seconds is about how long it took me to mount the stage and locate the highest position on the dais. Those six seconds took me from being just any competitor to the first non-European orienteer to win a world title, and the only athlete to ever win both junior and senior titles in the same year.

However, within approximately six seconds of the gold medal being placed around my neck, I had a sudden, maturing realisation. *I am still me. I am still Hanny.* With the same challenges to return home to. A frayed family. A home emptier of happiness. A half-begun medical career.

Harder still, while the success of accomplishing my goals felt ethereal and beautiful, it also already felt fleeting.

When I had been knocked down, falling into the deep hole that opened just seven months ago, my goals formed the superglue holding the pieces of me together. My dream of winning a junior world title, let alone this senior championship, had been my big, hairy, audacious dream that helped me steer a straighter route between life's controls in those past seven months.

But in this moment, that dream was realised. I felt suddenly jabbed by the fact that I had no clue what happens next. As I opened my mouth to sing my national anthem, I felt tears prickle the corners of my eyes and the words catch in my throat. I felt like a possum in the spotlight with no idea which way to run.

11

After delayed flights and some beautiful days loitering in Amsterdam and Singapore for our connecting departures, my mother and I finally touched down onto Hobart soil. Denmark and Lithuania were a world away. In Tasmania, it was springtime. I could sense the explosion of new growth about to happen, and somehow I felt confident that I was about to put up my own new shoots. I just needed to return to my home in Sandfly which formed my life's bedrock, to plant my feet, and then life could return to normal.

I couldn't wait to greet my father and be reunited with the excitable and now fully-grown brown and white ball of energy, Molly. I was eager to return to training and give Max a mighty handshake. And to once again roam my quieter stomping grounds of Sandfly. I was excited to begin reshaping the pillars that held me strong.

As the car cruised up the last narrow section of gravel road and our home came into view, I couldn't help but notice the carefully-mown garden. And the For Sale sign pegged into the eastern boundary of the property. For Sale?

The house still sat on its stone pillars but, internally, my pillars were crashing and crumbling. For Sale? Moments earlier, I had felt a sense of strength and certainty. Now, everything I had once known and loved was turning to dust. For Sale? I had always assumed that, no matter what adversity I was faced with, I could keep patching and fixing. I was rock-solid. I had an internal sense of resilience which I now know stemmed from the stability of my childhood and the home which encompassed the heart of our family. I will forever be grateful for this.

As I stepped from the vehicle, the smell of wattle lingering in the ripe air, I was still living in youthful innocence, with a false belief that the pillars of my childhood would always exist—that Sandfly would always support the integrity of the family unit, provide space, host friendships, support my mother, rejuvenate my father, nourish our bodies, inspire my brother, welcome us home from family adventures, and host my wildest dreams.

For Sale? That was the final gust of wind in the perfect storm. My youthful innocence finally blew down the valley and out into the Roaring Forties that swept across this island. We were imploding. Not just me, but all of us. A grieving mother. A confused brother. A healing father. They, too, were trying to catch the falling rocks as the pillars crashed down around our family.

Just like feet outgrow young shoes and young toes puncture holes through the ends of old socks, holes had begun to form in the family hub of Sandfly. I walked down the steps to the house's front door—steps that in a previous era I had helped my mother and father to build. Now I knew that even if I was internally crumbling, I needed to stay externally strong. So I pulled back my shoulders, held my head tall, and walked back into 'normal life'.

I SAT amongst my medical peers, willing myself to listen, learn and catch up from the six long weeks I had missed. Yet my mind was elsewhere, drifting somewhere between For Sale signs, my parents' separate bedrooms, my father's wound care and rehabilitation routines, Max's increased intensity about not dwelling on our successes, and a fatigue that ran so, so deep within me.

I was quickly finding out that life still happens to world champions. I was beginning to falter in my juggling act. Some days, I had an energy lifting me up so that I could perform forever, and other days, I would falter and watch the balls roll away from me.

The first ball to drop was my ability to look after my body. I still cannot identify whether this came from a combination of university, home life, and lack of insight into the caloric output of training, or if it was a subconscious plea for help: *I am not coping with these changes.* I certainly knew that, where once I had been a young woman with only small hurdles to jump over as she pursued her place in the world, I was now stepping over mighty hurdles every time I went out the door.

My morning runs became earlier. My training intensity heightened. One day, my sports doctor, who had helped oversee my wellbeing when the perfect storm was brewing, began to scribble in untidy handwriting about my decreasing mental and physical health. In quiet tones, he began to encourage me to consider getting an 'unreasonable to live at home' statement from my mother that would allow me to move into a share-house and a more stable home base with the support of the government. As I stood in the kitchen at Sandfly and watched my mother fill in the paperwork, I felt like I was being torn in two.

When the day came to move into my little share-house in Hobart, a cosy, albeit freezing, place nestled into the Hobart Rivulet and the flanks of Mt Wellington, my mother was a crying, hollow woman. As I packed my belongings into my little white Peugeot, I watched her walking up the road with my friends' mother by her side. She was too distressed to even be there to see me leave.

However, as the weeks passed, we came to a new state of stasis. And then there she was in all her beauty, standing at the front door of my humble new home, holding a large wicker basket containing her famous homemade bread, jams, and vegetables from the ever-producing garden now cared for by generous friends. We sat in my cold home, wearing down jackets, sipping tea, and watching my new indoor rabbit, Ernie, gaily leaping and scampering around the carpets. And on the evenings when my head threatened to burst, she would help me through the crux of my anatomy lectures. Within my own humble space which I shared with two friends, both of whom were also trying to find their feet, I began to slowly locate mine.

My memories of this time are blurry. I believe now that I lived these early, urbanised months with an underlying tone of 'just get on with it'. Lectures and phone calls home. Training and mountain missions. Mornings in the anatomy labs and evenings running around the hills of Lower Sandy Bay while Max hung his head from his car, the pompom of his beanie waving in apparently friendly camaraderie as he yelled, 'Move your bloomin' arse!' Sharing meals with my housemates and then burying myself in medical textbooks. It was a simple, humble life, punctuated by races. A trip somewhere, and then a return. Another trip somewhere, and then another return.

A phone call from my mother punctured my new equilibrium.

Later that day I stood on the front porch of her new home at Fern Tree, a wintry suburb nestled into the mountain slopes behind Hobart. A real estate agent with glossy red nails and white-blonde hair. A converted barn with orange and green walls, and a composting toilet. A loft bedroom, and a Harry Potter room under the stairs. A house that was not my father's nor a home that I recognised as my mother's. My first lie: 'Wow, Mum! It's amazing. When can you move in?'

Blurred memories, rising and then lingering, breaching before submerging … I was trying to reach in and grab hold of them, to identify, tag, and add them to the unfolding timeline. And yet they continued to feel elusive.

A SOLD sticker slapped across the For Sale billboard at Sandfly. Unwanted possessions gifted to friends. Boxes packed, some travelling with Mum to her new treehouse on Mt Wellington, and others with my father to his new rental property on Mt Nelson. More of my own boxes packed, somehow and by someone, and then tucked beneath my mother's deck as redundant. 'Come and look through them when you can.' Friendships shifted, my horses replaced by Ernie the indoor rabbit. Then, eventually, Molly went to live with a new family in suburbia.

BABY STEPS. *Just don't stop moving. Keep moving forwards. Roll with the punches. Rest my focus. Adjust to life in the 'big smoke'. Answer that lingering, burning question, what next?*

Turn a blind eye to the empty passageways. Turn a blind eye to the empty single bed resting in the corner of my old bedroom. Turn a blind eye to the scars beneath the hems of my father's shorts. Turn away from the lack of femininity in his new house.

Pay attention to the Krebs cycle and neuromuscular innervation of the pectoralis muscles.

Drive the winding route to my mother's new treehouse. Brave her dangerously steep and rutted driveway. Turn a blind eye to the orange and green walls, the composting toilet, and the taut smile of my mother grappling to also find her feet.

IT WAS my twenty-first birthday and I knew that I needed to keep inner positivity flowing, for fear that I would otherwise be buried by the landslides of change occurring around me. We celebrated this key life moment at the Cascade Brewery, and I laughed as my brother stood on a pillar, sharing quirky anecdotes of my childhood exploits with friends and family. Afterwards, he pulled me aside and suggested, 'Maybe you need a boyfriend?'

A boyfriend appeared. Then quickly disappeared.
Winning the Tasmanian Sports Star Awards.
Shopping for food that tasted bland.
Winning the Tasmanian Institute of Sport Athlete of the Year.
Trying medical parties and then realising I hated alcohol.
Winning the Tasmanian Young Achiever of the Year Award.
Another handshake with Max.
Another personal best time on the track.
And then … parental divorce?

IT IS easy to wish we could turn back the clock to those critical moments that lead to all the latter moments. Twelve years later, I wish I could wrap my younger, confused self in a hug and thrust a steaming mug of tea into her hand, and say,

Have patience Han, don't rush the next steps. It is okay to stand still for a while. Stare at the view and reflect on just how far you have come. Nurture yourself with what makes you feel strong and empowered. Be wilder, Han. Then, only once you have your feet back on the ground, begin to remind yourself of what brings you joy. Run on the mountain's convoluted trails for the pure euphoria that a sunrise can bring you. Visit your favourite places and find some new ones, too. Explore a little. Play in the rain and jump in the puddles. Rebuild your foundations and play wilder, Han. Only then can you lean into performance again. Only then can you stretch yourself to perform wilder.

Hanny, athletic success is not a way to judge your strength and character. Athletic success is never going to be the superglue, or the thing you are proud of when you are telling anecdotes in the retirement village. Life is not about winning medals, breaking records or receiving accolades. Nor will athletic success heal you or change you for the better.

True success is a willingness to put yourself on the knife edge and dance there for as long as it takes you to grow, whether that is winning or not. Failure is an unwillingness to walk in these brave shoes, shying away from the moment which requires you to stand on the precipice and lean into the wind.

Hanny, I can finally see that you were indeed a champion. However, it was not the gold medals that made you successful. It was your willingness to put yourself on the edge of your discomfort, to lean into the emotional and physical pain you experienced as you waded back from ankle reconstruction and the tearing heart of your family. Success was the bravery you showed as you re-entered the forests on a reconstructed ankle. It was your ability to switch back into daughter mode to support your healing parents. It was your ability to return to employment to fund your dreams, dragging shoeboxes and sleeping bags for retail customers while you were still wrestling with crutches. It was your willingness to lean into what felt like the irrelevant discomfort of university exams, when all you wanted to do was walk away from it all. It was your willingness to bravely approach the edge of your discomfort when you knew that your father was back home and taking his own brave steps in rehabilitation. It was your willingness to race with a humble, honest heart. It was those six higgledy-piggledy months when you first hobbled, then walked, ran, and finally thrived on the knife edge. Therein lay your success, Hanny. Success was *the journey*.

But Hanny, now that you have walked this narrow pathway and put every ounce of your energy into your dream, it is okay to take a step back, and nestle yourself into a safe hidey-hole. Snuggle in out of the breeze and enjoy the view for a while. It is okay to pull delicious delights from your pockets and refuel yourself. It is okay to sit still and even to close your eyes for a while. Take a rest! For what we have learnt from this journey so far is that we must *be more* to do more, rather than, 'I need to do more to be more.' For even when you strive to create meaning from purpose and ambition, it is okay to also sit still.

HOWEVER, rather than pause and let the enormity of the moment that had just passed sink in, I desired the stability of another big scary goal. I began to set my sights on both my orienteering and my athletic running. Almost as soon as my feet hit the ground I was on the go, from training to university, family to friends, and back to training.

The only sitting still that my younger self did was in front of the Dean of the University of Tasmania's medical faculty. Once again, I found myself asking for his permission: 'I wish to defer my third-year studies for a semester.'

A short while later and with a sinking heart, I left his grey office. Despite the kindness in his face and his desire to assist me with my ambitions, he had given me an ultimatum. 'Sadly, there really is no option other than to continue your studies.' Due to changes to the medical faculty's academic programs, there was no opportunity for students in my year group to take leave from the course without returning all the way to the beginning of the degree. This would take me from the end of second year all the way back to Day Zero.

I tried to reflect on the appropriate course of action but, each time I tried to think about staying on at university, an anxiety so scalding hot would wash over me. I felt myself shutting down, dreading each class, lecture, and especially the clinical sessions where we talked endlessly about the drug options available to patients. This was one aspect I had always found difficult to accept about the modern medical model. I was finding it increasingly difficult to feel empathy towards members of the community who had chosen not to look after themselves and thus ended up in a health crisis requiring medications to 'fix them'.

After much deliberation, I sat down with my laptop and logged into the internal university network. With one simple click of a button, I was no longer a medical student. What next?

TODAY WHEN PEOPLE introduce me as a world champion, I find myself wondering if they believe that it is the highlight of my career, the beaming bright light shining on a spectacular part of my life. My whole life.

Becoming a world champion was certainly spectacular! To meet a prince and realise a long-held dream is enough to still make me smile with a big, broad, goofy grin. To reflect on the richness of support networks rallying around me, and how our hard work culminated in that perfect day. And to know that in that one moment I had to perform, when everything I stood for counted, I made that moment perfect. That is definitely a highlight, and one I will always be proud of.

Today, when I watch other athletes perform with eloquence and see the sheer joy on their tanned faces as they lift their arms into the sky in exuberant glory, I feel their success. I read that moment as if I had been a character in their book.

And yet, at the same time, I know there is a more subtle story being told in that moment. A story that most likely involves heartache and hefty winds, discomfort and sometimes even despair. A story that is tucked away from the media and the intensity of the spotlight. A story that may never be told because of the vulnerability that comes when you do. During these moments, it is like running on a trail at night with your head torch running out of battery. You peer into the gloom and hope you have identified the obstacles. But from that dark trail, the true champion will eventually emerge into the golden colours of a new dawn, weathered but willing to now move towards the edge of their discomfort. Ready to perform on that edge, to push, to feel, to accept, and then to grow ... again. Rising above adversity. Growing with willingness. That is the highlight.

When I won my world title, I was strong. I was capable. And I was deserving. I had climbed out of the hole ready to stand high on a dais in a foreign country and sing my national anthem.

However, eventually my desire to keep running beyond the discomforts of the crashing pillars as they tumbled around me would catch up with me—a whole decade later when I least expected it. After my world title, dream-chasing transitioned from healthy ambition to fear-fuelled drive.

Little did I know that, when I won my world title, it would take years before I would come to a stop and learn to sit with the discomfort of emotions stemming from memories locked away in a dark basement. Memories and emotions that I could not see clearly and most definitely could not understand. It would take every ounce of bravery to allow myself to feel the writhing knot and surging fears of a young girl whose innocence abruptly ended as she was forced to become a woman and a world champion all at the same time. When I won that gold medal, little did I know that at thirty years of age I would sit in the corner of my kitchen, darkness heavy in the dead of the night, and quietly rock back and forward as the young girl within me finally grieved for everything she had lost so suddenly. By allowing herself to grieve, she was finally able to celebrate everything she went on to achieve.

Only then would this chapter of my life finally reach a natural end point. Planting my feet, dusting off the memories, reassuring that child within and then growing as an adult would finally allow me to put closure on the part of my life that I have named The End of Innocence.

PART III
LOSING MY FEET

2007–2009

Tuition at training with Max Cherry (Photograph: Sören Andersson, www.2see.se)

12

'Traumatised people chronically feel unsafe inside their bodies: the past is alive in the form of gnawing interior discomfort. Their bodies are constantly bombarded by visceral warning signs, and, in an attempt to control these processes, they often become expert at ignoring their gut feelings and in numbing awareness of what is played out inside. They learn to hide from their selves.'

—Bessel van der Kolk, *The Body Keeps the Score: Brain, Mind, and Body in the Healing of Trauma*

I always promised myself that when I wrote this book I would do so in an authentic, honest way. For me, it is really important that I use this process of writing to not only understand my own story and grow from within it, but to share these lessons with others who may also nod their heads and say with astonishment, 'Me too!'

I am really not proud of the era following my world orienteering title. It is a chapter where the pages became dog-eared and damaged, and at times went missing altogether. And I feel vulnerable. It discusses a time when I somehow slipped from my path, crashing down through the undergrowth, sliding, and catching my toes in every hole. Brambles caught in my hair. Thorns ripping at my confidence. Finally, I popped out onto a new pathway and tried to navigate out of the dark, confusing valley I found myself in. A valley so distantly foreign to the valley of my childhood that even my wilder spirit within began to hibernate.

I followed this new path and each time I felt like I might be about to break through onto the summit ridge, expecting to look back at the view and think, *Phew, what a ride!*, I would crest a rise only to find another hill, another descent, another climb. So I rose and slipped down, rose and slipped down … until I began to realise this wasn't my path.

At times I saw beauty—in intimate connections, foreign tongues, learning, running, exploring new landscapes and redefining relationships with my family members. But it was also a period where I was often living a double life. The confident Hanny would say to my increasingly estranged self, 'Follow me!' And then there was the other version of me who felt wildly outside my comfort zone, where old coping strategies could no longer serve me. Climbing trees, draping my arms around the neck of Humphry the horse, stomping off across the paddocks with gumboots flicking mud up the back of my legs and a dog happily in tow … these strategies no longer served me as I unshackled from my youthful innocence and wandered this new pathway leading towards a place called Adulthood. The path was too rough for training wheels, so I lurched and bumped my way forwards. And as I rounded each corner I found myself asking, *What next?* or, *How much further?*

My parents always have been and always will be there for my brother and me. But at that point, I felt that their headspaces were preoccupied with getting their own feet on the ground. Having grown up as a tight family unit in our little valley, they were the ones I would turn to first for advice, Dad with his more cautious approach, Mum with her vibrant energy and positivity. And yet, after I left medical school, when the *What next?* question loomed over me, I felt afraid to reach out for their guidance.

I had crashed off-course from an eight-year-old's medical dream. In my chosen sport I had gone from being an underdog to suddenly learning to be the girl that all the new underdogs were chasing. When I returned to orienteering, even at the local Sunday afternoon events, I felt like a rabbit in the spotlight. I was 'Hanny the World Champion', rather than 'Hanny'. When I ran in the local fun run, I was Hanny the World Champion. And without even realising it, Anorexia had sidled up next to me, a shadow amongst the shadows, and begun to whisper in my ear, 'I am here, Hanny. I can help you. Just listen to me and I can help you be strong. I can help you navigate through all of this.'

I feel vulnerable as I prepare to expose this friendship to you. Despite the repercussions, she became my friend—and yet it feels forbidden to utter her name. She is like the closed doors and long hallways of my youth. For as I learnt over time, even when Anorexia is evidently in a room with us, we try to look the other way. She will sit squarely alongside us like a pedantic, preening imp, and yet the topic of conversation will steer away from her. Until the two of you are alone and she makes herself the topic of conversation once more.

Together, we would enter the supermarket and pick up packet after packet of foods, turning them over and glancing at the nutritional display on the back. Anorexia would then put them down again, and we would wander onwards with a basket containing a couple of apples and some rice crackers. While some elements of my friendship with Anorexia were strange and warped, some of them were beautiful. Such as when we would rise early together, slipping out the door of a quiet house to run along quiet streets gently lit by streetlamps.

In fact, following my departure from medicine, there are many, many memories that I fondly reflect upon. Such as meeting my new boyfriend and sharing an adventure in the Flinders Ranges; moving together to New Zealand to study teaching; struggling to find somewhere to live and eventually buying a camper van in which we gaily trundled across the country during our leave breaks. Or returning to race abroad and teaching a classroom of eager, bright-eyed eleven and twelve-year-olds. Then, later, living with my brother in Melbourne. These are the strong, defining and beautiful moments in this chapter.

However, many are so tightly interwoven with my friendship with Anorexia that at times I cannot tell one story without telling the other. During this era of losing my feet, Anorexia accompanied me on every step of the journey, and I am not proud of holding her hand so tightly during this time. In fact, her presence creates a large shadow that overpowers the highlights. It pains me to have to relive this friendship again.

I am not proud of standing on a stool to reach the top of my host family's kitchen cupboards to where they stored the pick'n'mix sweet treats they bought at the supermarket. Somehow it didn't feel like I had eaten them if I didn't buy them myself. No, I am not proud of this chapter of my life where I walked a foreign route. And yet it happened. Sadly, it happened …

I attended parties, but so too did Anorexia. I am not proud of sneaking into a host's kitchen to lick the remnants of pavlova, cream and jam from the pots sitting beside her sink. But it happened! And I awoke the next day to run extra kilometres because I was too scared to let Anorexia invite Bulimia into this friendship with us too. It happened!

I allowed Anorexia to lead me by the hand, to have her shed any remnants of my youthful puppy fat until I was a minuscule forty-five kilograms, a running skeleton. Yes, Anorexia and I walked through three years of life together as best mates, shrugging off concerned looks from friends and family, before I realised that her friendship no longer served me.

Until the day when I sat beside my mother in the consulting room of a Hobart dietitian, having just consumed half a scone for lunch and Anorexia still dissatisfied with my discipline. Cutting through the noise of my internal critic, I heard the dietitian say to my mother, 'When Hanny gets angry or upset when you try to help her, it is not Hanny that is upset or angry, it is Anorexia. Anorexia is a disease.'

Something in this short statement cut through the fog of confusion. The overwhelming fear and loneliness that I had bottled away was finally allowed to flood to the surface. For the first time ever, someone had recognised that there were two people in the friendship—Hanny AND Anorexia!

When I had walked further and further with Anorexia on a pathway, I had slowly walked in the opposite direction to my friendships. And I had missed them!

I missed being able to run with a full tank of energy, or sleep warmly without a plethora of blankets piled over me. And more than anything, I missed my relationship with Happy Hanny, who had spent her younger years stuffing juicy, spurting berries into her mouth as she lay beneath dripping raspberry canes on the farm. Or eating her friends' meals so that we could return more quickly to the great outdoors to play. Or cooking beside my mother. Or making hefty chocolate cakes with my brother. Or simply sitting down at the dinner table without Anorexia sitting down beside me.

Removing myself from the toxicity of my friendship with Anorexia was not as simple as letting go of her hand and turning my back on her for good. She was my shadow lurking in the shadows. And even without her, I still couldn't see beyond the false summits to where my true north lay. However, I started willing myself to let go of her control. To become used to the feeling of being absolutely, undeniably out of control. To feel lost.

When I returned to my mother's house after meeting with the dietitian, for the first time in a long time I did not fight her when she put a small plate of food in front of me. Even as fear and a loss of control overwhelmed me and I wanted to push the plate away, I verbally agreed to allow the clock, not Anorexia, to tell me when to eat. I agreed to take baby steps alongside the support of my beautiful, caring mother, who came to walk on my pathway too. I made sacrifices, let myself be led during the times when I couldn't navigate myself, until finally I learnt to listen to my heart and not my head. To my own voice and not that of Anorexia's.

I learnt to be my own best friend, and to be okay hanging out with myself, and within myself, again. And as I did, Happy Hanny, with her ferocious maverick spirit and willingness to be a healer, emerged from the undergrowth to walk beside me once again. A little too thin, a bit bedraggled, wearing clothing that didn't look like hers. But by navigating her way through that adventure, Happy Hanny had grown two feet taller, had found her heart and her feet again, and in doing so, re-found her true pathway again.

She began to see the beauty in the small things, to marvel at nature, and to fall in love with Tasmania all over again.

This is my part of the story, a story of how Happy Hanny lost her feet. And I hope that you will not judge, as I try to explain the complexities of living with a best friend who didn't serve me, on a pathway that didn't fit me.

For I hope that by sharing my story, I can support any other individual who feels that at some point they too have lost their feet, and are now seeking them again. For our own unique reasons, many of us lose our steady footing at times. While understanding 'Why?' can be helpful, the most important lesson is: 'What can I learn from all of this?' Losing our feet is a process—not an identity. What should ultimately define us is how we find them again following these harder moments. This is the part that excites me. Sometimes, we need to be dragged down until we are forced to crack, to grow, to change. This is the part that comes next.

Thank you for listening. Thank you for allowing me to share this part of the story with you.

13

Max invited me to his house. On a shimmering spring day, wattles dripped over the highways and made the mountain look like it had caught a case of chicken pox. I drove over the bridge in my small white Peugeot hatchback with a sticker of a moose firmly attached to its bumper—a mark of my love for the Scandinavian forests.

I pulled up outside Max's weatherboard cottage at Lindisfarne. The neat garden and window shutters complemented his strong handshake and perfectly positioned tartan beret as he greeted me on the front porch. This was the first time I had visited Max outside of the training environment, and I felt almost nervous. He had this strong, bold presence. A gruffness that felt challenging to crack, his wisdom and strength zipped tightly into his blue and green tracksuit. He handed me a glass of orange juice. Orange juice. Max's beverage of choice.

We wandered inside, and he proudly waved his hands at the autographed Aussie Rules football memorabilia adorning his walls. I cooed respectfully, although I didn't want to deflate his bubble by saying that I had never watched football in my life. Nor owned a barbecue. Nor watched a live cricket match. In this way, I was very un-Australian.

I sat down next to him on the couch, sinking into the plush, tightly-knit brown cushions with a tartan quilt arranged neatly over the top. A cat rubbed against my leg as his wife Jo entered the room with more orange juice. He looked at her with absolute adoration, for she was his strength. The half that made him whole. But as Max began to speak, she slipped away, and we were left alone. He looked me deep in the eyes, 'What next, Hanny?'

I looked back at him, feeling like his wisdom was seeing right through me. To the small cracks that had formed in my confidence and resilience since I returned home from the world championships three months prior. Sensing my hesitation, he picked up my hand and gave it a squeeze, 'I think you have the potential to be an Olympian.'

Suddenly my mind travelled back to a moment on the farm at Sandfly, sitting on my bed with legs crossed and a journal open on my lap. Three goals:

Be an Olympian.

Live at the AIS (Australian Institute of Sport).

Become a Doctor.

I looked back at Max as his eyes searched through me. I felt a surge of purpose returning, like he was passing the Olympic flame to me. I had just won a world title. But an Olympian?

I left Max's house with a small white envelope, and drove the few short kilometres down to the waterfront. With a vantage point across the neck of the Derwent to the mountain slopes rising behind, I edged my finger through the seal and pulled a letter from the envelope's clutches. I began to read …

'Dear Hanny,' he began, 'I firmly believe in your potential.' Etched across the rest of the paper's surface in soft grey pencil was a step-by-step plan of attack for the Cadbury Marathon looming a mere three months away. Until that point, I had always sworn that I would never run the marathon. And yet here I was, a training plan in my hot little hands and Max's Olympic flame beginning to burn inside. For the first time in a long while, I could feel purpose and self-belief returning.

I STOOD on the start line of Hobart's local Cadbury Marathon, shifting from one foot to the other, nervously excited about what was to come. The rich smell of chocolate a gentle backdrop to the colourful scene of runners, mostly locals who make this pilgrimage every year. Nerves were not part of the equation, merely an excitement for embarking on something new.

Again, I felt like this race was not just for me, but rather for the dream that Max and I had sparked together. He was there today. A steady presence blending into the crowd of onlookers, hiding from the parents, with his trusty antique timing device hanging around his neck, his thumb hovering over the start button in anticipation.

Max didn't like fuss. He liked good old-fashioned hard work and perseverance. And I had given him that, and a little more. I stuck his handwritten plan on my fridge and executed it to a tee, adding extra morning runs and some gym work to make sure that when I stood on the start line, I felt ready. I also knew that in my toolkit was the knowledge and strength that came from my eighty-two kilometres down the Overland Track of Tasmania. And the knowledge of what it took to be a world champion. I had found myself drawing on these priceless experiences during Max's toughest track sessions and now, again, on this day. I was slowly learning not to say, 'I can't.' Max said there is no such thing as 'I can't'.

Just as we were about to start, I felt a small tap on my shoulder. Spinning around, I came face to face with a warm smile, a headful of red, tightly-curled hair and the question, 'I hear if I run with you, we might go under three hours?' Nerves coursed through me. I didn't know that anyone knew our plan. It was supposed to be a secret, but somehow the newspapers had caught hold of the excitement, and now my new friend was smiling back at me expectantly. I smiled back. 'Maybe ...'

We ran the first thirty kilometres together. We literally ran side by side, learning about each other's love of running. Then, as the glucose levels got lower, we learnt about each other's dreams, studies, and families. We held so much in common—a love of running and a love of the human body. He was a student of physiotherapy in Western Australia, and I had been a student of medicine. With each step, a friendship grew, and our competitive natures were left on pause until ... I heard the familiar rumble of the hatchback, then brakes applied, and finally the inevitable boom of Max's voice, 'Move your bloomin' arse!'

As he cruised alongside, I saw his pompom waving in the morning breeze, his watchful eyes monitoring our strides, and his heart urging me to keep moving. The chatting ceased, the tempo lifted and soon I was sweating inside my polo shirt and cotton bike shorts. My heavy training shoes suddenly felt heavier. That was another thing about Max. As long as we had done the work, it didn't matter how we looked or the professionalism of our gear. He simply advocated, 'Do it, believe it, achieve it.'

Discomfort was beginning to creep into my legs, and I focused in on absolutely every lesson that Max had ever taught me. *Run on eggshells … tuck your elbows in by turning your thumbnails to the sky … stand taller … hands brushing your hips … thumbs down, press forward …* Soon, I was floating, traversing the straighter and narrower streets, the River Derwent now far behind me. This was the first time I had ever run over eggshells, ever felt myself lifting as I pressed my thumbs down like a button. And then I was powering up the final hill, the collar of my polo shirt bouncing and my cap so soaked that sweat was dripping down my forehead. The finish line loomed, and I stretched out until I felt like my legs were being left behind. I felt like I had found my feet and I was thriving. The Cadbury Marathon of 2007 is still the easiest and most enjoyable marathon I have ever run.

On that day, Max and I shared a common goal of an inaugural sub-three-hour marathon. I crossed the finish line in two hours, forty-six minutes, twenty-seven seconds, setting a course record for women that still stands today. As I scanned the crowd, heart beating, breath catching, I finally found Max standing slightly off to the side, continuing to record his other runners as they approached the line. In his eyes, we were each as important. We were individuals, but we were also a team.

As I walked towards him, teetering slightly from side to side, he simply looked up at me, winked, and then in true Max Cherry style, held out his hand for his trademark handshake, a simple gesture that meant, 'You did good, Kid'.

Embarrassingly, I beat my new friend by a few seconds. In my heart, I felt we should have finished that run together. However, there was no defying Max: 'There are no friends in races.' As we shared a cool-down, I was surprised when he invited me to lunch with his family. Back on the tree-lined boulevard of Salamanca with him, I felt completely at ease, unaware that my new friend would become an important individual in my life for the next two years.

WHILE THE THIRD-YEAR medical students returned to university, pulled on their white lab coats, and picked up their scalpels to further explore the cadavers lying in body bags atop steel-framed trolleys, I pulled on my running shoes and big heavy backpack to return to the beaches of Maria Island as a hiking guide.

I loved this job, drenched in sunshine and bringing joy to the guests. I thrived on the responsibilities of preparing breakfasts, picnic lunches and gourmet dinners. I loved sharing stories, sitting on a bleached dune and describing the early explorers' first encounters with indigenous inhabitants as the guests lingered around smoky campfires. Or describing the whooshing spurts of the whales in nearby bays which kept the boys on their boats awake through the night.

And I loved the wide-open spaces! Rising early to tempo over the hills to the far end of the island, or to run barefoot on the beaches. I was back in time for a quick skinny-dip, then had the kettle whistling on the hob in the kitchen tent ready for my signature cup of tea in bed for the guests.

At the end of the four days, it was always hard to come home. In the quiet of Bernacchi house, a restored weatherboard cottage once home to Diego Bernacchi, an Italian entrepreneur who literally ruled the island through the late 1800s and early 1900s, I would tuck in the final hospital corners on the guests' four-poster beds before wandering down to the jetty. I would clamber aboard the small passenger ferry, and sit to the back as we chugged our way back to the mainland of Tasmania, watching the island grow smaller, and already hanging out for my next trip.

Between tours, I headed into the heart of Hobart where I enjoyed employment in a premium outdoor store called Passion8. My friend from my days of working at Paddy Pallin—Graham, with his brimming smile and keen sense of adventure—was sometimes rostered onto the same shifts. On these occasions, we would try to start or finish the day with a ride or run, all the while plotting and scheming, excitedly talking over the top of one another about what we would do differently if we owned the shop. Little did we know that one day this fanciful idea would become a reality. These early what-if scenarios were never meant to become deep, mature conversations around the dinner table, which in turn would evolve into emotionally laden questions while overlooking one of Hobart's local beaches from the front seat of the van: 'What are we doing?' I loved juggling the wide-open spaces of guiding on Maria Island with the dynamic environment of outdoor retail.

However, when a more operational role presented itself with The Maria Island Walk, I eventually felt compelled to leave the security of Passion8 and follow my growing love of ecotourism and Tasmania. It would be over two years before I caught up with Graham again.

On the cooler, sometimes damp, winter mornings, after an early training session, I pedalled down to my new job at Taroona, a ten kilometre ride through narrow suburban streets with expansive views across the mouth of the Derwent River. Tucking my bike behind the business owner's house, I would open a side door and let myself into the hive of the office hidden in the depths of his garage. Paperwork, magazines, rain jackets, backpacks and brochures lay in strategic places throughout the small space. All telling the complex story of what it is like to run a business on an island off an island off an island, and all from the garage of your family home. I loved listening to the pitter-patter of his children's small feet as they danced around his home upstairs. I fed off his enthusiasm and gratitude. That role filled me with such a strong sense of purpose that for a while I began to wonder whether my long-term place might be in the tourism industry.

However, deep down I knew that there was unfinished business at university. One day, I stopped outside the familiar doorways of the medical faculty and chained my bike to the grey metal railings. Pushing open the familiar door into the familiar grey office to be greeted by the familiar face of the Dean of the Medical Faculty, I shook his hand. Then I sat down in a grey chair and confronted the grey question that had been lingering in my heart since I left this place six months previously: 'How can I finish my degree?'

As I left his office, I was still not a medical student, but a student of medical science. He granted me the opportunity to finish my pre-clinical medical sciences so I could at least be granted a Bachelor of Medical Research.

It was a struggle to return to medical college for my third and final years of studies. Even though I went on to graduate after these twelve months of study, deep in my heart I knew that working in the research side of medicine wouldn't satisfy my personality. I was a wilder child at heart, and I had always felt propelled by the idea of problem-solving and performing medicine in remote area settings. I had always envisaged zooming around in helicopters and working in outreach clinics in the field. A life behind a microscope or playing with Petri dishes simply didn't make my toes tingle.

And yet I also knew that I was not going to be returning to medicine, not now at least. There was no way I wanted to enter first year medicine with students fresh out of school when I could have been starting fourth year. Looking back, I am sure there was ego tangled up in these decisions, but also a deeper desire tugging me in a different direction.

I had a profound sense that I wasn't doing what I was meant to be doing. In the heat of this moment of confusion, a medical career felt like glue that would hold me to my past. Finishing a degree, any degree, felt like a wind that could blow me forward towards my future.

And right then, in that moment, I was eager to be moving forwards. Because if I wasn't moving forwards then I was afraid of what might catch up with me.

Away from the formaldehyde and stifled lecture theatres of the university, I could feel myself beginning to bloom, like a bulb that had just been through the winter and was popping out new shoots. What was feeding my growth was a blossoming friendship with Jarrod, my Cadbury Marathon comrade. When his studies were completed, two months after we ran side by side along Hobart's marathon course, Jarrod moved back to Tasmania. Rather than returning to Launceston and his family, he chose to relocate to Hobart.

We had avoided the usual emails and long phone calls, instead choosing to write handwritten letters to one another throughout those two months. From this correspondence, I could tell that he was a special person, an individual who ignited something in me, and I truly felt he saw the same in me. This was the first time I had openly let someone else into my life without holding up walls to protect myself. I still felt vulnerable and exposed by my experiences in the dark basement of the Sydney Olympic Aquatic Centre.

During Jarrod's return journey to Tasmania we met up in South Australia, where I was racing at a large national orienteering carnival on the outskirts of the Flinders Ranges. Our friendship bloomed amongst red dust and dry creek beds, beneath towering river red gums and on trails that led to summits which looked out across expansive vistas. We would lie in the tent at night, using sleeping bags to ward off the coolness of the autumn evening, and listen to possums and pademelons bumping their way around the campsite. During the day, we explored until our legs became too weary, and then we sat on a rock and continued the conversation from where it had left off.

Jarrod sat tall and confident, thinking before he spoke. He walked slowly, rose slowly in the mornings, and prepared meals slowly in the evening. He was confident of his pathway and his role in his tightly-woven family. He was a son, a brother, and now a partner. And he adopted the role with gratitude and responsibility. When I hurt, he nurtured. When I played, he joined in. This was the friendship I had so desperately craved, the partnership that I didn't realise I needed.

Navigating the era after my world championship title alongside someone about whom I cared deeply, was both beautiful and exceedingly tough. My heart is still filled with gratitude towards the helping hands of all the friends who supported my family and me during the perfect storm which rose and collided with our individual journeys. Yet, as time passed, it was only natural that many of these friends drifted a little further away again. They moved to other states, met their own partners, became parents, or simply had to embark on their own journey to find their feet.

After the fragmentation of my family, I was acutely aware how hard it was on everyone who rallied around us—to know what to say, and how to support. After a while, words dried up, and hearts began to harden against further ache. I knew that every one of us needed permission to move on, to begin gluing the pieces back together, and so I tried very hard to maintain my independence and resilience. I often turned inwards to lean on my inner wild child, the one who never whimpered at the blackberry bushes as they tugged on bare skin, or who could fall from the heights of a tree only to bounce back up and keep running. I knew I had the strength. Max forever loved to reinforce this. And hadn't my recent Cadbury Marathon shown me this?

But when Jarrod came along, he was willing to just be alongside me, and that felt like a rare and beautiful experience. He willingly moved to Hobart and took employment as a physiotherapist at the local public hospital. For now, we were growing together beautifully. He encouraged me in my dreams, and I tried to reciprocate. When we played hard and fell deeply, I could feel my new growth stretching towards the sky, and a splash of colour filling my cheeks again.

Initially the emotions brought overwhelming joy. I was intoxicated by the relationship, and the beauty of 'first love'. However, as I allowed him closer and closer, I could also sense a greater level of vulnerability within me. This brought with it a swathe of unfamiliar emotions, and it terrified me! I failed to see this vulnerability and its associated emotions as an opportunity to grow stronger within myself and closer to those around me. It could have been the perfect opportunity to turn inwards, to confront, to accept, and then to reconnect.

But instead, I just kept running, because this felt like the more natural thing to do. Sadly, Anorexia had sidled up beside me and joined me on this run.

When I was stretched at university or overly fatigued from training, Anorexia encroached on my wellbeing. She sneaked up and began to demand my attention, praising me when I felt my tailbone pressing into the cool grey metal of the university lifts as I leant back for a rest, and urging me to keep up with the boys in training. She loved it when Max gave me feedback on my athletic development. She berated me on the nights when fatigue led to doubt.

In hindsight, I wish I had reached out for help to address the damaging beliefs and coping strategies that had begun in my formative swimming years and then developed more strongly in the wake of my ankle reconstruction and my father's accident. And when Anorexia joined me in my newly-forming relationship, it suddenly became crowded.

I was in full training for the World Orienteering Championships in the Ukraine, just a few months away. My return to the international orienteering stage was both nerve-wracking and exciting, all rolled into one. It was like sipping tea with milk, calming and yet invigorating.

News of my marathon debut had made it into the international orienteering media, and I was soon living under an intensifying spotlight. Two Swedish journalists and photographers travelled all the way to Tasmania to find the answer to the question on the tip of every orienteer's tongue: 'What is the secret in Tasmania?' For two weeks, they tailed me throughout the state, visiting Maria Island, and attending an athletics and orienteering training camp at which I was coaching younger athletes as well as preparing for my upcoming competitions. They came for breakfast at my mother's house, and followed me to university. And piece by piece, they slowly answered the question. The secret was that I trained hard in a stunning landscape filled with strangely wonderful mammals which had no Swedish language translation when they tried to complete their article. Tasmania was uniquely wild, tucked away from the rest of the orienteering world. As they quickly found out, it was a landscape that brought me great joy and belonging. It was the place where I played. Hard!

A few months before the 2007 World Championships in the Ukraine, a six-page article about my life in Tasmania was published in the world's largest orienteering publication, the Swedish magazine *Skogssport*.

Jarrod and I stepped onto the plane destined for Kiev. So did Anorexia.

I had reached out to the local orienteering club in Kiev to ask if I could be of any assistance coaching their members in return for a homestay arrangement. This is something that has always really inspired me about sport, how it can unite even the most diverse cultures. We were immediately offered the use of a family's home on the outskirts of Kiev, while they holidayed in Slovakia.

We were met at the potholed arrivals area of the Kiev Airport, then bumped and lurched our way through the wide avenues of suburbs and industrial Kiev. Thick smog belched from minibuses that scooted their way around one another, disposing of passengers onto cluttered sidewalks that doubled as the local refuse site. Eventually, we pulled up in a car park surrounded by the towering frames of Soviet-style, grey, sky-rise apartments.

Tugging our duffel bags from the depths of the van, we followed our kind, excitable host into the stairway, only to gasp and buckle in the humid, putrid air. The smell of rotting, decomposing matter thickly filled the stairwell, and accompanied us as we mounted the stairs to the first landing. I felt like I had been immersed in my father's compost heap. It was utter relief when our host twisted his key and pushed open the door into a neat, humble, one-bedroom apartment. Once the door closed behind us, the smells of the outside were replaced with that of freshly-baked cake. We were hustled into the tiny galley kitchen to meet five family members. A fresh pear torte sat on the dining table.

That first night, Jarrod and I were welcomed into the living room by our hosts, who helped us fold down the sofa bed, a ritual completed every night for twenty years by the mother and father of this family. For this living room doubled as their bedroom, while their three children shared the small bedroom next door. During the first night of our stay, our hosts insisted on sleeping beneath the kitchen table. Early the next day, they bundled and bumped their way out the front door to embark on a family holiday, and we were alone in the small apartment.

For three weeks this would be our home—one we would share with the stray cats who climbed in through the permanently open, jammed window. Our days were filled with training in the nearby forests, trying to avoid the large gullies that weaved like fingers into the suburbs and were the extensive rubbish dumping grounds for local residents. I navigated exposed heaps of jagged glass and burning piles of rubber as Jarrod trailed behind me—my athletic, red-haired bodyguard. After training, we held our breath and rushed up the flight of stairs until we were safely back in the apartment. The stench was getting worse. Every second day, we filled our arms with empty plastic water vessels and rushed back down the stairs, lining up behind small women doubled over at their middle, their head scarves wrapped tightly around greying buns. We helped them to lift and push, raise and suppress the heavy metal arm of the water pump. Clear, fresh water spurted into their vessels and then ours. This water pump was the hub of the health of the families who lived here. The innocently-flowing water from the taps was too unsafe to drink.

Jarrod and I shopped at the local markets, and filled our bags with fruit, vegetables and freshly prepared salads. We picked up hefty baguettes from the older male squatting on the sidewalk, and not once during our first few weeks in the Ukraine did we get sick.

However, Anorexia didn't fare well away from the normal routines of home. She found it difficult to manage the increased training load and the inability to stick to her safe routines. She felt the pressure of the upcoming competitions mounting. Only when we were out exploring the beauty of the eighteenth century Ukrainian Baroque architecture of central Kiev did she relax.

Until I lost Jarrod.

As the local orienteering event drew to a close—our last practice session before competition week—I handed my belongings to Jarrod in preparation for running back to the centre of town with some Kiwi friends. I waved him goodbye. 'See you outside the McDonalds at the station really soon!' Jarrod was experiencing a few niggles that day, and so had opted to walk with our belongings the short distance back to the station while I ran with my peers as a cool-down.

I arrived at the McDonalds and began stretching in a corner. I began to cool down, but having nothing with me I soon opted for wrapping my arms around me rather than overstretching. I watched as floods of people came and went, descending into the depths of the central station, disappearing into the bustling streets, and licking squelchy ice-creams from cardboard cones. I watched the light transition from noon to afternoon. Watched the short sleeves of the tourists replaced by the grey suits of the workers. And I watched the clock, with each minute bringing on a fear so terrifyingly real that eventually I found four hours of bottled tears begin to stream down my face. A concerned onlooker offered me his phone, but I had no number to call other than my parents back home. And what could they do?

I had no phone, no money, no passport, and absolutely no idea what the name of our suburb was where we were staying. Just as the panic became so real that I felt like ants were crawling beneath my skin, Jarrod appeared, running from the depths of the subway. Perhaps my panic was disproportionate to the occasion, but I was so profoundly aware of the feeling of loss that I shook for hours. 'I am so sorry Han, I am so sorry. I got lost.' Lost. Jarrod had tried to speed up his return to the station by jumping on a bus which had taken him to a different train station altogether. In the depths and complexities of Kiev's underground, he had eventually become so baffled and lost in translation that it had taken him five hours to find his way back to my tear-stained patch of pavement outside McDonalds. I had always hated McDonalds and this moment only heightened the dislike. When I was in the depths of this fear, it made me realise just how close we had become. Our relationship had transitioned from a small shoot to a young seedling, and it made me realise how important Jarrod was to me now. For the first time ever, safely back in the confines of our apartment, I told him this.

When we moved to the official race hotel, we dined on more familiar western foods in their restaurant, and drank bottled water. But by the time the competition came around, I was sick. My stomach was swollen like a beach ball. Anorexia rejoiced in the discipline of avoiding meals. I ran through the entire competition week like a scared cat, chased by the media and hounded by my own internal pressure. I made errors, but ran quickly to make up for them, finally flopping across the finish line with a podium result in the long-distance event. However, around the hilly parklands overlooking the tiled roofs and grey Soviet apartments of Kiev, I panicked my way into ninth place in sprint distance. I couldn't help but feel disappointed by this result.

I nearly cried with relief when our aircraft finally lifted from the Kiev tarmac. I was ready to go home. However, we had already planned a short, two-night stay in Kuala Lumpur, where we roamed the streets without the looming pressure of competition. I felt more capable of tucking Anorexia into bed and playing hard without her. On our final morning, we roamed the city streets one last time, picking up a few final gifts for our families back home. We quickly ducked into the supermarket in the basement of our hotel to grab some provisions for lunch. The lift was full as we ascended to our hotel floor and it was a relief to shut the door of our hotel room. I picked up the internal phone and dialled reception, 'Can you please order us a taxi to the airport?'

I am not sure when Jarrod suddenly realised that our sole credit card was missing, or how long we searched his pockets, our bags and amongst shopping for it. We raced back down to the supermarket and then lurched our way back to the room. The deadline for departing for the airport was fast approaching, and we had at least ninety kilometres to travel there from the hotel. It was a public holiday and, as we found out when we approached the taxi rank, there was also a taxi strike at play. With no money, and only a few gifts still wrapped in tissue paper, we had little leverage for a lift.

Perhaps he could see the panic or hear my heart pleading to return home, but one kind male finally opened the back door of his taxi and ushered us inside. Hanging from his rear vision mirror was an elephant. I couldn't take my eyes off it as he drove us along broad freeways, pulling money from his own wallet to pay for the excessive tolls. The elephant wobbled and jiggled its way to the airport with us as this generous, gently-spoken individual welcomed us into his life with a plethora of stories. 'I believe in karma. I can sense that you two are beautiful people, and that one day you will return this gift of generosity to others.'

I WAS RIDING out of the bike saddle, working to match the power of the Tour de France rider alongside me. In fact, I had been out of the saddle for three hours. Our mountain bikes were mounted onto a rickety rail cart. As we pedalled, the cart moved painstakingly slowly along the steel railway tracks. Around us, the valley was filled with mist. Occasionally, heavy droplets of water fell from the leaves of the myrtle trees to land with a 'twang' on my helmet.

I was so fatigued. We had paddled through rough seas before running and navigating back to the docks of Strahan—a small, isolated town on the wild west coast of Tasmania—in time for a quick lunch break. I had fought off the frigid cold that ran so deep I was unable to think rationally as I stood shivering in my wet, salty clothing on the Strahan wharf.

Managing discomfort is the art of adventure racing, and a huge part of the challenge that brings competitors back time and time again. I have participated in a few events on the Australian mainland, mountain biking, navigating and kayaking, all while warding off the sleep monsters—the gremlins of fatigue commonly experienced by adventure racers.

This event was different, however—the brain child of Australian Formula One driver, Mark Webber. Tasmania had crawled under his skin, and he saw this wilder landscape with its crashing west coast ocean beaches, remote and muddy South Coast Track, and jagged eastern granite mountains as the perfect place to conduct a charity-inspired adventure race. His professionalism and authenticity were a magnet, and this challenge had attracted the imagination of the media as well as some top-class athletes. I had been roped into the adventure of it all, and my role was to safely navigate a team of Australian sporting icons to the finish line in Hobart. The team constituted three supremely strong, professional male athletes at the top of their careers—Tour de France rider, Matt White, top-class distance runner, Craig Mottram, and Australian Olympic mountain biker, Sid Taberlay … and me!

So there I was, buried in the depths of Tasmania's west coast wilderness, with Matt casually pedalling beside me. Looking over my shoulder, I couldn't see any other teams on the long straight tracks of railroad behind us. We knew there was no-one ahead, as we were the first team to embark on this bizarre leg of the challenge, the aim of which was to cover a distance of thirty-two kilometres to Queenstown through the dense west coast rainforest. If we were going to reach the stage's finish, it was essential that I matched Matt's power output to prevent the cart's scary habit of dismounting from the tracks. If that happened while crossing one of the many bridges on these rail tracks, the cycling challenge could well have ended up as a swim.

So, I stood and pumped my legs up and down. I could feel my triceps burning as they tried to hold the weight of my body evenly over the pedals. As minutes turned to hours, adrenalin was replaced with glucose lows, and we began to enter deeper conversations. I found myself asking Matt about his experiences racing on the pro cycling circuit. I had just finished reading *Breaking the Chain: Drugs and Cycling – The True Story* by Willy Voet—a haunting account by Team Festina's masseuse. I was interested to hear Matt's views on drugs in cycling. Without arrogance or ego, Matt didn't dismiss my recounting of the book. He simply closed the discussion by saying, 'If you don't do it, you don't keep up.' To me, this was a big, bold and confusing statement at the time, and it wouldn't be until May 2013 that Matt would make an official statement about his use of performance enhancing drugs during his racing career.

That conversation with Matt was my first confrontation with the concept of drugs in sport and, to be honest, it terrified me. While I was frequently required to undertake drug tests, it never occurred to me that athletes may actually be using drugs to enhance their performance. I had seen the lengths that athletes took to keep ahead of the tidal wave of internal and, on some occasions, external pressure … to keep ahead of their dreams and remain on the knife edge of performance. I had observed many of my Australian orienteering teammates give up their entire professional careers in the pursuit of their orienteering goals. I had seen a Russian athlete consume only a bag of iceberg lettuce the night before the long-distance orienteering final of the World Championships, because somehow he believed this could help him to win. I had admired the lean and mean Simone Niggli-Luder as she won her way to multiple consecutive orienteering titles. Gosh knows, I had even found a friendship in Little Miss Anorexia now tucked in beside me on the rail cart.

Yes, athletes are certainly driven to make difficult decisions, because our dreams can take such a stronghold on our hearts. But performance-enhancing drugs? For the first time ever, it raised the question for me: what was the price of success?

As the event drew to a close, we washed the last of the mud and ocean salt from our bodies and gathered in the banquet room of Hobart's Wrest Point Casino. I had visited this room on a number of occasions—to huddle in a corner and two-step my way through school formals, or feel the nervous pulse of stage fright when my name was called as the winner of a sporting accolade. But that night I was able to just be, to enjoy the company of the comrades I had participated alongside.

During the event, when I had felt my team no longer needed my navigational services, I dropped to the back and supported many of the teams who needed the moral support more. Individuals had pushed aside their desk jobs to challenge themselves through some of the least-visited parts of Tasmania, including the underground stormwater drains of Hobart. I found myself so inspired by their humility and playfulness, I fell in love with helping these everyday individuals striving for extraordinary things. Helping everyday people play and perform wilder would later become a marker stone in my approach to Find Your Feet.

Jogging alongside these teams on the trails felt like a very natural place for me to be. It was a great surprise when, at this celebration to mark the closure of the event, Mark Webber sidled up next to me. Steering me gently into a crowd of unfamiliar faces, including the CEO of Foster's Brewery, the marketing manager of Telstra, and an elite physical preparation army officer from the UK, he then released his grip. 'Hanny, when I was starting out in my career I was given a helping hand, just like the one you've shown to many of the athletes here in this room. Today, in the true nature of the promise I made to the person who reached out to me, I now want to pass this gift forward to you. We would like you to accept this as a token of our appreciation and belief in you. All I ask is that, when the time comes, you pay it forward.'

Later that evening when I returned to my share-house in South Hobart, I opened up the envelope he had given me. Inside was $3000.

As I crawled gratefully into my bed, Ernie the rabbit snuggling up beside me, I promised then and there that I would always do my best to pass on the baton.

14

Sunshine on a crisp October morning. I was tucked in behind the two petite female leaders of the 2007 Melbourne Marathon. While I ran in my bike shorts, t-shirt and training shoes, they each sported skimpy racing undies and crop tops. Twenty kilometres in, I certainly didn't expect to be up in this position, watching from behind as the girls pumped their arms, chests pressing forward, feet flicking up behind them in determined competitiveness.

We approached a small bump in the road—a slight incline as it rose up and over a sand dune. I recognised this place immediately. For many years of my childhood, I crossed this exact section of road at this exact set of pedestrian lights to walk down to this exact stretch of coastline I was running parallel with. My aunt and uncle, and now my grandparents too, lived there in that suburb of Brighton.

I saw the water shimmering. I heard my deep breathing and that of the girls in front. And I heard, 'Go Hanny! Go girl! Go Baby!' And then footsteps. Long, heavy footsteps cantering along behind me. And there was my uncle, his normal calm, cool, businessman's composure broken by the excitement of this moment. I lifted, stretching into a longer stride, relaxing through my arms, dropping my hands to beside my hips, holding myself proud while I ran on eggshells. Max would have liked that, and I could imagine his pompom leaning out of the window of his hatchback, gaily waving at me. I could sense his wink. 'Nice work, Kid.'

I lifted again, and soon I had clean, fresh air and daylight around me. I suddenly felt more at home. The tranquillity suited me, and I began to fall into a quiet, patient rhythm. This was still only my second marathon, and I was unsure what pace I should be holding or how I should be feeling. So, I ignored pace. I ignored the result and merely focused on the rhythm. *One, two, three, four … step, step, step, step …*

'Hanny?' A surprised voice pulled me back to my senses and I realised I was now running in tandem with another Tasmanian. A very confident, competent Tasmanian who held running records around Tasmania and was known for his adventurous spirit. 'Wow, what time are you hoping for?' I hesitated like the container ships in their holding bays out on the harbour, waiting to dock and unleash their cargo. 'I have no idea.'

Now we were spinning around the halfway marker and heading back towards the distant skyline of Melbourne's CBD. After a few minutes, we passed the girls still coming the other way. 'Well you must be … prepared … because if we keep this up … we will … be … on target to … run under three … hours thirty-five … minutes ….'

I fell in beside him, my head whirling in confusion. I was only here for Grandpa's eightieth birthday!

Memories of the previous night's celebration, at the prestigious Australia Club in the heart of Melbourne, came to keep me company. Watching my grandparents sitting side by side, so absolutely, totally in love with one another even after their long lifetime together. My heart skipped a beat as the memory rose, surfaced, and then disappeared. Thoughts constantly do this when I run. And then a flash to the plateful of confit duck with a side of blanched string beans. The speeches. The long, late night with the walk home to our hotel. Sitting on the carpet in the hotel, pinning number bibs to my racing t-shirt while I munched on a white bread and apple sauce sandwich. The clock striking 11 pm. And then 4 am. Rising early with the street cleaners, and dodging evidence of Melbourne's revellers and their overconsumption of alcohol as I completed my routine twenty-minute jog. Showering. A cup of tea and a white bread and honey sandwich.

And there I was, thanks to a spontaneous decision to have a run. Because it was Grandpa's birthday and I happened to be in Melbourne. Yes, I was there. Running a marathon. Just because …

The leader's motorbike scooted alongside me. I avoided looking into the lens of the camera and instead dropped my gaze to where its rear tyre met the hard bitumen surface. I registered that I was completely alone, and a quick look over my shoulder informed me that somewhere in the midst of recalling birthday balloons and tender speeches, I had dropped yet another companion.

The city loomed closer and I passed the thirty-kilometre mark. I found myself wondering how Jarrod was going in his half marathon. And Mum for that matter. Both had eagerly toed the start line that morning, although I knew Jarrod would have loved to be out here with me today. I wish he was. My legs felt heavier. *Has the leader's motorbike sped up?* And the crowd's cheers seemed quieter. My vision became narrower, and while each rise of St Kilda Road led me closer to the finish line at the Melbourne Cricket Ground, I felt like I was climbing mountains. My pace dropped and whether or not it was the escalation of my depleted glucose state, I felt fear and dread creeping into my stride. I hadn't stopped at the aid stations properly—finding the water sachets more akin to a sprinkler than a refreshing drink. My solitary glucose gel, consumed ten kilometres ago, was now but a sticky residue on my mouth. Salt crusted onto my forehead and around my sunglasses. 'How far behind?' I bleated towards the camera crew dangling from the lead bike. It was lost in the noise of the moment. I felt lonely.

Finally, the cricket ground became visible and I lifted, trying to stride my way up and over the pedestrian bridge that would lead me back onto the concourse surrounding the stadium. Beneath the large inflatable sponsors arch I ran, 'Great! Only one kilometre to go.' The crowds were deeper here, and I heard the noise emanating from the stadium too. I tried to lift again, but by now my hip flexors were like taut rubber bands. I pressed my thumbs down for Max. I tried to stretch up tall for Max, and all the while I wondered, *Where the bloody hell is the entrance to the stadium?* I eventually reached a dark passageway that took me down and then up again onto the grass. And by then I was desperate, running with all the will and gratitude, confusion and fatigue, and best of all, the support and love from my family and friends there to greet me.

What I thought was my last kilometre was actually nearly two. I had been deceived by the placement of a sponsor's archway over the course —it remains the longest kilometre I have ever run. But when I crossed the line all these thoughts were forgotten. I was almost immediately engulfed in excitement. A microphone was thrust into my face. 'How was your race?'

Between shallow breaths, the first word that came to mind was, 'Lonely!'

THE 2007 MELBOURNE MARATHON was when I transitioned from being an orienteer to being a runner. As the media reported in the aftermath of the race, 'Only her second marathon attempt ever, Hanny Allston has quickly established credibility as an elite runner on the Australian athletics scene. With 664 females registered in the 42 km marathon, the field was anticipated to be highly competitive and did not disappoint. Australians took out the trifecta, with Hanny Allston (TAS) first in a personal best time of 02:40:34, Helen Stanton (QLD) second in 02:41:51 and Belinda Schipp (NSW) third in 02:42:22.' I had also just run an official Commonwealth Games qualifying time.

My grandparents and their friends, my mother and her friends, and Jarrod were all in the stadium as I stood on the dais that day. With a trophy under one arm, a cheque and a voucher for a forty-inch Samsung television in the other, I couldn't help but wonder, *Now what?* I couldn't help sensing that I was on track and, when I returned home, I dug out Max's letter. 'I think you have what it takes to be an Olympian.'

Sadly, when the new light of day came and I should have been recovering strongly, I experienced a discomforting pinching in my groin. Rest didn't help. I found myself once again in a surgeon's consulting room staring down the barrel of uncertainty.

I had frayed the ligament that connects the head of the femur bone to the hip socket, an injury which causes a very uncomfortable pain referral into the groin. I was almost certain that my companion in crime, Anorexia, was behind this injury. Her subtle taunts to be leaner and meaner, as well as the increased aerobic training load, had resulted in a lot of muscle wasting that had left me less stable and strong through my core. Forty-two kilometres and forty thousand steps without adequate core stability was only asking for trouble. My name was added to the surgeon's waitlist.

In the interim, I shook Max's hand each evening, returned to university, and sold the Samsung television. I wasn't going to need it. Because, with the support of Jarrod, I had decided that at the beginning of the New Year, just two days after my upcoming surgery, I would be moving to New Zealand. I had come to believe that my calling was to be a teacher. Somehow, the land of kiwifruit and campervans felt like the place to do my one-year degree in primary school education.

MOVING to New Zealand was exciting in its conception, challenging from the moment we got there, enriching in the course that I studied—and nearly broke me by the end. It became a year of running more pavements than trails, and more marathons than orienteering courses. I thrived in the playful education classes, revelling in the tasks of learning to paint, add and subtract numbers, write poetry, learn survival backstroke, dance wildly, and learn how to spell … all over again. Jarrod landed on his feet in a private, sports-focused physiotherapy clinic. Although we were eternally grateful for the hospitable friends who initially put a roof over our heads, we set about trying to find somewhere to live.

'MEET me at two this afternoon at the Turkish pizza kebab shop on the corner of Epsom and Remuera Roads.' This bizarre invitation was the answer to our enquiry about a rental listing. It landed us and our new vintage campervan on the corner of two jostling streets not far from the university's grounds. Shortly after the allocated time, a dishevelled ute pulled into the dishevelled car park with a dishevelled arm hanging out of the open window. 'I'll just go and ask him if he wants us to follow him to the house.'

Instead of prompt action, I found myself exchanging pleasantries with a dishevelled, sweaty man. Jarrod eventually joined me. It appeared this gentleman loved small talk. Eventually, the conversation turned to the real reason we were all there in a dirty car park smelling of kebabs.

'So, about the house. I just have a few curly questions for you. To begin with, how open-minded are you?'

I looked at Jarrod and he subtly smiled back. I could sense his humour egging me on: *Go on, your turn.* 'Well,' I started, 'I think we are pretty open-minded.'

The meaty gentleman wrung his oversized hands. 'Ah, good, good. Well, about the house. There are three people living there. First there is George. Lovely guy, lovely guy, lovely guy. He is an aircraft engineer, but he is currently out of town.' He looked between us and then continued on, 'And then there is Suzie. Well, let's just say that she works in the sex industry. Lovely girl, lovely girl, lovely girl.' I felt myself going red, joining our new companion in a light sweat. He looked between us and then continued, 'And then there is Dominique. She is … a … dominatrix. Lovely girl, lovely girl, lovely girl. But I know you are going to love the house! Modern, sunny, lots of space! Do you want to take a look?'

We clambered back into the van. I don't know who nodded or said what but, somehow, we found ourselves tailgating this odd character into the suburban streets of Auckland. I finally broke the silence. 'Um, Jarrod … what is a … dominatrix?' Soon we were hooting, hanging our arms out the window and laughing until our bellies hurt.

Soon after, Jarrod piped up, 'How open-minded would your Mum be when she comes to stay?'

All I could think was, 'I don't think it's *my* Mum we have to worry about.' Until then, whenever we visited Jarrod's family we had been asked to sleep in separate bedrooms, so I was not too sure how they would feel about a dominatrix in the room next door.

We pulled up behind the ute in a surprisingly pretty street. Jarrod stepped down from the van and quietly uttered in my direction, 'Let's just get this done and get out of here.' But our new friend had other ideas. We loitered once again in the shade of the unfamiliar New Zealand trees that created a subtle avenue up the street. We appeared to be waiting. And waiting. And waiting.

Eventually, a dark car with tinted windows descended down a nearby driveway and revved off down the street. After a short pause, we trotted behind Mr Dishevelled, trying to avoid tripping over his slow waddle. As though we were his two bodyguards, we tailed him up the inclined driveway and waited as he knocked gently on the door. Then he let us in. 'So, here you are!' he boomed proudly. He waved around the room and then called into the silence, 'Suzie? Dominique?' He then waved towards a door. 'That room will be yours. Suzie and Dominique have decided to share a room given they work different hours.'

I heard Jarrod quietly mumbling at me, 'Don't say anything. Don't say anything.'

Then we waddled towards the door he had just introduced us to, and our eager host knocked quietly. After a rustle, bump and, 'Hang on, I'm just cleaning up!' the door swung open. Hot, humid air escaped and swirled past us. I looked into a room filled with what looked like gym machines, and yet I was aware there was something very odd about that. I stepped backward. Jarrod did too. Mr Dishevelled spun towards us. 'And now the kitchen!'

WE TURNED down the offer of living with George, Suzie and Dominique. We eventually ended up living a block away in the home of a middle-aged Indian body builder whose house was completely maintained by his ageing parents, who themselves lived just around the corner. His stooped, bustling mother let herself into the house each day to deliver his washing, make his bed, and fill the fridge full of food he never ate. He didn't need to cook, when he went for dinner at their place every night.

Our other housemate was an Australian girl of similar age to me.

She smoked like a chimney and swear words frequently belched from within her. But we tried to make it home, filling the yard with potted vegies and basking in the tranquillity when the others were out. We helped ourselves to the Jamie Oliver kitchen utensils and to the food in the fridge. For a short while, everything felt normal.

On the weekends, Jarrod and I rose early and pulled on our running shoes, setting off on a one-way adventure to some place new. When weariness enveloped us, we turned towards the nearest coffee shop or petrol station, and tapped on the shoulder of the individuals with the friendliest faces. 'Can we have a lift home?' With delivery men, fruit and vegetable trucks, and kind triathletes on their way to training, we bumbled and lurched our way back from the hills, and on every occasion made it home safely.

Some weekends, we braved the Auckland traffic and turned our campervan with its single wooden bed and plastic wine glasses towards the south. Our favourite destinations were Lake Taupo, stinky Rotorua, or the Coromandel Peninsula with its hot water beaches. We worked hard and played hard, jumping out of aircraft, hiking mountains, and roaming new trails. And yet, so too did Anorexia.

While injuries plagued Jarrod, Anorexia gripped my willpower tighter than ever. No matter how fast I tried to outrun her, she just wouldn't let go. As my grandmother once stated, 'Guests and fish have something in common. After a while, they both start to stink.' This is how I began to feel about Anorexia. She was becoming an unwanted houseguest in our relationship.

We weren't a couple anymore. No, there were now three of us in this relationship, and it was only a matter of time before one of us cracked.

MY RELATIONSHIP with Anorexia was like an unhealthy relationship with a new friend. Such relationships begin slowly, and then subtly start to alter the way you behave. You act more alike, dress more alike, and be more alike. You begin to talk over the top of one another and think that you no longer need your other friendships. You begin to withdraw into yourself, and your friendship with her, so that one day you realise you are on a completely different pathway.

That was what happened to me in New Zealand. I boarded the plane to Auckland with all the greatest intentions and love in my heart to be a loving partner to Jarrod, and a dedicated student of my teaching degree. I believed the change of scenery was going to serve my ambitions.

However, Anorexia took me in another direction. I became unable to feel love from others because I couldn't feel love for myself. I wasn't able to remain in the present because I was always listening to what Anorexia wanted me to do in the future. I became like a caveman, searching for food and developing an obsession with roaming the shops to look at all the delicacies Anorexia wouldn't let me buy. I distracted myself with studying, becoming a straight-A student. However, I felt like I was on autopilot.

I continued to run, and joined a new squad coached by the legendary Barry Magee, a fine coach and a taskmaster to fill the big shoes now vacated by Max—still back home in Tasmania. And yet I was plagued with back pain. I lacked a solid understanding of the importance of post-surgical rehabilitation, and my hip joint was more unstable than ever. On our exploratory drives through the rolling New Zealand countryside I frequently had to ask Jarrod to stop, so that I could crawl down from the lofty heights of the passenger seat and lie flat on my back at the side of the road.

But I was too afraid to stop running, for fear of what might catch up with me. I was too far down a path that didn't feel like it belonged to me, and I was terrified.

And it was this same fear, and the intoxicating, interwoven friendship with Anorexia, that led me to push Jarrod away.

Even though Jarrod is no longer the love in my life, this doesn't mean that the love we felt for one another during the depths of our relationship wasn't real. Jarrod was, and still is, a beautiful soul who helped to pull me back onto my feet. He knew how to nurture, and how to make me laugh. And in return I taught him to play wilder. Our love was young and very real. But in that time together, there simply wasn't space for three of us, and Anorexia was incredibly convincing.

I was taken in by a loving and excitable family, who lived very different lives from everything I was used to. They slept in and went to bed late, laughed loudly and watched horror movies. Thanks to their generosity, I was able to remain in New Zealand to complete my studies. They turned a blind eye to my pedantic habits. They allowed me to prepare my own meals and study at their kitchen table through the early hours of the morning. And I turned a blind eye to their New Zealand humour, such as the evening when I emerged from my bedroom to grab a glass of water and found the three of them, mum, dad and daughter, sitting on the sofa watching a movie with a pair of brightly-coloured cotton undies on each of their heads.

It was into this unusual dynamic that my mother came to visit. She was horrified. She had received my increasingly desperate phone calls, and understood my desire to return home, but I don't think she was prepared for the skin and bones that greeted her at the airport.

She whisked me away for a break and, in the beauty of the Coromandel Peninsula, broke the news to me.

'Max is dead.'

WHEN MAX unexpectedly suffered a heart attack and died during an everyday coaching session at Sandown, I was stranded in New Zealand, separated from him by the Tasman Sea.

Days rolled together, and in between walks on the beach with my mother, I slept. I slept so long and so deeply, making up for lost time.

And soon it was the eve of his memorial service and, coincidentally, the New Zealand Marathon Championships. I had not planned to run this marathon. In fact, thin, gaunt and in the grips of my darkest days with Anorexia, I had begun to fall out of love with running. While I had found some groups to participate with in Auckland, I missed the grounding presence of Max. I missed his beret and watchful eye. I missed his handshake. And the wink ... oh, the wink!

Over the years, Max had become a rock in my world. The thought that I would never return home to Tasmania, stare into his deeply-penetrating eyes and feel the strength in his handshake as he egged me on ... the thought of this simply tore through my heart. I knew I needed to do something truly memorable to say farewell to Max, to show him just how much he meant to me and just how much I had learnt.

On the day of Max's memorial service in Hobart—an event which overflowed with admirers—I became the New Zealand Marathon Champion in Rotorua, crossing the line in two hours, forty-three minutes.

The race was not pretty, but it felt painless. Despite needing a bathroom stop at twenty-one kilometres and confronting a headwind on the way home, I felt like I was running over eggshells, an analogy that felt very fitting as I breathed in the heavy, sulphurous, rotten-egg air. I felt tall, proud and empowered as I ran down lonely roads towards the finish.

It was an honour to run for Max in an event that he had loved. And it was the event in which he saw the Olympian in me. It was the appropriate comma in our story; while it would become the last road marathon I ever ran, Max's story and teachings continued on far past the end of this race and his death.

Throughout the most challenging and confusing ups and downs in my life, Max Cherry stood alongside me. He had trained under the watchful eye of iconic endurance coach, Percy Cerutty, and alongside distance running legend, Herb Elliott, on the sandhills at Portsea in Victoria. Max's own coaching methods became all about, 'Go hard or go home!' Dragging me off the Hobart Domain Athletics Track as I ran past him, he would poke his beautiful, etched face into mine and near-spit, 'What was that?'

Dripping with sweat, fatigue coursing through my muscles with the lactic acid, I would automatically begin saying, 'I can't …'

Like oil repels water, Max repelled unnecessary weakness. 'Go home!'

However, Max always knew whether it was punishment or encouragement that we needed. On some of my hardest days he surprised me with a hug—a big, tracksuit-filled, beret-topped, white-haired hug. Sometimes this would extend to an invitation back to his home to sit on his couch and listen to him retell stories of training with sand between his toes. Max invited me to believe in my running ability. His wink said it all: 'I believe in you, Kid.' He frequently slipped a handwritten letter to me at training, crafting each physical training session—which I followed, most of the time. Each one of these letters has been tucked safely into my journals, a record of Max's love and lessons that I now try to pass forward to others.

Losing Max taught me that you cannot replace a rock. The replacement will always feel too sharp, too big, too small, or the wrong colour. While the world lost Max, I never lost the memories, teachings and life lessons that I still carry in my pockets to this day, pulling them out and dusting them off when I need them. Max carried the baton on from his coach, Percy Cerutty, when Percy passed away. When Max passed away, I reached behind me, clasped the baton tightly, and have carried it carefully ever since as I strive to help others to also find their feet.

I CAME 'HOME' from New Zealand on a short mid-year semester holiday. Tasmania was wrapped in the loving arms of winter, and frosty fingers of fog were extending down the Derwent River from the mountains each morning, a phenomenon fondly nicknamed 'Bridgewater Jerry'. Between this, my low body weight, and the icy air swooping down the gullies off Mt Wellington, rolling across and into the cracks of my father's weatherboard home in South Hobart, I was freezing.

While I had been desperate to return from New Zealand for a break, in some ways I had been terrified of this trip home. Because where was home? My mother was now away travelling in the depths of China on a cycling tour. My father had recently purchased an old weatherboard cottage. The stove in the kitchen was a homemade brick contraption with a rickety, twisting chimney extending up through the ceiling. A laundry chute dropped into the basement from beside the kitchen sink. Mustard yellow carpets. Peeling paint on the exterior. I wondered what in my father's right mind had possessed him to buy this place? This wasn't home, was it?

The other dramatic change was that there was a new woman on the block, and she wasn't my mother. In New Zealand I had been able to turn a blind eye to this. In Hobart, it was reality—the women's clothing I would occasionally find amongst Dad's washing, or her spontaneous arrival into the peace of an evening meal with Dad, as she bounced in the door holding a hefty bag of browning bananas high above her head. 'Look what I bought! One dollar!'

I wasn't sure I was ready to spend a few weeks in this changed family dynamic, and yet the trip to Tasmania was a beautiful, healing experience. We lay around in the cosy living space playing board games and sharing stories. I came to know Janeil as an extraordinary lady, a strong, compassionate and exceptionally giving woman, albeit one with few domestic skills. Despite her and my mother both being medical practitioners, the contrast couldn't have been more pronounced—and yet amazingly I found it easy to let Janeil into our world.

No matter how challenging I found my parents' decisions, I wanted a relationship with both of them. I needed a relationship with them. And I knew that one day I wanted them to have a relationship with my children, and my brother's children. In my eyes, once a family, always a family. And Janeil became an important member of our family too.

However, in my heart I knew I was lost. For the first time ever, I felt like all my rocks had moved. Where was home? What did family mean? How could I find my feet?

Without discussing it with anyone, and before returning to New Zealand for the final months of my teaching studies, I made another appointment with my sports doctor in Hobart. My palms were sweating when I walked into his room—a cold, gaunt young woman beginning to search for answers. There was so much I wanted to say, that I was going to say. And yet, as I sat in his room with his kind, soft-featured face looking back at me, it was as if my throat was muted. All I managed to discuss was the hollowness left by Max's passing and how my family's health was now. I left with a phone number and an intense recommendation: 'Jackie Fairweather.'

From the tranquillity of my father's rickety balcony overlooking the gurgling, cheerful chatter of the Hobart Rivulet, I dialled Jackie's number. And so began an intense one-hour discussion, and a relationship with a woman who would radically influence my life. Days later, I boarded the plane for Kiwiland with an increased sense of direction, and willingness to finish what I had started. Teacher and Olympian. Jackie was definitely the woman to help me get there.

For the first time ever, I began to want to lose my Anorexia. I tried to run faster than her in my training sessions, and to lean into Jackie, who I came to learn could absolutely empathise with my experience of losing my feet. She allowed me to be honest by demanding honesty. And in return she gave absolutely nothing less.

Jackie was an extraordinary woman. A world champion triathlete, Commonwealth Games marathon bronze medallist and Australian Institute of Sport High Performance Administrator, Jackie had respect from the Australian sporting community wherever she went. She had raced as a professional triathlete for eight years, becoming the World Champion in 1996, and setting a championship record in doing so. Later that year she went on to win the World Duathlon Championships, becoming the only person to ever win both world titles in the same year. In the lead-up to the 2000 Sydney Olympics, Jackie had been a near-certain member of the Australian triathlon team, and was the name on the tip of everyone's tongues to win the prestigious home-based Olympic title. However, Jackie not only did not win, she did not even make the team. She had become so involved in the pursuit of Olympic glory that she later admitted to overtraining, eventually fading to twenty-fourth in the qualifying race. An incredibly determined, strong-willed woman, she immediately turned to Commonwealth Games marathon running, winning a bronze medal in Melbourne in 2006—the same year I won my own world titles.

Remarkably, she became my coach. I admired her honesty and strength. In fact, I rose up to that challenge. My connection with Jackie allowed me to relegate my connection with Anorexia to the back porch. She no longer held such a grasp on me. Soon, my training sessions were tougher than ever before—two hours of leg-searing tempo-running tough. In those last few months in New Zealand, I fell in love with the sport all over again, recovering quickly, and because of this, beginning to run better than ever.

On a brief trip to help coach the national junior orienteering squad in Canberra, I visited Jackie and her husband—the Olympic archery gold medallist from Sydney, Simon Fairweather. We sat around the kitchen table, laughing at their stories and their love affair with Porsches. Jackie giggled like a young child as she picked at the vegetables in the curry Simon had made us, and then got exceedingly excited by the apple crumble I contributed. Red wine and fun banter flowed through the evening, although later I found myself trying to marry 'Coach Jackie' to this 'Free-spirited Jackie'.

My last five months in New Zealand were a mixture of gritting my teeth as I reached for the finish line of my degree, and then finally the excitement that I would soon be returning home. I began to share the dark, early morning training sessions with a new friend, whom I had met doubled over and vomiting at the side of a trail-running racecourse. 'It was a big night,' he later explained. He wasn't that kind of guy, but rather a chiropractic student who was more eager to play wilder than he was to study. He made the early mornings fun, travelling for up to one hour to meet me at five-thirty for a run.

He pulled up at the new house I was residing in, a stout, proud mansion whose broad windows peered down the nose of Remuera into the Bay of Auckland. Here, I had become nanny to an eight-year-old girl who hated being outside, and whose mother had recently lost her husband to cancer. Each day, after my final teaching placements in the girls' school over the hill, I met her and walked her home, while she dragged her heels and pleaded for lollies, or chocolate, or to watch television. We were polar opposites and yet, when the day finally arrived for me to say goodbye, she cried into my chest. My heart cried with her, for I was her fifth nanny in just a few years. And the next day her sixth would arrive, eagerly standing on the welcoming doormat and trying to navigate her way around the kitchen and the heart of an eight-year-old who simply wanted to be loved by her mother and deceased father.

In New Zealand, I had come close to despair. Anorexia continually gripped my hand, until out of desperation I began to Google inpatient treatment centres in Auckland. But I could never dial the number. Because when Jackie walked beside me, I somehow felt like I was going to be able to beat it once and for all.

15

I only moved back to Hobart for a short while, joining my mother in her treehouse in Fern Tree, and celebrating Christmas tucked beside a roaring fire, a pile of presents dwarfing the small decorated Tasmanian pencil pine straggling from its pot. My mother and I have always loved presents. Loved to pick them up, run our hands over the surfaces, try to guess, then eventually give up and tear through the bright wrappers to unearth the carefully-considered gift.

As January rolled around, I began to gather my belongings in preparation for relocating to Melbourne.

Two months before, on the side of a snowy mountain towering over New Zealand's Queenstown, I had paused while above me, my father and Janeil climbed on ahead, maximising their time during this precious visit. Running shoes clawing into the grassy hillside, I answered the phone and took a job interview for a prestigious girls' school in central Melbourne. Throughout the call, I watched the world unfold below me, the sheep wandering across the browning landscapes, the wind whipping up the lake's waters. I discussed the pedagogies of teaching young girls and the values I would endeavour to bring to the classroom, while silently revelling in the icy wind in my hair, the dampness of my feet, and the feeling that I was closer to the pathway to exactly where I wanted to be. Later, reunited with Dad and Janeil, we lumbered back down the mountain together, my fingers crossed all the while.

In mid-January I drove onto the ferry in my little Peugeot, and once again waved goodbye to Tasmania. I was off to be a primary school teacher.

UNTIL THAT MOMENT, my wardrobe predominantly consisted of running attire, some outdoor accessories, jeans and plenty of warm jumpers. Most of it hung like a limp chaff sack on my petite frame. So, in preparation for the well-to-do parents and prestige of Grammar's long hallways, my aunt bundled me into the car and beelined for Chadstone Shopping Centre. Black dresses, smart jackets, stockings, white shirts.

I exited the building feeling excited and with the underlying question: *Oh, is this who I was meant to be?*

In Melbourne, my brother and I moved in together. While we had become emotionally closer in the era after the Perfect Storm, this was the first time we had lived together since he left home six years earlier. It was perfect, and there wasn't a day that went past that I didn't look up to my brother. I admired his tenacity at work, and his dedication to his friends and our family. He wrapped me in hugs, and nurtured me through the challenging beginning of my new role. And while we were opposites, we were always able to meet in the middle. I loved the mornings and he the evenings, but we lived harmoniously, preparing dinners, baking his butter-filled peanut choc chip power cookies, and creating our herb garden masterpiece in the miniature backyard. Our little house shook with the trains as they roared by towards the city, but the house was filled with a peacefulness ... and so was I.

However, from the word go I found the teaching world confusing. I had an amazing mentor in the librarian but, rather than a bank of physical resources at my fingertips, I just had a whopping big budget and no idea how to spend it. I tapped into online resources, tried to calm the parents who carried high ideals for their daughters to attend medical or law school, and filled the day with classes that I hoped would be educational and entertaining for the girls.

I got into trouble when the girls dug holes throughout the school gardens as we learnt about how hydro dams were built, made sure I was on time at seven-thirty in the morning, and tried to teach the girls about the real world. I dashed down to the local markets with my wicker basket, and returned with an abundance of ripe, vibrant vegetables. They filled the classroom with colours and aromas so foreign to these girls that, when I quizzed them on where and how they grew, a few girls thought that carrots grew on trees. I was horrified.

Adding to this confusion was the plethora of nannies who dropped the girls off outside the front doors, and who greeted them again in the afternoon. When a nanny attended a parent-teacher interview on behalf of Mum and Dad, I couldn't help but notice just how far I was from living in alignment with my wilder child. Through all this confusion, it was my growing bond with my brother, my running, and the tightening relationship with Jackie that kept me strong and empowered.

On many evenings, after the school day was done and the last piece of paper prepared for the next day, I wandered down to the train while conversing via phone with Jackie in Canberra. She egged me on during my good days, tried to encourage me to eat chocolate frogs for breakfast like her, and promised that this time she would definitely come to my race—the upcoming National Cross-Country Trials to be held in Melbourne in a few weeks' time.

But, just like each of the previous promises she had made, when race day rolled around she didn't show. I began to feel confused by her lighter and darker moods that had begun to rear in conversations. I could feel my running ping-ponging in harmony with these moods too, as if even from Melbourne I could sense something was out of kilter. But I continued on with my running, winning the Melbourne Half Marathon in a new personal best time of seventy-four minutes, and running a thirty-four minute ten-kilometre road time.

I also returned to race-orienteering overseas for the first time in two years, travelling into Hungary where the world championships were being held. However, I felt fragmented, like I was neither a runner nor an orienteer. My coach was training me to be a runner, the orienteers were happily discussing maps and route choices, and all the while my head was halfway between my school classroom and the finish line of my orienteering events.

I was aware that I was a favourite for the races, and yet somehow I didn't feel attached to the results. It was as if I wasn't sure that I was following my path. I felt distant from the excitement of my team, like I was looking into that world from the outside. When I read the athlete's oath at the opening ceremony of the championships, I was hugely aware of this honour, and said the words with weight, but couldn't feel my heart in the occasion.

The pressure I was allowing myself to feel from returning to the international orienteering spotlight had allowed my friend Anorexia to creep back into the scene. Thanks to 'Little Miss Pedantic' encouraging me to tighten the reins on my nutrition yet again, I faded in both my races to scrape into the top twenty.

On the journey home to Australia, I stopped in Hong Kong, and then Taiwan for the World Games—the Olympics for non-Olympic sports. This time I was determined to enjoy the experience, and to make amends for my distant headspace in Hungary. I was also determined to leave Anorexia hungry in Hungary.

I loved Taiwan from the moment I got there, with the jovial faces of the locals, the athlete nations' flags lining every inch of the city, and the vast backdrop to the mountains. I rose early, roaming the hills and pausing at the small shrines nestled into the hillsides. I joined locals for green tea at small teahouses, before running back to the hotel to meet the team. There, I was able to play wilder, and in doing so, was able to find the truest version of Hanny. By playing wilder there in Taiwan, I found a way to align my heart, head and ambitions. I boarded the plane home with a gold and a silver medal, awakened to the simple fact that when you are brave enough to play in your own style, to play wilder, you can thrive.

Jackie excitedly welcomed me home. So too did my brother, who engulfed me in a huge hug, and instantly made the world feel more real and bright again. I loved his bear hugs, his broad presence, sleepy morning mumbles, and loving gratitude when I made him dinner in the evening. Weekends were my favourite, when we sat on brown stools at the brown 1970s kitchen bench top and ate raisin toast that we bought from the local baker after our morning jog together. Somehow, our completely-at-odds lifestyles fitted together, and it was healing.

Perhaps I really was starting to find my feet here in Melbourne, and not just as a runner or an orienteer, but as Hanny. My black work clothes didn't feel so foreign, and the rocking and rolling of the train home each evening became meditative. Home. I felt safe in this world and alongside the strong presence of my brother. Home.

I PICKED UP THE BOOK, waiting patiently for the girls to wrestle into their own quiet bubble of space on the carpet in front of me.

I loved each of these girls, energised in their youth, and fair in their opinions of me. As one parent informed me at the recent parent-teacher interviews, 'My daughter thinks you are scary but nice.' Yes, that was fair. I demanded a lot from them, reflecting my belief that we achieve what we strive for, but I tried not to inflict my own ambitions on them. We are each on unique journeys, and the only real way to learn is to find out what makes us tick, and how to channel our strengths and weaknesses. As their teacher, I felt like my role was to help steer them on a straighter pathway, to provide them with skills and knowledge that could potentially be added to their growing toolkit of life. I wanted to shield them from unnecessary discomfort, but not to protect them from failure, for from my own experiences, even while racing abroad in Hungary and Taiwan, I was reminded that failure is where we can truly grow. From the disappointments of the World Championships in Hungary I had found strength for my goals at the World Games in Taiwan.

I smiled as I recollected those recent events, and knew that I could help these girls find their own pathways and thrive. In that moment of quietness that took over from the frenzy of lunchtime, I opened the book and began to read.

We were deep in the midst of our three youthful heroes searching for treasure in the depths of sea caves, a book that grabbed my attention at the very same age as my girls, when the door quietly opened. The assistant principal moved gently into the room and waited until she had my attention. 'Miss Allston, there is a phone call for you. Perhaps I can continue the story until you return?'

We exchanged places and I let myself out into the hallway, making my way along the grey corridors lined with vibrant artwork, Picasso-like in their bright lines and spots, until I reached the front office. I was handed the phone and couldn't help but notice the door being closed behind me. When a phone call requires privacy, I know there is something wrong. I could feel myself bracing, tensing somewhere deep beneath my skin, as if I was toeing the start line of another marathon. My breathing became shallower. As I heard the voice of my mother's friend, a shaky whisper on the other end of the line, I knew that my world was about to change … again.

'Han, Han … I am so sorry to have to call you at work. Your mother has found a small lump in her breast. It is probably absolutely nothing, but the doctors have decided to operate to remove it. They did a biopsy and it came back looking normal, but they don't want to take the risk.'

I hung up the phone and took a moment to collect my senses. While my body was physically located in that small, grey office, my heart was with my mother on my island home of Tasmania. When I returned to my room the girls were all peacefully reading their own books, so I took a moment to step back out into the corridor with the assistant principal. We huddled together into the unknown. 'I need to go home to be with my mother.'

Later that evening, as James and I stood in our small kitchen, slicing into the strength of carrots and stirring aimlessly at a pot of bubbling pasta, we discussed this turn of events. We were united in devotion to our mother and the need to be a family in this moment of fear. We came to a united agreement that, for this moment, until more was known, only one of us needed to return. And for the first time in our long brother-sister relationship, he uttered the simple fact that we had always known to be true: 'Your mother needs you, Han. Only you can really help her through this.' This was not stated out of favouritism or jealousy, but rather a deep-seated knowledge that when father and son were united, mother and daughter were too. When son struggled, father gave strength. When daughter required it, mother wrapped a protective wing around her.

And in that moment, as the tides of adulthood continued to ebb and flow around us, it was time for a daughter to rise up and provide strength once again to a mother so that she, in turn, could regain her own strength.

When the plane touched down and I stepped onto the metal disembarkation staircase, I was hit by an icy southern blow. It whipped in off the sea a mere kilometre from where I stood, a direct affront from Antarctica. I was poorly insulated for this, and wrapped my coat more tightly around me. As usual, I carried my airline snacks in my pockets. Maybe later, I promised myself, knowing only too well that later rarely comes.

I was met off the plane by a family friend. United by love and loyalty, we piled into the Subaru station wagon—car of choice for Tasmanians—and beelined for the hospital. The light was dim, and fishing vessels moored at the docks of Hobart danced gaily in the icy breeze. Pedestrians leant into the night, halting at traffic lights or walking briskly along the wide-open pathways lining the famous water frontage where stunning vistas exposed the towering Mt Wellington tucked behind the city. We headed towards the mountain's steady presence, shadows blowing across her face, before pulling up outside the hospital just before the road kicked up onto her heights. We would go that way soon, navigating carefully up the rising road while watching for the wallabies as they darted in hysteria in front of our vehicle. But first we needed to pick up another passenger …

We walked into my mother's room. Her eyes were closed, and her face barely stood out from the stark whiteness of that room and its empty walls. The television was black, offering no sense of vibrancy in the sterile space. Mum barely looked at me, instead reaching for my hand and then going limp as I placed my thin fingers into hers. She let out a small weep and, in her weakness, I found strength.

'Come on Mum, let's go home.'

16

We sat on the couch together. A mother and a daughter. A medical professional and masters athlete, and a world champion and teacher. Both as competent and yet as lost as one another. Mum cried—quiet, heavy sobs that emanated into the small glass sunroom, an elevated space looking out into the stretches of trees as they reached for the sky. As if feeling our sadness, they swayed in the breeze like distressed souls who teetered with emotion. And yet they were calming—tall, solid species that had stood the test of time as fire threatened this mountain time and time again, as human footprints crept onto its flanks, and as developments tried and failed.

This was my mother's home now. This was her mountain hideaway, a place where she could unwind before preparing to put on her baggy green doctor's uniform and plug the holes and heal the pains of her patients in the emergency department. It was her home where she could welcome her growing bounty of friends, whipping up strawberry, blueberry or apple muffins and an oversized pot of tea before sitting in this very sunroom to share her view. It was a home which welcomed strays, cycling tourists, her son, and in this moment, her daughter. And yet it was her salvation, her very own home in which she could enclose her hurting heart and give it the time and space to heal. From here she could tug on her running shoes and head for a trail, ducking and diving beneath the drooping man-ferns before finding herself on a straighter and narrower pathway, perhaps a beautiful metaphor for where she aimed to be?

That day we sat on the cool leather couch staring out into the heightened depths of the vast vista before us. We watched the light brighten and dim, brighten and dim as each individual cloud whisked across the sun, tracking its way towards the horizon and the expansive sea cliffs of the Tasman Peninsula National Park. I observed the light dancing at the mouth of the Derwent River where she met the sea, having traced a path from the heights of the central Tasmanian mountains all the way to the ocean. Then, when the light began to fade with the advancing evening, I returned to the present and the quiet discomfort of my mother.

Suddenly, I couldn't breathe. I felt a boiling of emotion so intense that it grasped at my chest and my throat. I leant in to give Mum one last hug before darting out the door, dragging on my running shoes and brushing past the straggling natives along the back path to the mountain trails. Then I was running, running as hard as my body would let me, feeling each foot strike the compacted earthen trail, bending and curving my way towards the body of the mountain's trails. I felt the cool, damp air coming into my chest in short, sharp breaths, each one cooling the heated emotions somewhere deep inside there. I was on edge, each foot exploding onto the trail in a desperate need to escape that discomfort.

Soon, I was climbing, powering and pushing, tugging and pressing my palms deep into my defined quadriceps muscles. Press and step, press and step, doubled over in the effort to climb this mountain. When I reached The Springs—a favourite picnic area for locals and tourists with vistas up to the exposed rocky outcrops highlighting the mountain's summit—I found my rhythm on the flatter paths as they curved around her vast slopes. I ran with a rhythm and intensity normally reserved for races, finding comfort in the sensation of the vegetation and boulder scree fields as they whipped past me out of the corners of my vision. Then I turned to my right, snaking along a short, very narrow trail until I stood on a stumpy sandstone outcrop with the whole world laid out below me.

And there, with my breath coming in shortened bursts, I yelled my emotions to the world—explosive frustrations, wails of pain and whoops of elation, an eclectic string of highs and lows, celebrations and frustrations, stemming from the depths of emotions that until then I had buried in the deepest layers of my soul, never to be felt or heard. Tears streamed down my face. My body shook with the intensity of the sobs that emanated and fell out over the cliff. The animal-like wails disappeared out to the vista, to Hobart with its dancing fairy lights beginning to appear in the darkening evening, to the blackness of the Derwent River snaking between her urbanised shores, and to the layers upon layers of rising and falling hills as they disappeared into the distance. Memories ran before my eyes—a swing, bright lights and hospital rooms, crutches and puppies, a sea of faces, the handshake of a prince, a Sold sign on a farm fence, packing boxes, and an obituary for Max. A sliver of apple, a lolly jar on a top shelf. White sheep in a green paddock. A plane ticket home. So many memories, so many emotions, leaking into the void until there was only a void left within.

Then I sat, peace falling around me like the night-time. Crickets squawked their awakening, a faraway currawong bird called into the night, and slowly I realised, this was the first time I had felt such tranquillity. I stood up, cold hands pressing into cold rock, knowing for the first time in a long while that I was finally ready to move forwards once and for all … to find my feet.

When I walked in the door, my mother was up, moving slowly around the kitchen preparing dinner. This is her love language, a need to provide and show her love and devotion through the art of doing. I walked towards her, observing a hollowness and yet tranquillity in her. It was like I was walking towards a mirror, reflecting the same emotional release that I had experienced, a hollowness that comes when two people have united to share and then overcome the pain they have shared, but never voiced before. Until that moment, we had pretended our strength, finding outlets of distraction, ways of running ahead of our pain until we couldn't run any more.

We had thought we were on our path, when really we had just

crashed off-course only to stumble onto the slightly overgrown route we were meant to be following.

Now we were together, arms wrapped around us, knowing that two souls are stronger than one. And strong we would be. Stronger in our vulnerability and honesty.

Conversation flowed easily that night. And as we stood brushing our teeth in the small bathroom, watching the lights of suburbia dancing far below us, stars lingering in a vast sky, we knew that whatever would be thrown at us, nothing could take us lower than the hole we had begun to climb out of together.

What was the first step? In the depths of my heart I knew that the only way for either of us to move forwards with leaps and bounds was for me to unshackle the friendship with Anorexia once and for all. Until I could find honesty in the sneaky licks and picks when no-one was watching, until I could find peace in the aisles of a supermarket or at a cafe table with friends, until I could accept dinner invitations to the home of a loved one without panic rising through me, until a mother could look at her daughter and not see a hollow, unsmiling ghost looking back, neither mother nor daughter could navigate their own pathways.

I HAD RETURNED to Hobart from the bustling Melbourne metropolis assuming that I would come home to support my mother through a benign breast cancer scare, before returning to my classroom of vibrant eleven- and twelve-year-old students. However, in the light of day that followed the depths of confrontation with a challenging past, nothing about this plan felt right. When I snuck out the front door the next morning to go training, thinking I would sneak in one last run on the mountain before being reunited with the urban concrete jungle, I felt like a ton of bricks.

After the outpouring of emotion the night before, I felt so empty and hollow, and so damn hungry, that it was impossible to move even slowly along the flattest trails. And so I returned to Mum's cosy treehouse, quietly kicked off my shoes and tiptoed into the bathroom. I stripped down to my thin nakedness to stand under the beating shower, dipping my head to watch the water stream over my face and fall onto the unusual bed of river rocks that lined the shower's floor. I could feel each rock poking up into my feet, the heat of the water soothing a body so fatigued I could barely stand upright.

Normally when I towelled myself down, I avoided looking at the mirror, not wanting to confront the thin, gaunt girl who looked back at me. I was never afraid of seeing fatness, but rather I was avoiding looking at her thinness. For I knew she was thin, and I knew that she had been on an unsustainable path. But now I knew in my heart I had finally, truly stumbled onto the right path, however overgrown and mossy it had become. So, on that morning, I met her eyes, observing the dark lines buried beneath them, and the grey, hollowed face staring back. I observed the poking rib cage and the protruding hipbones. And as I looked at this person that I no longer recognised, I knew there was no way I wanted to live even one more day like that.

Little did I know that I was then consciously embarking on the hardest training routine I had ever experienced. Little did I know the frustrations I would feel with myself, the obstacles that would be hurled at me from random angles, and the pain I would inflict on others as I began to wrestle to shrug off my protective best friend, Anorexia.

But at least I had found the commitment within myself and was ready to take the baby steps required to find my feet. At least I was finally able to ask for help and, thankfully, I had a family willing to help.

My mother's results were blessedly benign, and I returned to Melbourne—but not to my classroom of shining, expectant faces. Rather, I returned with a letter of resignation and a car full of packing boxes. Waving goodbye to my brother and the life we had grown together is still one of the hardest things I have done. Every moment that we created together, growing in our strength and spirit beside one another, sharing imaginative dinners derived from his love of cooking, and baking his power cookies, a dough concocted from hefty hunks of butter, peanut butter and sugar, are memories that I will hold close to my heart forever. I will never forget him wrapping me in a huge hug on the doorstep with tears in his eyes and a lump in my throat.

'I am so sorry. I am just so sorry! What will you do now, Big Brother?' In that moment of unity, I pressed my head into his broad chest, feeling his strong arms wrap me in his trademark bear hug. Despite his strength, his heart was transparent, available for the whole world to see. I knew right then that it was cracking with loneliness and confusion, perhaps even frustration that he had not been able to completely help me patch the cracks in my own internal being.

'I am going to find a replacement you.'

It would only be on his own return to Tasmania years later that we would be able to begin gluing the pieces back together. But for now, as I turned my little white Peugeot hatchback towards the freeway and the Spirit of Tasmania ferry, towards home, my heart and relationship with him felt stretched and then finally torn apart.

17

Twenty-four years of age and sitting in the dietitian's waiting room beside my mother. I could not help but feel embarrassed, like control was slipping from my grasp. However, deep down, I knew I was never in control. I felt silly, like a bright young child who rebelled despite knowing better. I was there because I knew I needed to be there. But I was also there for Mum. I loved her and knew how much discomfort she had already overcome.

She certainly didn't need my anger every time she tried to make me eat more; my tears when I was scared of my own anger; my fears of leaving the house and my questions of how I would ever find my feet again. I knew that seeing the dietitian and seeking her assistance was going to be a huge step forward. When Maree took us into her consulting room, I felt somewhat comforted. She was extraordinarily beautiful, a tall mother with strong features and an athletic physique. I felt like she was someone I could trust. I had seen her before, but this time was different. This time, for the first time, I was ready to admit to my weaknesses and commit to getting better. This time, I wanted to find my own feet, to get stronger, to feel playful, wild and resilient once again. And, for the first time ever, I knew that I couldn't rely on others to do this for me.

In that hour, I admitted to not having had a period for over four years, and prior to that only an intermittent one since I was thirteen years of age. I admitted to no longer knowing what a normal meal was, and to not loving my sport in the same light anymore. I agreed that I was afraid of living like this, and that I wanted to find my own strong, playful feet once again.

In that moment, every wall that I had built about me came crashing down. And in that same moment, Maree turned to my mother and explained something, making it more understandable than anyone had done before. 'Julia, you need to realise that there are two individuals here today. First, there is Hanny and then there is Anorexia. When there is anger and frustration, rebellion even, that is Anorexia talking. And then there is your daughter, Hanny.'

At the time I heard what was said, but it wasn't until later, alone on a trail, that I finally comprehended what was spoken. It was this moment of clarity that ultimately helped me to take leaps and bounds forward. As the weeks rolled past, I began to learn that I was living with an illness and that the illness was not me. The Hanny I identified with most strongly, the child who roamed the hills, the rebel in the school classroom, the wilder free-spirit and the strong athlete in her prime, she was still there. She was just sick. With that understanding came only one obvious solution ... to get better.

SLOWLY, slowly I came to realise how Anorexia had grabbed me so strongly by the hand and led me down a frightening path. I was the girl who, when told, 'You can be anything,' only heard, 'You have to be everything.' I had tried to juggle all of the balls with competence—medicine, world champion, family, friends, teaching. I had thought that by achieving outcomes I was maintaining strength and competence. I had also become very good at putting on my brave face to weather the weather.

Yet the perfect storm had still hit me—and with such ferocity that I didn't realise just how far it had blown me off course. During my latter coaching studies I was reading deeper into the achiever mindset, a frame that resonated so strongly with me. I read how the greatest risk for the achiever archetype is that we are often in a headlong rush to achieve whatever we believe will give us more purpose and make us more valuable, to ourselves and others. In doing so, we risk becoming so alienated, even from our own self, that we no longer know what we truly want, or what our real feelings or interests are.

However, no matter how difficult the journey was after I lost my feet, I am still hugely proud of what I achieved and grateful for the lessons I gained. I do not believe that I would be the person I am today, nor be able to empathise as strongly with others, if it hadn't been for those turbulent times. I became a world champion, completed my degrees, ran qualifying times in marathons, and grew as a young adult thanks to discipline, self-belief and working hard. I was willing to listen to the experience of my mentors, to ask questions, and to adopt advice. I was always willing to turn weaknesses towards strengths, learn from setbacks, and rise above adversity. And I was able to be honest. So damn honest!

However, where I went off course was when I continued to hear my heart saying to me, 'You have to be everything.' The winds of life buffeted. Insecurities were fuelled. These arose from deep-seated beliefs instilled in me at a young age—the bullies, the sexual abuse, the fragmenting family, the external spotlights, and the internal pressures. I now believe that these insecurities manifested from confusion and a sense of isolation, eventually leading to a very disordered approach to nutrition and, ultimately, a friendship with Anorexia.

If I could change one thing about my journey, it would be to give myself an internal awareness of the grasp this illness had on me at that time. That I could have seen one piece of toast was not enough to refuel after a hard morning's training session, or that grazing from one small bite to another, unable to wander through a supermarket without feeling like a hungry scavenger, was not a normal mentality for an athlete. But initially I didn't have this awareness. Even when I finally began to see how anxious I had become while I lived like this, Anorexia had grasped my hand so firmly that she led me to believe that the results I was seeing were all due to her pedantic demands.

As I began to heal, I was immersed in the elite Australian running scene. I couldn't help but feel that it was acceptable, even normal, to be rake thin and running on empty.

I was invited to a national distance-running camp. Many of us were already exceptionally petite, and yet we were still constantly given messages about the importance of 'healthy nutrition'. Fat was bad, protein was great. Girls were returning from long, hard runs to a breakfast of spinach leaves, a sliver of leftover steak and a glass of diet Pepsi. One girl vocally discussed how some of her teeth had fallen out, and another how she was only allowed to run if she ate.

I spent each night on the phone to Jackie in streams of tears. Through her own experiences it appeared she could empathise with my fears surrounding these circumstances, reassuring me that I was deserving of my place to be there. Together, we continued to hatch dreams of representing Australia at the London Olympics in the marathon, if not the upcoming Delhi Commonwealth Games.

However, deep down I knew that my path was diverging once again. When I tried to peer down the one leading towards the Olympic marathon, I wasn't sure that I could see beyond the confusing undergrowth. In my heart, I wasn't sure that it was the right path for me, and my results began to show this fear. And yet, without having reached a place of clarity about my future in running, I continued to persist.

In the new year I boarded another plane, this time to Sydney, hoping to be greeted at Arrivals by Jackie leaning out of her sporty Porsche with a cheeky grin. She never showed. With a friend's assistance I caught a train to the Olympic Athletics Stadium and began my warm-up for the New South Wales State 5000 m Championships.

IT WAS A STORMY NIGHT. The lights of the Sydney Athletics Track shone across the shimmering surface, reflecting off large puddles that had formed on its synthetic surface. That track was fast but brutally hard, and on this night I knew we were in for a challenging run. Not for the first time, I wished Jackie was there. Wished for just one time she could watch me run.

However, as I warmed up, I pinched myself because I had her as my coach. She was so transparent with the lessons she had learnt from her own story, so vulnerable about her rise to athletic fame, so giving of her rich knowledge base. She understood the complex world of internal pressure more than anyone. And on that night, even though she was not there to cheer us all on, I was under her tuition and running with gratitude. I really, really wanted to toe the start line.

Moments after crossing the finish line—just outside my personal-best time of sixteen minutes and four seconds—I was reunited with girls from Jackie's Canberra training squad. We shared a few congratulations and excited gossip, then began to jog down. Round and round. Around and around. Around. Until there was just myself and my dear friend Hannah remaining. She pulled me to a stop, turned to me with grave eyes, her damp hair clinging to her open, honest face. 'Jackie didn't come tonight because she is sick. Really sick. Han, she is in hospital. She tried to take her own life ... again.'

The conversation hung in the air, a thick statement so incomprehensible that I was unable to acknowledge it. Hannah had momentarily driven a wedge between Jackie and me. I bent over, hands on knees and released a whimper. 'Nooo ...' Jackie was my rock, the one I turned to when I felt stuck in the mud. My dreams were visible to her and together we had a plan.

I did not return home to Hobart the next day. Instead, I clambered into the back of Hannah's car and went to Canberra with her. Walking into Jackie's hospital room, I was only too aware of the symbolism of that moment. She greeted me with her usual cheekiness, her girlish laugh and enthusiasm. 'I don't need to be here! Come on Han, get me out and we can go for a run!'

Instead we headed towards a café, where she ordered and then pushed the food away. She talked about everything other than the elephant in the room, and became frustrated when I failed to commit to taking her for a run. Deep inside, I was panicking. I couldn't do this again. I was all too aware that I was instantly and incredibly fragile, a mere millimetre from the edge, and so for the first time ever I admitted to my vulnerability and I turned away.

I AM NOT proud of how I reacted that day, and I frequently find myself wondering how I could have responded differently ... if I could have that moment again. But blow by blow, accident by accident, death by health scare, home by new home, I had been whittled down to my rawest, most vulnerable self, and I just didn't know how to confront that scene all over again. I didn't yet realise that when you finally admit your vulnerability, you are ready to bloom again.

I never spoke freely with Jackie again. I returned home and laid my relief teaching work aside. I found myself responding to the curious media and friends, 'I am just trying to find my feet.' I continued to dabble a little in my running, tried on a few new coaches for size, but none could refill the vast shoes of Max on my left foot and Jackie on my right.

I WAS WEAVING BACK up the mountain roads to my mother's house. I had just left work at Passion8—the outdoor athletic store where I first found employment, where I returned after my father's suicide attempt, and where Cheryl and Nigel had opened their arms to me again.

There were lots of familiar faces, including Graham's—he had migrated back to Hobart after skiing all over the world and thinking maybe he needed to get a real job. I admired all these individuals, and I especially admired Graham's tenacity in following his heart, for he is a skier at heart. He had let his heart rule his head, and to me that is still amazingly inspiring.

The car window was down, the breeze cool on my face. I couldn't help but notice all the lonely souls plodding up the road. Their gait rigid, their grimaces, too. I wondered what had possessed each of them to enter the upcoming Point to Pinnacle Fun Run—which takes runners from the Hobart waterfront to the summit of Mt Wellington.

Perhaps, just perhaps ... I could teach them to run, to play. To meet like-minded individuals and make the process of striving for their goals more enjoyable. It would be a chance to bide my time while I let my heart, not my head, determine the *What next?*

By the time I pulled up in Mum's snaking driveway, bundled myself from the car and jostled in through the front door, I knew exactly what I was going to call my new hobby. Bubbles of excitement. A smile which felt so authentic and genuine that for the first time in four years I was able to identify with the real Hanny.

I whipped out my laptop and Googled 'Find Your Feet'.

An error. An empty screen.

Then, a signal!

And so, Find Your Feet was born. As easily as that, I knew I would finally begin walking the right path … my path. And for the first time in a long while, I was willing to let my heart lead the way.

PART IV

BAREFOOT

2009–2017

A wilder summit, Mt Anne, Tasmania (Photograph: Graham Hammond)

18

November 2009. A whipped-together business logo like a thrown-together dessert. A business registration and domain name, but no business plan. An A4 laminated sign nailed to Mum's fence. Would it capture the attention of the runners who jogged past each day?

I visited the local running shop in town to ask if I could host two running sessions a week from the doorway of their store. Hand-printed flyers left on their counter: 'Join us for running games and education in the parks of Hobart. Meet 5:30 for a 5:45 pm departure. Mondays and Thursdays. $5. Just turn up.'

Day One arrived. A mishap—it was a public holiday. I sat on the steps of the closed athletic store and wondered if anyone would turn up. I glanced up and down the empty street. The clock ticked past 5:30 pm.

And then she arrived. A single car. A woman I had met earlier that morning as she jogged along the Pipeline Track. I had watched from behind as her heels struck the earth with force, her arms held a little too high, her shoulders tense. *I can help you*, I had thought.

A tap on the shoulder. An exchange of names. A nervous invite that lead to Heather becoming the first member of my Find Your Feet community. I was too embarrassed to accept the flimsy five-dollar note she waved towards me.

Day One. Zero dollars.

I NEVER, ever believed that Find Your Feet would be anything more than a handbrake while I worked out what I wanted to do. I re-sat my medical entrance exams and was accepted back into medicine. Tears of excitement flowed when I opened my acceptance letter—but days later, I declined the offer. I had promised myself that I would no longer let my head rule my heart, and somehow my heart was saying to me, 'No, No, NO! Wrong way, Han, this is a one-way street!'

At every Find Your Feet session I met someone new, someone else with a story, someone else grateful to run beside other individuals also on the journey to finding their feet.

As I listened to their stories, my own story began to grasp me less strongly. Helping others was helping me to put more and more space between myself and Anorexia, although recovery was certainly not a straight line. On the days when I felt the most confused about my *what next?*, I found Anorexia continued to offer a helping hand. I became more adept at fobbing her off, but the wrestle to resist her friendship could occasionally feel exhausting. It was the wise words of a Find Your Feet member that continued to bring me back to my steadier place: 'Han, it doesn't matter how incredible the gift you are trying to give to us is, if all we see is someone who cannot return the same gift to herself.'

That statement was so achingly true. It was filled with such honesty. At the time, it took me back to Jackie's hospital room in Canberra. Her thin frame sitting on the edge of the bed, trying to tug on her running shoes. Rather than turn away, could I have offered those same wise words to her: 'Jackie, it doesn't matter how incredible the gift is that you are trying to give us, if all we see is someone who is not returning the same gift to herself.' Could I have then listened, and stood by her side until she too could find her feet again?

Through Find Your Feet I began to realise that I was not my endeavours. That is, I began to understand that I was not 'a runner', but rather Hanny, with thoughts, emotions and deeper layers, albeit a young woman who loved to run. I was not my parents' daughter; I was me. I was not a teacher; I loved to share my knowledge and thrill for life. I was not my achievements or my failings, but rather the sum total of my experiences. And I was certainly not my story. The question that started forming inside my confused head was, *So how do I find my feet from here?*

In a moment of intuition and spontaneity, I signed up to an Advanced Diploma of Life Coaching with the Life Coaching Academy of Australia. The course was literally life-changing. Through that education I came to identify that we all have stories, that we all have moments which will bring us crashing to our knees and questioning how to stand again. But these stories do not define us, and life is not about striving for success or happiness. When the day came to put the final touches on my thesis, *The Art of Happiness*, I was finally able to understand that success and happiness are both processes. They are a journey, not an outcome. And I was finally able to acknowledge, understand, and then treasure each of the successes that I had experienced to date.

Find Your Feet became a vehicle to self-discovery. My clients and I would buckle in and embark on continually-evolving journeys together. From trail running festivals on Mt Wellington to camping trips on Maria Island, from primary school running games in Hobart's parklands to a very soggy, stormy interstate journey to the Victorian Alps, we ran to connect with others and ourselves, all the while sharing our stories and learning to realise that the beauty was in the process and not the outcomes.

19

My father and I cycled side by side. We were so close that I could reach out and touch him, and yet our legs spun at different cadences. We were out of sync and it felt awkward, clumsy even. In many ways it had been like this ever since the Perfect Storm, and the days afterwards when I helped to rub moisturiser into his healing wounds. We drifted together as we spun around a corner, and then we drifted apart again on the wider, open roads.

'Han?'

Dad's quiet voice cut through the whistling wind and the noise of my thoughts. I looked across at him. His face held a seriousness. Beyond him, the Derwent River glistened as it reached the sea and yawned into the great Southern Ocean. This autumn was crisp, a tranquil bleed of colour into the approaching winter. It is still my favourite season. And I was cycling with my favourite father. We may be out of sync, but we were still there together, and that is the beauty of family.

'Han, I am thinking about asking Janeil to marry me. I am wondering what you think?'

Silence held. The landscape continued to pass, a blur of autumnal apple orchards with oceans behind. But my internal world was suddenly spinning faster than my legs, as if my brakes had been released and I was flying down a hill too fast. I could feel the breath catching in my chest and my hands gripping tighter to the handlebars.

'Han?'

And still I paused, before finally choosing my words carefully.

'You have my full support, Dad.'

Because he did. While my inner child was begging me to try one last time to glue the fragments of our old family unit back together, my maturing adult could find the strength to look over to her father, lock eyes for a brief moment, and utter those words of support.

Janeil is a beautiful woman, rich in empathy and zest for life. She had made my father smile again and brought out those chortling laughs in us all. My mother had also moved on, surrounded by undying friendships and a gratitude that we were all slowly getting back on our feet. So, however hard my heart momentarily ached, I knew this road was definitely the right one for us to be riding along. With the question then asked and the answer given, we had closed the gap.

A father and his daughter, not quite so far apart.

MY FATHER WAS MARRIED under the domed ceiling of the Baha'i Centre in Hobart. A small ceremony filled with a sea of friends. Barn dances and jovial festivities followed. Or so I am told.

While the night unfolded, I was slowly rising from a deep slumber in a family-run pension in Austria. My mother knew that I was still on the journey towards finding my feet. Having already booked a European cycle touring holiday for herself well before the wedding date was set, she continued to drop offhand comments. 'Maybe you could come with me, Han?'

One by one, I rejected the comments. Shoulds and musts flew around in my internal world: *It's my Dad!*

My head said to stay ...

but my heart said to go.

And I had learnt to listen to my heart. So, eventually, I chose to ride through the rolling green pastures of the Austrian countryside, one bike length in front of my mother. I knew my father understood that even though I wasn't dancing on the wooden floors of the Sandfly Hall alongside him and Janeil, celebrating their union, I was there in spirit, two-stepping awkwardly as I tried to overcome my fear of dancing. As the Austrian light changed from dawn to midday glow to dusk, my heart beat in tune with his. And, when a busker sang a beautiful ballad beneath the archway of an historical church that evening with my mother standing quietly beside me, I knew I had made the right decision. This was the closest I had felt with both my mother and father, perhaps ever.

For ten weeks, I cycled around the striking green landscape of Switzerland, Germany, France, Italy, Austria and the Czech Republic. Four of these weeks were in the nurturing company of my mother. Within days, I realised how much we had both missed true, uncomplicated maternal joy in our lives. We had both crawled into our crab shells after the events of 2005. Only now, five years later, were we both reappearing into the big wide world and realising we had a whole lot of playfulness to catch up on.

Each day we excitedly jumped onto our bikes, roamed at large on a route to somewhere unknown, ate baguettes and cheese, drank *sturm*, the young wine in fermentation, and downed pizzas in the evening sun after a long day in the saddle. One week in, my bottom ached from saddle-sores, and yet I felt freer than I had for nearly ten years. Somewhere between Zurich airport and the foothills of the *Schwarzwald*, or Black Forest, of Germany, I turned a corner and found clarity.

I was ready to step back from elite competition, to put my racing shoes down and say to them, 'Not now.' From then on out, mornings would be opportunities rather than routines. Exercising would be play, not training. I was learning to be wilder and to play wilder, and it felt so damn great!

The trip was not without its complications. I was the fearless navigator out the front, my mother the brave bodyguard behind. When I said 'follow me' it was coming from my explorer archetype but also the grateful daughter who wanted to repay her mother's love in a rubber-tyred, vista-filled adventure together. In my truest wild spirit, if the signs pointed one way then I always assumed there must have been another. Under this fateful guidance, my mother and I ended up on a glorious country footpath winding its way along a small Italian brook. We rode gleefully—my ego puffing out my chest, proudly congratulating me, 'Aren't you clever, Hanny!'

Concentration wrapped in ego.

An unsuspecting ditch.

A quick grab for the brakes.

A mother colliding with her daughter.

A twisted knee unwilling to hold a mother upright.

We climbed back onto the bikes and braved the way forward, silent tears of pain creeping down my mother's face. And then a cobblestone Roman road led up towards the heavens. Pushing heavy bikes one painful step at a time. Then it was my turn to weep, tears of guilt finally washing away the ego.

Eventually, these tears turned to hysterical laughs, belching out into the unfamiliar countryside. We put down our bikes, sat on the cobblestone street, and laughed at the silliness of our predicament. For what else could we do?

We eventually pulled up outside a hotel in the sleepy city of Cremona, and were greeted by a fragrant Italian man with wildly-waving arms. He led us into the cool interior of his guesthouse before leading us, painful step by painful step, to the very top floor. We showered, lay on our beds and contemplated our fate, until our stomachs could no longer resist the Italian aromas seeping into the room. By the time my mother reached the bottom of the stairs, tears were cascading down her face.

Our host's jovial face turned to utter concern, and his waving arms pushed my mother down into a seat in the restaurant. He disappeared out the front door in a waving, babbling Italian hysteria. And then he returned, arms still flapping, but this time with a spray can. He reached my mother, rested his hand gently on her shoulder and then took two giant steps backwards before enveloping her leg in a thick fog from the contents of the spray can. The can's contents were a chilling, ice-like substance supposed to cool and numb the area. By the time the mist cleared, he had placed before us bags of ice, brimming wine glasses, and a packet of foreign drugs which he popped open and forced into my mystified mother.

The tears cleared.

The pain disappeared.

And thanks to his assistance, we kept on riding for three more weeks through alpine passes and Italian motorway tunnels, little suspecting that my mother had a torn ACL ligament, ruptured cartilage and generally buggered-up knee.

AT THE BEGINNING OF 2011, I returned to tertiary studies in the form of paramedicine, using the slowly growing pennies from Find Your Feet and my casual retail jobs to fund my studies. While I loved propping with my mother, in my heart I knew that if we were both to continue on the journey towards finding our feet, I needed to move out of my mother's house.

I moved out to live with a nurse and a call centre employee. Two girls, one a junk food addict, the other a Weight Watchers fanatic with two freezers to store all her frozen meals.

Living in the heart of the city was like trying to keep a wombat in a cage. I could feel myself trying to dig beneath the concrete jungle and escape to where the grass was greener. When my father offered me the opportunity to rent his quirky house on the banks of the Hobart Rivulet —a glorious place in summer and a damp, cold house in the depths of winter—I readily agreed. I felt freedom rising in my veins. A great friend moved in, and together we made delicious, wholesome dinners, studied at the kitchen table, ran on the trails, and felt the pulse of Mt Wellington just beyond our front door.

Isn't there a saying, 'life is what happens to you while you are busy making other plans'? When I began to drop the plans and lean into the everyday moments, I was suddenly able to let relationships and opportunities catch up with me.

The most important was a friendship with Graham—my long-time friend from the Passion8 retail store. Our friendship grew amongst the down jackets and tents of that very same store where we were both still working, and blossomed further on the trails of Mt Wellington. It fed on laughter, the 'imagine if' conversations, and an insatiable desire to live every day to the full. It giggled as we jumped in the puddles during an early morning run, squealed as we bombed down a steep trail on our mountain bikes, and held us in excited anticipation when we began planning a holiday escape to Borneo … just as friends.

We shrugged off the knowing looks from family and friends who suspected more from the friendship, until eventually we couldn't deny it any more. While friendship formed the deepest, most important core of our relationship, love had indeed snuck up and wrapped us in a tight bear hug. As we stood on the beaches of Maria Island, the Milky Way igniting, phosphorescence sparkling in the shallow waters of the bay, our athletic fingers interlocked. Two hearts hoping for a shooting star. A squeal. A long, deep hug. A wish. A kiss. Gratitude.

I admired every element of Graham. He was kindness to his core and did not have a competitive bone in his body. Every day I marvelled that I could walk beside him through playfulness, business, and the adventure of our relationship, our steps falling into a quiet rhythm together. He was quite the opposite of the person I saw myself wanting to be alongside. After the brief relationships I had with other athletes, I thought my perfect partner might be a big, fat, overweight musician. Oops!

He was so content in his own shoes, and playful at his core, which made him a wonderful role model for me. Eager to explore hard and then rest hard later, he appreciated the simple things in life. A mountain peak, a new trail. Fresh snow and the sound of rain on a roof at night. A tub of yoghurt, and Nutella, too. Peanut butter and honey sandwiches and a hearty bowl of pasta. Vegetarian, a three-meal-a-day kind of guy with a soft spot for lying in the sun just because he could. He allowed me to be my truest, most authentic self, and it was ultimately my love of Graham that allowed me to explore my greatest me.

Anorexia did try to break into our duo on a couple of occasions, and

I wondered if I would ever completely be able to turn off her whispering voice. Walking alongside Graham helped me to learn how to change the radio channel. There was certainly no space for her in that relationship.

Today, I quietly joke with Graham that I also fell in love with him because of where we were renting—The Barn. This beautifully renovated residence was once the oldest barn in Hobart, a rickety jumble of sandstone blocks and broken windows. We would ride our bikes up the long driveway, toss them aside, and then close the door with a loud thud. Inside, it was purely still. Light filtered in through the high slit windows and the stone gave it a steadiness that mimicked our relationship. It felt like home, and even though I had planted my feet, I knew that I still hadn't answered that underlying question of, *What next?*

I found myself writing an application for an Athlete Supervisor job at the Australian Institute of Sport in Canberra.

THE PLANE TOUCHED down at eight o'clock in the morning. It was minus-eight degrees. The light was grey. The grass was grey. The mist over Lake Burley Griffin was grey. The car that met me was white, and the lady who drove it had hair that was dyed white. The arrival hallway of the Institute of Sport was a breath-steaming grey, and the key that unlocked the plethora of barred doorways and eventually my grey front door into my grey apartment was also grey. My pleading, frightened phone call home to Graham was grey too. 'What am I doing?' I said into my black mobile phone.

I lay down on the grey carpet, observed the black furniture devoid of any softness, and plucked up the courage to dig around for my running shoes. I exited the building onto the grey cycle path and followed it into the frosty, grey bushland. I ran in a quiet haze, with foggy tears blurring my way through the tightly twisting mountain bike trails.

I found myself entering a tunnel of gratitude for everything that I had left behind. For Graham with his ever-positive enthusiasm for my wild ideas. For my mother who had helped me back onto my feet. To my brother who was living abroad in Germany, chasing his own dreams. To my father who was always there for support. And to Janeil, who had joined our family too.

A splash of colour. A tuft of yellow wattle sprang into my peripheral vision. A lace of purple creeping through the grey undergrowth. The brilliant brown of drying sprigs of grass. The blue of young eucalyptus leaves, round and plump. Slowly, slowly the world felt a little bit brighter.

WHILE GRATITUDE DIDN'T INSTANTLY MELT the frost, over time the greyness dissipated and my new world in Canberra came to life. I was ready to embrace my new position, living alongside the Paralympic and Olympic athletes as they built towards the 2012 London Games. I was beginning to enjoy living in the athlete residences, checking on their needs through the day and night, and driving them towards airports, appointments and, for the younger ones, their school classes.

It wasn't the hardest job in the world, but it gave me a fascinating insight into the incredible support networks these athletes performed within. With scholarships worth in the high tens of thousands of dollars, they ate, slept and breathed sport, under the brilliance of coaches and support personnel.

During this time, I laid down my running shoes completely, and threw myself with excitement into the world of mountain biking. The city was prime for it, and the vast network of friendships that formed around the dusty, rocky trails of Canberra gave me a pathway into the underbelly of the city. Graham regularly flew up to visit, and together we explored the camaraderie as well as the trails further and further afield.

When the day came for him to fly home, we would sit side by side on the shores of Lake Burley Griffin and try to will time to stop. But it never did. If anything, it sped up. It was getting harder and harder to say goodbye.

Until one day he visited and didn't go home. He arrived in a flurry of duffel bags and Easter egg wrappers, strewn across the floor of his old Subaru. The year apart had tested the strength of our relationship, and it was rock solid. In fact, it was diamond-tough. We needed to be together.

He took up employment as the manager of a local Australian outdoor retail store, which strangely happened to be adjacent to one of the famous sex shops in Canberra.

When I moved to Canberra, I never expected Find Your Feet to follow me, and yet somehow it did, via emails from runners and event organisers alike. Opportunities to continue coaching individuals, and rapidly-growing events such as The North Face 100 km, now the Ultra Trail Australia series, kept manifesting—and somehow it always felt right to say yes.

The ever-growing numbers of athletes with whom I worked were often starting from a very low base-fitness, and yet were setting extraordinarily high goals. One athlete proudly exclaimed, 'I've entered the 100 km event because I feel really fit!' Excited for him, I asked what was behind his fitness. 'I am a body builder and I run five kilometres a week on the treadmill.'

Not only did I marvel at how stretched many of these athletes' goals were, but I was also perplexed by how little support there appeared to be for them. The athletes I worked with at the Institute could all perform with more agility, competence and stamina, but I kept coming back to the simple fact that a goal was a goal. It shouldn't matter how fast we can run, or how bravely we can descend on a mountain bike. We are all striving towards goals because they are meaningful to us and, therefore, shouldn't we all be entitled to the same elite knowledge that can help us?

The more I observed the AIS and elite sporting world in action, the more perplexed I became about the breadth of knowledge held within this elite tier of sport. Effectively, if you weren't participating in an Olympic or Commonwealth sport, and if you weren't seen to be of champion-level performance, a lot of this world was out of reach. The longer I stayed at the AIS, the more I felt a calling to share that elite knowledge with the rest of the world.

So, after twelve months and the conclusion of the London Olympic and Paralympic events which I watched on television, I submitted my resignation letter. I took casual employment as a project and event manager for Pedal Power, a not-for-profit cycling organisation based in Canberra.

When I wasn't working on cycling-related projects, I began to dabble more and more in opportunities to assist recreational runners. I consulted on the phone with recreational athletes around Australia, drew together training planners, freelanced for magazines, worked on my blog, hosted running camps and clinics, and eventually reached a point where I couldn't keep all the balls in the air. One evening, Graham and I looked long and hard at my bank balance and concluded that I had to be brave. There was never going to be that 'right time' to throw in the security of someone else paying my income.

With Graham's unwavering support, as soon as I jumped in the deep end with Find Your Feet, the ball rolled wildly. While there has certainly been a fair share of challenges, and on one occasion I just wanted to send a letter of resignation to my own email inbox, I have never doubted the decision I made to pursue Find Your Feet. For, at the end of the day, I feel compelled to assist people like you and me to find our feet.

GRAHAM and I purchased our first home on a whim. With Canberra rental prices burning a hole in our lower-income pockets, and returning each evening to a single room, top-floor apartment in a mostly treeless suburb, I once again felt like a caged wombat prowling around a concrete pen.

I found a small ad tucked in the corner of a real estate magazine. I went online to have a look at the pretty pictures. Except that they were not so pretty. The only thing that was pretty about this uninspiring property was the price tag. It was not-quite-but-nearly affordable, and so I made a sneaky, solo visit to the property. I peered in through dusty windows and fell in love with the cockatoos who screeched and pooped their way across the sky overhead.

Before Graham had even entered our flat that night, I bundled him back out the door. We were the only potential buyers to arrive at the arranged property inspection. In hindsight, I am not surprised.

Following the shuffling gait of the agent down the flat concrete pathway through the tumbleweeds of the front garden, we had already decided it would be a downright no. Leaves protruded over the building's gutters, the windows were a murky shade of grime, and the front door housed an orange glass arrangement that shed a strange light onto the porch.

As the front door swung open to reveal a thick, dirt-crusted shag pile carpet and a comprehensively brown kitchen, we turned to one another in dismay. With every blind closed, a mirrored sliding door reflecting our horror, brown wallpaper covering every blank wall space and an odd blue plastic sheet covering the rear porch, it was like stepping back into the mid-nineteenth century—but with the lights dimmed.

The agent hesitantly informed us that the property was a deceased estate, and had sat vacant for three years awaiting the grandchildren's decision on how to divide the asset. We found ourselves transported into the former owner's life. A brown, wood-like television stood on three metal legs, a plethora of ornaments and floral platters adorned the shelving, and every single piece of the previous owner's life sat in its rightful place, right down to her crockery, underwear and as we later found out, the enormous cupboard designated for her delicious homemade port.

It was Graham who first realised the property's ultimate potential. As we wandered around the small museum in a baffled daze, I heard a whisper. 'Hanny? Hanny!' I wandered into the bedroom, its single bed covered in brown blankets, a bedside table still hosting her books and water glass, and found Graham scrabbling at the windows that looked out into a lush internal courtyard. As he removed a pair of oversized, scrunched-up undies from a crevice in the lower half of the window, a sheet of chipboard came away in Graham's grasp to reveal full, floor to ceiling, glass windows. We stood transfixed, knowing that the soon-to-be-retired agent waiting outside for us knew nothing of this hidden potential. That residential monument, a tribute to 93 years of life, was actually constructed like a glasshouse.

We moved into our new home at the beginning of December 2012. Piling our relatively small number of possessions into a few vehicles, we trundled towards the leafy suburb of Cook and our new home, oblivious to the disarray soon to greet us. Once again, we shuffled behind the agent down the concrete pathway towards the orange-glassed front door. Our excitement resonated with the jingle of his keys. Handing us a bottle of celebratory champagne, he then turned the key in the door and gave it a light shove.

The door swung open to reveal that, despite the requirements of the contract, not one plate, not one teaspoon, not one pair of undies had been moved. The life of a 93-year-old lady sat there, laid out before us. And so started the trade of one life for another. Plate by plate, mug by mug, clothes pile by clothes pile, we traded her dust-covered possessions for our clean, modern ones.

At 10:30 pm that evening, we stood alone in our new home, eating bread and cheese in our brown-benchtopped, brown-tiled, brown-wall-papered kitchen. The brown shag pile carpet had already broken two vacuum cleaners. The smeared, hardened patch in the middle still looked like a dog had died on it.

Outside sat an overfilled skip bin—a spontaneous welcome present from the real estate agent, to go with his bottle of champagne. Despite the darkness of the evening, the house was filled by the glow from a moon sitting low in the sky and shining through the smeared windows into our glasshouse. Our feet were once again able to sense the ground beneath them, and the sliding doors remained open into a rear courtyard now devoid of blue plastic.

I knew then and there, munching on cheese sandwiches, that for the first time since leaving the farm, I had finally found home. We named our glasshouse 'Base Camp', as it was from the safety of its brown walls that we would play and love with wilder hearts.

BETWEEN VARIED ADVENTURES, Base Camp slowly evolved into a gleaming, soft-toned, modern bungalow. The interior sparkled, and Graham and I learnt to garden just enough to host a fantastic parsley patch enjoyed by the possums. Friendships blossomed around our large carpenter-style table, including one with our adjoining neighbour and caretaker to the local possums. As we changed shag pile for muted grey carpets, so too did Chris. As we replaced brown benches with stone tops, so too did Chris. When we replaced the hideous front door on Christmas Day using a blunt chisel and a hammer, Chris was the first person to knock on it. And when we finally pulled out a few weeds, she was the first person to offer to water the young replacements when we were away playing.

Base Camp was our rock, and from that solid foundation Graham and I began to also dust ourselves off, wiping clean our adventurous spirits, polishing our relationships with family, and uncovering even more gems in our own partnership.

Once a skier, always a skier. When summer rolled around again—a furiously hot one at that—Graham packed his warmest winter gear and took off for ski-guiding work in Japan. While he dazzled and roamed in the powder playgrounds, I sat in our unairconditioned home in my bikini. Between consults with clients, I plunged into a bathtub filled with cold water. The heat lingered and lingered, until I felt as stressed as the sagging forest trees. The sight of the shrivelling garden and the stressed native animals lying like living corpses in the bushlands was enough to break my heart. As much as I loved Canberra, I couldn't adjust to the extremes. The ravaging summers and the frozen winters. Tasmania was beginning to pull at my heartstrings.

What was also becoming a stress was the relentless hours I was beginning to spend on the telephone and emails. If I wasn't life coaching or performance consulting with athletes on the phone, I was churning out weekly training programs. This was partly due to the great demand from the recreational trail running community. But it was also due to business advice that I had been offered. Out of the blue, a member of the running community had sent me an email offering to help me lift Find Your Feet to new heights. Having never considered Find Your Feet a business, but rather a service to the adult recreational running community, I was pulled up short. *Maybe I do need a business plan?* I engaged his services, and a few weeks later I held a sharp-looking business plan in my hot, sweaty hands.

For twenty-five dollars a week, I would write training programs for adults using online coaching software. Once a fortnight, I would email them. Once a month, a short phone call. I would initially build to fifty clients, and then once I had mastered the art, raise this to one hundred.

However, the plan was short-lived. By forty clients I was seeing stars, and by fifty I was a puddle of tears each Friday as I anticipated the sheer volume of work I had to create before Sunday night. I had a cheat sheet on my wall reminding me of the athletes' names, their chosen goals and any titbits I knew about them.

The tears also flowed from fear. A deep, unrelenting fear that someone was going to get injured because I had failed to see the warning signs. I later realised that this fear was also stemming from a subconscious knowledge that I was moving in the opposite direction to the values which created Find Your Feet in the first place. I was no longer helping, educating and empowering individuals. I was telling them what to do and allowing them to mindlessly be led.

Living in Canberra so easily surrounded by beautiful bushlands and playful community, as well as striving to empower others, led me back into the running world. In the depths of another winter I gratefully ditched my bike and laced up my running shoes again. When I headed out the door for my first run, I assumed I would run to there, over that, around this and then back again. I didn't even reach 'there'. After a couple of kilometres, everything was aching. Despite my mountain biking fitness which had led me onto some elite teams and a few local podium results, my chest was heaving, my calves burning and my movements as uncoordinated as a baby pademelon learning to bounce.

I wobbled home in a humbled, sweaty mess. I had always assumed that once a runner, always a runner, and yet it would take me two long years of hard work before I found flow in the sport again. That small lesson not only gave me great empathy and insight into the athletes whom I coached, but it also gave me the feeling of being back at the start of a long climb. It was intoxicating to be there, and I was more ready than ever to run again. Furthermore, with Canberra being the home of orienteering, I sensed a deep calling to return to this sport too. I ran with two questions in my heart. *Was 2006 just a fluke?* and *Was it possible to return to that level in a healthy, playful manner?*

CANBERRA WAS a city planned to be beautiful, with its artificial lakes and swathes of bushland bordering each individual suburb. Bike tracks were built before roads and trees planted before houses grew. The city was purposefully designed for active living.

However, active doesn't foster wild. While I loved running along the twisting trails around the city and growing even more connected to my like-minded friends, in Canberra my muscle for wild adventures began to waste. I was sure it was already weakened from the previous years of living in bigger cities and pursuing road running interests and, to be honest, I had not noticed the encroaching weakness.

Then Graham and I embarked on a road trip to the Flinders Ranges in South Australia. Seeing the sun beginning to dip and knowing that meant kangaroos were about to appear on the roads, we needed to find a campsite. Instead of stopping at an idyllic, free, 'sneaky camping' option where the sunset and night sky would no doubt have delivered, I insisted we continue to drive. Hours passed as we peered through the windscreen for frightened kangaroos, until we finally found ourselves wedged between two enormous motorhomes in the Broken Hill Caravan Park, streetlights creating an artificial glow through the tent walls as we listened to our neighbours discussing the bowel habits of their pet cats.

A few months later, we returned to Tasmania to visit our families. We always aimed to find an adventure, but this time, bound for the broad plateau, rising trails and rocky upper slopes of Mt Anne, I felt unprepared. Where had my adventure muscle gone? Despite carrying strong fitness, the right equipment, and an unwavering trust in Graham's experience, there lingered an honest sense of unpreparedness. In simple terms, I just didn't trust myself.

I desperately craved the confidence to play wilder again.

A DARK DAWN LINGERED. Clouds on the horizon held the night to ransom while, overhead, stars dominated the skyline, vaguely silhouetting Cradle Mountain. I took hold of Graham's warm hand and give it a firm squeeze. One of those 'I feel scared' squeezes.

We were in this event together, thanks to a spontaneous moment of insanity two months earlier. It just so happened to be an eighty-two-kilometre dash down the Overland Track, an ideal saunter for your first race in over three years! Somehow, and just a few months earlier, we had bumbled our way through the qualifying requirement of sixty-five kilometres in a local event in Canberra, and later wound up sprawled on our couch thinking, 'What have we got ourselves into?'

From the moment the starter announced, 'Okay, you can go now,' I felt the fear dissipate. A profound desire to be out there encompassed my whole being. I knew I needed to be there. For that is the thing about fear, it simply exists to highlight what is really meaningful to you, and the only way through it is to wade right into it. I tucked in behind the boys, and made chirpy chitchat while trying to avoid the worst of the black ice lacing the famous Tasmanian duckboards—narrow segments of wood strung together by wire. We slipped and slid, our head torches cutting into the gloom, and then finally ran in silence, gaps widening and tranquillity settling over the field.

Memories of my eighteen-year-old self running this very same event encompassed me. I was still just as naive about how to fuel and hydrate myself, and I was very aware that my body was nowhere near full strength for the event. Recently, Graham and I had embarked on a spontaneous trip to an adventure race in China, filling in for injured teammates. Amongst unexpected snowfall and under the domineering demands of our team leader, we battled until we didn't want to battle anymore. At some point, amongst the outflows from piggeries and in sheeting rain, I crashed my knee into a rock, later discovering that I had put a hairline fracture through my patella. Even though the injury was out there with me this day on the Overland Track, a niggling discomfort underneath my right knee, I gritted my teeth. I just wanted to absorb the sheer thrill of being back in the Tasmanian mountains. Out here, I felt at home.

Approximately fifty kilometres into the trail, I passed into a clearing where one of the five hikers' huts proudly sat. Each of those huts marks one day of hiking for the trekkers who take up to one week to complete the track, and yet today the field's lighter-footed trail runners would be covering the entire distance between dawn and dusk.

As I departed into the cooler shadows of the rainforest once again, I observed a familiar, balding head atop an exceedingly athletic body, bouncing along the track in front of me, the bright red and white of his Salomon running kit in vibrant contrast to the grey dolerite landscape and dark hues of the trees. I was perplexed, and instantly ... terribly afraid! This man was one of my idols. I had marvelled and drooled over his schmick website, and read about his running and coaching exploits in many trail running publications.

What on earth was I doing near him? For a while, I threw out the anchor, trotting along behind him and chatting in friendly introductions. He gave little away, which only led to further doubt. Had I gone out way too hard?

Then I could feel him lifting, his pace quickening to match the wind which was gently picking up as we crossed the pass between two proud peaks. As we began to descend, I could feel the clear air growing between us, and relief washed through me as I said my farewells. 'I will see you at the finish!'

Then I was alone, watching him run off into the distance as I fell into my own rhythm once again, bounding down deep steps. I felt good, gliding along the track, the presence of the mountains always nearby. But what was that? A flash of red, a shiny scalp? Once again, I found my wagon hitching onto his engine, and we began to run in unison once again.

'Are you okay?' I asked, my empty question hovering in the air as he pulled off the track. I paused but he told me to keep going while he ate a leaf. Did I hear him correctly? Eat a leaf?

Eventually, I heard familiar footsteps behind. As I pulled off the track, he greeted me cheerily. I quickly felt my wagon disengaging from his strength, the gap ever widening until I yelled into the distance once again, 'See you at the finish!'

An empty trail. A space for reflection and downtime. And then another flash of red. A bald spot now tilted downwards with a head hanging in greater defeat. A crumpled posture, shortened strides, an individual humbled by the challenging sport of ultrarunning. He explained that by eating a leaf he was reconnecting with the landscape and the moment—a distraction from the physical and mental discomforts he was experiencing. I tried to interpret the unusual psychology, but eventually found my head returning to a calm, quiet space. We ran together in this silence, the camaraderie of the moment adding strength back to our weary bodies until we gratefully crossed the suspension bridge and ran the final kilometre to the aid station at Narcissus Hut. We had now covered sixty-five kilometres.

I paused, picked up some watermelon and handfuls of jelly snakes. In my weary haze, I gazed around, wondering where Mum—my avid support crew—was. Time was passing quickly and I could feel myself cooling down, so I grabbed a few more munchies and headed back onto the trail and towards the final nineteen kilometres. I warned my head not to say the dreaded words, 'not far to go!'

My new running comrade was nowhere to be seen, and he ended up reaching the finish line around ten minutes in front of me, his interesting choice of fuelling strategies enough to hold off my strong finish.

In fact, I had run so strongly that my support crew had not been able to arrive at Narcissus Hut in time to meet me. Mum only just made it to the finish line to greet me—as I set a new women's record by over an hour.

FOR ME, that whole day just felt so good! From start to finish I thrived, loving every step I took through the Tasmanian mountains. That was where I felt most at home and through that day I knew the running was purely my mode of transport to see and immerse myself in the landscape.

Despite the constant pain in my knee, I felt calm in the darkness of dawn, energised by the first rays of sunlight, meditative when the clouds rolled in, frisky with the developing breeze, and then contemplative as I wound my way through the ancient forests along the lake edge, all the way to the finish.

I still hadn't mastered the art of fuelling my body, and experienced ferocious cramps after I crossed the simple finish line—a scraped boot mark etched into the car park's gravel.

But I had not just survived, I had thrived. To date, that is still my best race, and it became something of a turning point in my athletic career. It gave me the confidence that when I was healthier and engaged in a dream which stemmed from tingling toes, that was where I would find my flow, and my belief that I really could do anything I set out to achieve.

20

Sweat. Dripping from my nose, dribbling down between my breasts and soaking into my undies.

A few months into my return to running I walked subconsciously back into the athletics world and into the circle of friends I had met through training with Jackie. Every night, the girls met at the athletics track. For ages, they eagerly encouraged me to join them.

The thought provoked so much fear in my bones. I wasn't sure that my steely willpower was strong enough to avoid the quiet quips of Anorexia, who had seemed to thrive in that world once before. Furthermore, I was confused as to what might happen if I was to try to return to something which had once brought me such joy. Would it feel the same?

Knowing that fear merely highlights what is important and that leaning into it can spark great growth, I launched myself back into athletics training with its personal bests and head-to-head competition. It felt clunky and foreign, and at times I wondered if I was trying to turn back the clock. However, I felt the bud of the sport once again poking through into my heart cavities and I knew deep down that if I wanted to let it bloom, I needed to simply lace up my shoes and have a try.

Through dusty days on dusty trails, on training camps and dusky dawn runs, Jackie was always there with us in spirit, running with us girls as we pushed ourselves up and down hills or around lap after lap on the track. We trained, travelled and encouraged one another, each striving on our own journeys.

Dripping profusely, on one of these scorching summer days I stood in my own pool of sweat. Only a few weeks earlier I had proudly and playfully crossed the finish line of another hilly trail marathon—only my second since returning to running—in a sharp three-hours, and now I was already back at training. However, tonight my body felt hollow. My legs felt uncoordinated, my movements mechanical. Perhaps it was due to the residual marathon fatigue or the heat of this still summer's night? However, I had felt that lethargy frequently in the twelve months since I started running again. I was struggling to find a spring in that defining moment when your foot hits the ground.

The coach for this night's training stood surrounded by a few other athletes when I wandered over. I held back until there was a pause in the conversation. I still didn't quite feel like I fit in. The training felt foreign. The hills felt shorter and steeper than I was used to, and the pace of this particular group was elite. I knew that Max would tell me to give it time, run on eggshells, stand tall, thumbs down. This coach's manner was more edgy, more eagle-eyed, and yet somehow less educational. While it made me nervous, I craved guidance, so, when there was a pause in conversation, I took my chance.

'Um, can I have some help? My running is feeling a bit mechanical. I feel heavy when I'm running. I was wondering if you could look at my running and give me some tips?'

The coach looked me up and down. His eyes roamed from my feet to my eyes and then back down to my thighs. Then he leant forward and pinched my upper thigh, gripping a fold of skin just beneath the line of my shorts.

'Well, for a start, you could lose a bit of that.'

The group around him turned their faces away, embarrassed for me. I ducked my head and returned to untying my laces, hot tears threatening to join the sweat seeping down my hot, fatigued body.

I was all too aware that my body shape had changed, but I also knew that I was healthy, as evidenced by blood spots once again appearing on my unsuspecting undies. I was more womanly, with curves and a few extra bumps and lumps—but by no means was my mountain biker's body overweight at sixty kilograms with a body mass index of nineteen.

This coach's comment polarised me.

A huge part of my heart wanted to run the other direction and never return.

But the burning question of whether it was possible to return to the pinnacle of elite sport in a healthy manner still plagued me. I could feel the layers of dust slowly disappearing from my skills, and my orienteering and running coming back to life. My heart was still happy, and my relationship with Graham ensured that the playfulness component of the dream certainly held true.

So, I turned a blind eye to his comment and kept turning up. I was willingly walking along the edge of discomfort, to prove to him that it wasn't about how I looked, but rather how I performed. And it felt so damn good!

RETURNING to elite sport was a motley process. What made it so challenging was the intensity of my inner competitor, who sought to benchmark myself against my old self. In my mind's eye I could clearly see what I had once been capable of, which willed me towards believing that was where I should be … now!

Contrasted to this was my heart quietly reassuring me, *Take it slower. Don't force it this time. Establish your foundations first.* Each day, I was in this juxtaposition as if the hands of the clock were paused between where I used to be and where I wanted to go.

I returned to the World Orienteering Championships five years after my previous attempt in Hungary. I felt like the rookie, standing in a Finnish forest surrounded by wild blueberries, raspberries and strawberries. It was not lost on me how beautiful this region of Finland was, with the Arctic Circle so close you could almost touch it. The daylight hours lasted through the night, casting a blue hue into my white room located in the heart of the sporting academy residences that became our home for the competitions.

For the weeks prior to this, I had stayed with a young orienteering couple who lived in the nearby region. This was always the way I loved to orienteer—to see it as part of a grander process to learn about the landscapes, cultures and ways of life that made these communities tick. In those weeks I was easily able to forget about the reason I was there, as I revelled in the friendships and experiences that fed my adventure bug.

Eventually, the competition week rolled around and, while I was hugely excited to be back, it was hard to escape the spotlight. The media frenzied when they saw my name on the start list. For even after seven years, I was still the Down Under novelty, the young girl who planted her feet on top of the dais to become the only world champion from outside of Europe.

I tried to block out the television cameras and the hype, but I knew in my heart I was not at the prime fitness I had been in back then. My return to orienteering felt clumsy and awkward, and my return to running even more so. I couldn't believe how heavy I had felt when I first tugged on my shoes and tried to head out for a casual jog. Each step was a weighty surprise, each arm swing a clumsy rag doll. My inner child, who had feared dancing classes because it was so hard to coordinate her arms and legs, was suddenly fumbling with an unfamiliarly-familiar dance. Further to this, my skills were dusty. For five years they had been pushed into the corner of my cupboard, kept for that rainy day when you think, *Actually, maybe …*

My results in Finland highlighted these insecurities. They weren't bad, but they certainly weren't amazing. What let me down more than my weaker fitness was my inability to control my inner critic. I allowed my inner imp to chip away at my confidence. He told me to rush when I didn't need to rush, told me to push on, when I needed to stop. He also invited Anorexia to join me for a while, and while she didn't get the better of me in the dining room, she liked to infer that I was too fat, too weighed down. In hindsight, the only thing weighing me down was that internal baggage.

When I returned to Canberra, the bright blossoms were shifting the grey forests from winter to spring. I vowed to myself then and there: it was the last time I would allow my internal critic and the unwanted guest at the table—Anorexia—to control the outcome of my dreams. There was no space left in my life for her friendship.

ON MY RETURN FROM FINLAND, I willingly pushed myself back into uncomfortable situations, embracing a few local fun runs and trail running events. I knew I needed to overcome my insecurities. By placing myself in challenging situations, I could practise turning up the positive internal radio channel and, in turn, drown out the chatter of my inner imp. My plan became about harnessing my mind games, playing wilder, and utilising every opportunity available to me.

Over the next twelve months, Graham and I took our Find Your Feet coaching to regional communities, including Wagga Wagga, where I attempted another trail marathon, finishing in just over three hours on a hilly course. Graham accompanied me on the bike, and the whole experience felt light and freeing. It also highlighted that my perception of my fitness in Finland was nothing other than perception—an interpretation, and a relatively incorrect one at that.

Back home in Canberra, I found less and less joy in my day-to-day Find Your Feet work. I spent hours alone at home, tapping away on my keyboard while the days passed by outside my study window. I was preparing up to sixty training plans each week, using my cheat sheets stuck to the wall so I could remember who each of my athletes were. Not only did I begin to resent the lack of interaction with living, breathing human beings, but I was constantly terrified that one of my athletes would become injured.

From the outside looking in, Find Your Feet was a healthy little business. But, deep down, I knew that the coaching structure—carefully documented in business plans and spreadsheets—had taken me so far from my values for starting Find Your Feet in the first place that I began to question whether I still wanted to coach at all.

After the trail marathon, we travelled into the heart of the Flinders Ranges in the northern region of South Australia, camping on amber dust under darkening skies as stars appeared in the expanse. Spending two weeks in a tent with no pressure to write training programs or hang from the end of a mobile phone felt liberating.

Lying in the tent each night, I sensed the stress that I had been carrying ebbing into the ground. I could feel it seeping out of the distal tip of my spine where my sacrum poked into the hard earth, the negative energy leaving and clarity taking its place. I didn't want to coach this way. Rather, I wanted to educate, and allow my athletes to navigate their own pathway forwards. I was happy to guide and support, but I could clearly see that if I was telling them what to do every day, then I was clipping their wings. I was holding them back from playing wilder, from the freedom of lying under expansive skies, their tent flapping gently in the breeze while they dreamily wondered, 'Wheee! What will tomorrow bring?' I just didn't yet know how to escape this daily grind.

With a series of trail running camps and small local races that we had hosted together behind us, Graham departed for casual ski instructing in Japan over the Australian summer. I felt inundated with work, and my inner thermostat was rising. I had nearly reached boiling point.

Added to the stress was the heat of a ferocious summer. While the thermostat plummeted into the negative twenties for Graham, it rose into the high forties Celsius for me. I was melting in my own house, consulting in my bathers and plunging into the cold water of the bath between each client. On my morning runs, I watched native wildlife spread lethargically across the ground, distressed and dehydrated. I would return teary and confused, pining more than ever for Tasmania, with its cooling forests and people-free beaches. There you could escape the intensity of the summers.

That particularly brutal Canberra summer was like a wildfire, assisting the germination of my internal Tasmanian seed. It would be another few winters and a house renovation before the seed became a seedling and wrapped its growing fronds around my Tasmanian heart.

As the 2014 World Orienteering Championships in the Italian

Dolomites approached, I was very prepared. Invited to join an altitude study at the Australian Institute of Sport, I had been able to prepare for the expected altitude of the racing areas. Graham and I inhabited a small bunk room for three weeks, and escaped the cold rage of the Canberra winter where temperatures easily plummeted into the negatives.

At the end of the first week of sleeping and working long days at a simulated altitude of 3100 m, where nitrogen was pumped into the small internal kitchen and bedroom spaces to reduce the oxygen content, I spontaneously decided to run the National Mountain Running Championships which were visiting the Australian Capital Territory.

I rocked up, shorts and singlet barely shielding me from the crisp morning, and collected my race bib. When the starter's gun went, I suffered instantly, heartbeats exploding with my ragged exhales, sucking air in gasps to fuel the searing discomfort in my legs. I struggled upwards, hands pressing into concrete quadriceps until slowly, slowly I stumbled onto the summit.

Returning to the altitude house, I was surprised to find that each of the other runners had also suffered that morning. Those who tried to participate in a local fun run ended up glumly plodding across the finish line, while those who embarked on their regular weekend long run returned early with crushed confidence. And yet, when we returned to training the next day, there was no sympathy. We were told it was all a coincidence and to lace up, toughen up and strive upwards. So, despite the aching fatigue in my limbs, I did just that.

That was the thing with some of the squad training I became involved with during this period. In my heart, I knew I was playing with fire and forcing my body to progress faster than it probably wanted to progress. But if you backed off you felt like the weakest link. If you skipped a session, then the next time you set foot on the trail or the athletics track it was as if you were invisible, a ghost. You would run your heart out, your watch recording your piston heartbeats, only to find a coach's back turned to your searching eyes. Unlike when I worked with Max, I was struggling to find encouragement, or any insights into my improvements.

What this taught me, however, was to look for encouragement deep within myself—to listen to my intuition and trust that I would execute to my best. When the niggles set in for perhaps the first time in my entire running history, I initially dismissed them. 'It's just fatigue. It'll pass.' But when they lingered longer than I wanted, I knew that something needed to change. For the first time ever, I was becoming far more in tune with my body, listening to her quieter whispers. It felt so good.

I began training more on my own again, hooking up with my friend, Hannah, for early morning tempo-running sessions around the bushlands or the grass running track out at the Stromlo Forest Park. We ran side by side, honest camaraderie and conversations fuelling us through some gritty sessions, while hot air balloons rose into a duck-egg blue sky, dancing a tango around one another as the sun's rays melted the frosty dawn. It was some of the most beautiful running I had ever done, and together we felt our bodies thanking us for this changed attitude and approach.

To top up our experiences in the altitude house, Graham and I sifted through the internet's fluffier travel guides, seeking an altitude base camp suitable for the final preparations in Italy. Dismissing Spain and a destitute ski village in France, we settled on a random hotel on a random pass in the middle of the Italian Dolomites. Excited to be experiencing Italy together for the first time, we set off from Milan Malpensa Airport in our little cupcake of a car, turning onto the backroads as soon as we could. Where was the joy in following open freeways when you could weave through the picturesque valleys and quaint towns of northern Italy?

Twelve hours later we crept up the mountain pass. The drive through desolate towns suffering a severe case of Sundayitis left us uncomfortably wriggling in a mess of stiff, raw emotions. Welcome to Italy! The weather mimicked our emotions—billowing, grey storm clouds predicted the imminent arrival of tears. Shuttered hotels sat silent and empty, car parks were void of any life, human or other. The towering mountains hid behind the weather, and darkness was rapidly encroaching. As we rounded the last of the plethora of switchbacks, the silence in the Cupcake said it all. *What have we done?*

However, opening the front door of the hotel we were welcomed to a shaft of light, a cheerful Italian family and a blast of warm aromas from the kitchen. The winding staircase led to rooms where fluffy doonas lofted on spongy beds. Shuttered doors with love hearts etched into the timber opened onto small balconies that in turn opened into expansive vistas.

As the rain lashed down, the room became cosier. Unsuspectingly, we had literally driven to paradise. In the morning, marmots awoke us from our slumbers and the sun poured into the cosy room. The mountains shed their blankets and beckoned us. We raced to tug on our running gear, jiggling with a sock, frustrated with singlets and shorts. Our hearts were yelling, *Come on!* but it was as if my clothing was signalling a warning, *Not so fast!*

We tore off down the mountain, legs brushing through garden-like meadows, marmots squealing as we excitedly dashed past in a flurry of arms and legs. We ducked beneath picture-perfect Christmas trees, drank from the streams, and ran along trails so pristine it was as if they were created by gnomes. I was madly, deeply, head-over-heels in love with the landscape and the person I was sharing it with.

Eventually, we turned for home, aware that breakfast was beckoning. We found a straighter trail arching up towards the blue skies, and began to shuffle and squiggle our way back up. I could sense the stiffness in my legs from the thirty hours of plane travel, the twelve hours locked into Cupcake, and the hour of solid downhill running. *Never mind*, I thought, *it'll loosen up.* And then ... TWANG!

My knee felt like it had ripped into two pieces, a jabbing pain so intense I dropped to the ground to clutch at it. Graham was still somewhere further down the trail and my fearful yell felt out of place in this beautiful landscape. When Graham finally reached me, he could sense my panic.

'It's as if it needs to crack back into place. I can't bend it. I can't.' We wrestled it on the ground, trying to twist and pop my knee back into some place I knew it needed to be. However, it stubbornly jabbed, grumpily refused to walk up the hill, and eventually I was resigned to the fact that I would have to wait for Graham to retrieve the car. Cupcake to the rescue!

The rest of my preparation time before the World Championships was spent marching between non-English speaking physiotherapists and others who wished to rub magic gels over my knee. My mother, now joining us from Australia, suggested splinting it. I spent long hours wading in the cool waters of the lakes. I tried a little orienteering training, managing to complete a few short sessions while Graham tailed me like a security detail. But my internal alarms were blaring, *Warning! Warning! Warning!*

The sprint event of the championships was to be held around the bustling streets of Venice, a city so unusual that most tourists end up peering at upside down maps and wondering where the hell their hotel is. Through torrential downpours, we practised our navigation and the art of darting between toppling ice creams, umbrella fronds and draping washing lines.

My knee strained to perform on this flatter terrain and, slowly, slowly, I felt a glimmer of hope returning. However, when it came time to wave Graham goodbye, his leave now expired, I was in a flood of terrified tears. 'None of this was part of the plan!' Our trip had been scarred by the injury to my knee, which I would later find out was an acute burst of ITB Syndrome caused by a tightening of the tensor muscle in my hip, thanks to the hours and hours of sitting we did at the start of our holiday. Rather than wave him goodbye, I longed to be back up in the mountains with him, running freely. Instead, I was days away from lining up on the World Championships' start line, the second since my return to the sport.

In Italy, I definitely took a huge step forward. While I had absorbed the lessons from Finland, I still felt disappointed by my races at these championships. Surprisingly, my knee was almost entirely better by the time I raced, but I had let the final weeks of disrupted training chip away at my confidence. If I could have removed myself from the emotion of the moment, I could have seen that a few weeks of disrupted training is a mere blip in the grand scheme of two consistent years of running since my return. But, once again, my inner imp won the argument.

Following the competitions, I travelled to Bulgaria, where I took on the role of assistant coach to the Australian Junior Orienteering Team. Without the responsibility of being the athlete, I felt myself relaxing into the environment, sneaking off in the early mornings to run through the mountains where ageing moss dripped from the long limbs of the pine trees. And despite a severe bout of bedbugs, I was able to channel my unresolved dreams from Italy into the ambitions of these younger athletes. And they thrived. We returned as one of the most successful Australian Junior Teams ever. It was highly rewarding and fired me into thinking, *Next year* ...

21

We kicked off our running shoes. Cool concrete beneath our feet. A sweaty hand turning the doorknob to Home. An arm brushing beads of sweat from a forehead as we entered the glowing white heart of our renovated Base Camp. We stripped off damp running clothes, lingered under a hot shower and let water vapour fill the bathroom to the sound of a kettle boiling.

I loved Sunday mornings. The world felt peaceful. Standing in the kitchen, basking in a post-morning-run glow, my hands were cupped around a steaming mug of tea. It felt like even the birds flew more slowly, that the clouds lingered, and toast took longer to pop from the toaster. Yes, it was as if the morning was still in its pyjamas, as Graham and I lingered over our breakfast, chewing slowly, chatting quietly, feeling deeply. This morning was particularly sacred. For it was the last morning we would ever eat breakfast at Base Camp.

Piles of boxes lay around us, some tightly closed as if holding back the emotions, others bursting open stubbornly, rebelling against leaving. We had literally sold our Home, our precious Base Camp, and had nearly completed packing everything into boxes. Boxes lying face down in the hallway. Sticky tape sealing off one life, preparing to transport it to another. We awaited the removal company's arrival by brewing more tea, and then lazily stepping out into the sunshine on the back porch. Waiting, waiting ... waiting.

We finally stood back and watched three chirpy males carry first our sofa, then our bed, and finally our two dozen boxes into their van, before driving off into the curving, roundabout avenues of Canberra. We were left standing on the steps of what used to be our home, locking the door for the last time, hugging our teary neighbour, and then levering ourselves into the heights of our Volkswagen ute. After reversing out of the driveway, I avoided looking in the rear-view mirror. I was finding it hard to say goodbye. Instead, I lowered my sunglasses to my face and looked through the windscreen as we turned in the direction of Tasmania, all the while wondering, *Are we doing the right thing?*

RIGHT FROM WRONG. Success from failure. Start to finish. What lies in the middle are experiences, and that is exactly what Graham and I turned towards as we left Canberra for the very last time.

The outdoor retail industry had been weakened by a few national chain stores closing their doors. Graham found himself answering phone calls from concerned suppliers who had lost their footing in Hobart, the outdoor capital of Australia. After years in the industry, he had become well-known and well-respected. So it wasn't completely surprising when they asked the question, 'Would you be interested in opening a retail store in Hobart?'

This question had reignited the *what if* conversation from our Passion8 days. Graham and I threw the idea back and forth around our dining table, sometimes alone, and sometimes with family and friends. The idea gained traction, the scribbles and handwritten budgets grew longer, until the day came when we arrived at the realisation ... there was no other option.

En route to our new lives in Tasmania, we travelled down the New South Wales and northern Victorian coastlines, before pausing in the leafy valley of Bright. We punctuated our journey to Tasmania with a

Find Your Feet running tour in the Victorian Alps, reuniting with friends in a large, holiday rental house at the foot of Mt Feathertop.

WE WERE there to participate in the Bright 4 Peaks running competitions, where we would climb four peaks over four days. The weather was glorious, and each day, after the runs, we wandered down to the nearby river to leap from the rocks into crisp waterholes. Goosebumps crept across our bodies as we lay in patches of dappled sun, watching wispy clouds dart across a sky framed by mountains.

On our third and final evening, I lingered by the river with my eyes closed, feeling content in the simplicity of the moment. Suddenly my phone began to vibrate. I fumbled beside me, finally picking it up and squinting at the display. I was surprised to see the caller was Hannah—my Canberra running buddy—for we rarely called one another, instead relying on text messages to confirm our early morning runs together. While we loved to share our stories and the human experience, we always left this to the moments when we were rolling around the bushlands together. The further we ran, the more our words could unfurl. Or not. Running does that. It helps to clarify the words that need to be spoken, and those that are best left unsaid.

I answered the phone.

'JACKIE IS DEAD.'

Suddenly the clouds were moving faster. The breeze felt colder, and I needed to flee. I pushed myself to my feet, wrestled with my thongs, and left the smiling faces of unsuspecting clients for a place somewhere else. Graham jumped to my side, sensing something was wrong. And as I listened to Hannah explain the suicide—which was not her first attempt—I could feel all my internal walls crashing. Graham grabbed my hand, holding it in a firm embrace as if saying, 'This time, we are walking this road together.' And then Hannah's wobbly voice was leaving me. While the mountains stood still, I was shaking. I turned to

Graham, finding it difficult to meet his eyes, and yet dragged my damp ones up to meet his. 'Jackie is dead.'

Ever since meeting her in the hospital in Canberra and learning about her deep internal sadness, I knew that Jackie was still trying to resolve a past that couldn't be resolved. She had known she was destined to be an Olympic champion and that the Sydney Games in 2000 was going to be her year. Yet her desire to reach the top had been her downfall, the pushing beyond and a little too far, and no shoes ever felt like they fitted perfectly after that.

Jackie had left behind her husband, Simon, Australia's first gold medallist at the Sydney Games. With a slight dent running down the middle of his nose where he used to hold his archer's bow steady, I knew from my own experiences that nothing could hold him steady in the waves of grief that would wash over him.

'Jackie, it doesn't matter how incredible the gift is that you are trying to give us, if all we see is someone who cannot return the same gift to herself.'

Jackie had all the gifts in the world to give us. She showed us the art of running fearlessly while remaining smart in our preparations. She taught us how to see the silliness in ourselves and to giggle at our imperfections. She knew how to play wildly and was never afraid to break the rules, especially when she was driving her Porsche along the open freeways of Canberra or coaching us to our individual endeavours. She demanded honesty and begged for openness.

And yet, underneath all these beautiful gifts which she extended so willingly towards us, she was unable to extend the same gift to herself. I believe now that she hid her sadness and grief behind a veil constructed from a willingness to help us, as well as other less-healthy coping mechanisms too. It doesn't make me think any less of her or see her as weak, by seeing deeper into her imperfections and the vulnerability of her final moments. Quite the contrary—I believe that Jackie was the embodiment of strength. I imagined her as her younger self, scribbling in her athlete journals: 'I want to be a World Champion.' I truly believe Jackie knew she was capable of reaching the moon and, in her haste to get there, fell into the traps of the aspiring human's experience. If only she could have known that, medal or no medal, she was a world champion in our eyes. She always will be.

In her death, I lost a mentor, friend and role model. I knew how much strength and purpose the coaching gave her, and I have no doubt how much our relationship meant to her too. I will always carry a sense of guilt that I had not found the strength within myself to stand next to her in the depths of her pain. I know I cannot turn back the clock, but I will always wish that when Jackie had asked me to take her for a run, her inner child reflected in her large, pleading eyes, I had said, 'Not now Jackie, but I will always walk beside you and am willing to share your discomfort.' I will always be left wondering whether, if everyone around her had done so, Jackie could have learnt to look in the mirror and see the champion and the beauty that we all saw.

After Jackie's death, I staggered, wobbled, and tried to crawl back onto my feet. As much as my heart didn't feel like it had the strength to run, I made myself lace up my shoes and feel what I needed to feel. Jackie would have wanted me to do that.

Doubled over, hands pressing into thighs as I climbed upwards through the mountain ash forests of the Victorian Alps, I gasped for air to help lighten the discomfort of my grief. At times, my tears contributed to the sweat running into my eyes, and my vision blurred then cleared, blurred then cleared. I would blast snot from my nose, longing for it to remove the clogs of anger, sadness and grief that would bring me to a crumpled halt beside the track.

But Jackie would want me to keep running and so I did, staggering back onto the track and running, running, running. In my head I could hear her giggling behind me, 'Thanks for taking me for a run, Han.' In my heart I knew I needed to run, not away from the internal gnawing, but rather in tune with my feelings. I allowed myself to feel my grief and, in doing so, find the lessons within it.

At the end of the four days I was crowned the Queen of the Mountains, celebrating alongside the Find Your Feet crew. Each of us had been on our own journeys. One friend ran in a chicken costume up the final mountain, Mt Buffalo, as she shed her childhood feathers to embrace the next step in her adulthood—wife. Others were learning the art of playing wilder, shrugging off their corporate personas to put on their running shoes. And others were wondering if they still had the strength within them, having watched birthdays continue to pass.

Over these four days, it was our journeys and our willingness to embrace the edges of our discomforts that were our successes, and I knew that both Jackie and Max would be proud of that.

As we clambered back into the ute, and waved our goodbyes to the mountains and our guests, I sensed it was time to close the doors. Once again, we turned toward the freeway. It was time to go home.

22

We drove off the ferry into Devonport and through the rolling potato, poppy and dairy plains of Tasmania's northern agricultural region. We rolled down the ute's windows and breathed in Tasmanian dampness, laced with a tinge of cattle and ocean.

We pulled up outside a newly vacated retail store in the heart of Hobart's CBD, turned the key in the door, and gingerly took our first steps into the world of outdoor retail.

We gazed around the small, 70 m^2 premises, still strewn with the remnants of its previous life as a bike store. Every cent of our home in Canberra was going to be invested into this new and unpredictable retail venture. We took a deep breath and wrapped an arm around each other, standing in silence while shifting from one foot to the other, taking in the enormity of the project ahead.

There was no turning back now.

DESPITE HAVING WORKED IN RETAIL, the step up to running our own business was enormous. While Graham already had a firm understanding of the technical nature of outdoor retail, I was like a starry-eyed kid standing in an ice-cream store and wondering which flavour to try.

When we decided to open our store, we turned to our community for guidance on what it should be called. 'Find Your Feet!' we heard. We listened to them, but as I watched skilled men mount new signage onto the facade of the building, deep down my heartstrings were crying, *Find Your Feet doesn't sell people stuff! We deliver services to help people find their feet!* It has taken me years to come to an organic understanding of our business values. I now firmly believe that providing access to high quality equipment and apparel for everyone's playful adventures is an important part of helping people to find their feet.

As the business began to take shape, I wrestled with imposter syndrome. I couldn't see myself as a businesswoman. Running a retail store had never been part of my grand plan! It wasn't until Find Your Feet and I were named the 2015 Young Businesswoman of the Year for Tasmania that I really awoke from my stupor. Even if my purpose was not financially driven, I was a businesswoman, I am a businesswoman, and it was time to emotionally commit to this journey.

However, I pined for my home in Canberra and, in some ways, I still do. Base Camp was a first love, and we all know that our first loves never completely fade. I missed the stillness that came from closing the door as you walked inside, and knowing it was yours. Or taking a hammer to a nail and gallantly whacking it into your plasterboard. I missed the four walls that enclosed two hearts and how, when you went to the letterbox, you knew that the letters addressed to you signified home. Base Camp was our launching pad, but it was also our landing place. While I was gratefully embracing the new life in Tasmania ever since leaving Canberra, I felt like I had been constantly in flight. 'Rocks,' my father would say. 'You need a rock.'

We threw everything we had into our new retail venture. We knew we wanted to be a big player in the outdoor industry, influencing Australia with well-made products from ethical brands, presented in the European style—colourful, lighter-weight and sexier. Trail running, hiking and light-weight travel. We felt empowered to share wilder lifestyles with our Tasmanian community and the travellers who visited our homeland to adventure and explore. In our eyes, when we tugged on our shoes and moments later found ourselves exploring the mountain trails behind Hobart, we lived in the Chamonix of Australia ... the outdoor capital. Our eyes wide open, our toes tingling with the excitement of sharing our joy ... but our budget was only a few pennies in our shallow pockets.

We quickly outgrew our small store, a long, squiggly building housing an internal staircase that led to an upper level. We were so confined by our pockets and the size of the premises that we began flip-flopping between consolidating our ideas, then expanding them again ... consolidating and expanding. We were indecisive over the future direction of the business, the only certainty being our desire to continue operating the trail running tours and coaching arms, both of which were beginning to expand into more exotic destinations such as Italy and Japan. Despite those early indecisions, we continued to pack products into the space until it was exhaling garments and gear onto the footpath outside.

Graham and I lived like nomads after moving back to Tasmania. From parents' homes to the converted basement garage of a friend's home. From house-sitting to spare rooms, and even homeless nights in the back of our van at the local waterhole. Without the security of salaries and with the overheads of starting a retail store, we were never going to be welcome customers in the eyes of mortgage brokers. Our arrival back in Tasmania was also perfectly timed with booming rental prices and dire availability, so we washed up on the doormats of friends and family who graciously allowed us to call their place home. For this we are eternally grateful. Many of these friends admired our bravery, saying, 'I would never be brave enough to do that!'

We never thought about it that way, because we both felt an incessant calling to grasp the opportunity to share the joy we found in playing wilder. Lessons were learnt and lessons could be shared from exploring, living and breathing a more adventurous lifestyle. If the whole experience turned to mush, we knew that we still had each other, a van, and a very privileged island to call home. Yes, we could always start again.

It is never lost on me how fortunate a life I have lived. Both in the people I have met and the experiences I have had. Since my first overseas trip to Finland at seventeen years of age, I have travelled to thirty-five countries. Almost all my travel has been through the opportunities of elite sport, and two parents who were willing to let their small blonde daughter roam the world at large. From racing in the high mountains of Switzerland to the sweltering tropics of Borneo; from living in the soviet-infused Ukraine to the schmickness of Norway; from the upset bellies of Nepal and China to eating cake for breakfast in Italy.

The opportunity to travel the world was one of the motivators helping me grit my teeth on wintry mornings when the last thing I felt like doing was pulling on my wet shoes for another training run. Whenever I now leave a foreign journey, I become more and more excited about the prospect of returning home to our island Down Under. As my father so beautifully put it at my brother's wedding a few years ago, 'When the plane touches down on the tarmac in Hobart, and you walk down the steps of the aircraft, the smell of the salty air hits you, and you feel like dropping to your knees and kissing the ground in gratitude that you live here.' Like father, like daughter.

The more I have travelled, the more I have come to realise the extraordinary beauty of our island home. Remote stretches of untouched wilderness, small cities, quaint towns and rich, fertile soils. I am most at home, when I am at home. As the *Hobart Mercury* newspaper wrote about me when I was relocating back to Tasmania, 'Hanny Allston is a homing pigeon – a young individual who leaves the nest and eventually returns.'

When I returned home, I still felt a deep longing to pursue my running and orienteering endeavours, to use them to explore the corners of the globe and the corners of my own potential that remained untapped.

THE TASMANIAN ORIENTEERING World Cup was just around the corner. It presented a unique opportunity to race on home soil, but for the months leading into the competitions I found myself wrestling with guilt. When I was training, I felt distanced from the infant business. When I was at work, I felt guilty that I wasn't focusing more on my training. Graham stood firmly by my side, encouraging me to lace up my shoes on the days when I felt too afraid to feel selfish. For we both knew that the opportunity to race for your country and chase a dream was a rare and special gift, which also presented an opportunity to learn, grow and explore, to uncover more lessons to share with yourself and others.

Ultimately, a lot of what I know about running has come from chasing such dreams. A lot of what I learnt about humanity has come from living a rich life. Graham recognised this more than anyone, and so he willingly picked up my bucket when I was too nervous to pick it up myself. Later, when the northern hemisphere winter rolled around with its skiing opportunities for Graham, I was able to willingly pick up his bucket in return.

From when we arrived back in Tasmania, we had worked hard, trained hard, played hard and loved hard. And when the World Cup competitions rolled around, I raced hard too.

The World Cup Orienteering Carnival hit Tasmania in 2015. I felt the eyes of my Tasmanian orienteering community watching me, when all they were really doing was watching the excitement of international competition unfolding in front of their eyes. Racing for my home, on the soils of my home, felt unfamiliar, and I ran like I was afraid. While my body felt strong, the voice of my inner imp still floated to the surface. *You are fit, but not as fit. You are strong, but not as strong. You are capable, but not as capable as these girls who are training in the Scandinavian forests all the time.*

So, I ran through the World Cup carrying the weight of fear. Because I didn't believe I deserved to perform, I undermined myself at every step of the competition process, resulting in underperformance. While I walked away with tenth place in the long distance, I was disappointed. When I look back at these results, I am ashamed that I let my inner imp get the better of me. In hindsight, I was supremely fit and strong, and what had let me down was my deep internal criticism.

Once the buzz and internal pressure subsided, I knew I could not end my orienteering career on that note. I could sense that the upcoming World Orienteering Championships in Scotland heralded the end. While the flame was definitely still alive, it was dimming. I wanted to leave the sport with a bang and answer the still-lingering question: *was 2006 a fluke?* I needed to rise above my insecurities.

I felt my resolve strengthening me from the inside out, keeping this fire burning in my belly. It was time to get serious, to once again see myself as an athlete. It started with maximising my hormonal health and sense of vitality, which felt slightly degraded from the relocation to Tasmania, long hours of beginning the business, and training for the World Cup. As my best friend and training partner would say, it was time to turn on beast mode.

It wasn't like things were going badly. Quite the contrary. I had competed in many big races this year already, including the World Cup Orienteering and then the Buffalo Stampede SkyMarathon, which doubled as the Oceania SkyMarathon Championships, where I finished second to sponsored American athlete, Stevie Kremer.

Then there was the Six Foot Track Marathon in the Blue Mountains.

This event was especially meaningful to me. A year before, in my first attempt, I had joyfully crossed the finish line, only to learn I had just missed the race record set by Australian mountain running legend, Emma Murray. In the year she set that record—which happened to be the year I also won my 2006 World Orienteering title—she went on to win the World Mountain Running Championships in phenomenal style. Some people, myself included, wondered if that record could ever be broken.

I threw every ounce of myself into my second attempt at the race, running in a bubble so intense that nothing could penetrate it. Unlike the first year, the scenery remained a blur. I buried myself during the ninety-minute climb out of the Coxs River. I was so fearful of the performance expected of me in relation to that record, that I literally dug myself into a cave and ran solo through it.

With ten kilometres to go I allowed myself to look at my watch, but I couldn't make sense of my pace. I was in a lactic acid rage and a glucose-depleted low. I ran careering down the hill, my bubble bouncing along with me, surprising a few male athletes and some of the local marsupial population. While I felt strong, my toes felt fragmented from my body. Something was not right with them. The new shoes I had so bravely agreed to try, despite never having worn them, felt foreign and awkward. With six kilometres to go, it was not the time to be worrying about that.

With three kilometres to go, quadriceps beginning to seize, I rounded a corner to see Graham's face lighting up the track. That smile, that excited, loving look, burst through my bubble like a knife and sent my heart sprawling onto the track. Tears began to pour from my eyes, obscuring my vision. Immediately I was aware of the searing pain in my toes. I could feel shards of my toenails clawing at the ends of my shoes. With Graham careering down behind me I began to squeal, 'My toes! My toes!' In isolation I had been strong, but in love I was weak at the knees.

I fought my emotions down the final flight of stairs, spinning around the bottom railing and plunging towards and over the finish line. My bubble lay in a burst mess around me as I buckled forward, head on knees, trying to claw the shoes off my feet. Ripping bloodied socks from bloodied toes, I was oblivious to the commentary. But as my heartbeat began to subside, I wobbled back onto my bare feet, searching for Graham. And with his look … that look … I knew I had done it. I had won, setting a personal best time and a new course record.

The emotions surged again, relief washing over my fatigue. For in that moment I knew I had finally returned to where I knew I could be. I was definitely back at my best.

23

Sally called me into her consulting room. Adorning the walls were motivational posters proclaiming the benefits of home-grown food, gut health and, especially eye-catching to me, vitality. I sat down, unsure what to expect, but excited to finally have an opportunity to tap into Sally's wisdom.

Sally was a medical practitioner specialising in women's health and holistic practices. She and I had spoken alongside one another as keynote speakers at a health and wellbeing forum in Hobart. In intimate and occasionally gruesome detail, Sally discussed the tight link between gut health and hormonal production, and how medical testing could reveal areas for improvement. That afternoon, I felt like I was the only audience member in the forum as Sally peeled back my layers to reveal what I needed to action. Cycling back home after that presentation, I looked deep inside myself with the greatest honesty I could muster. Yes, I was still dragging baggage that was holding me back from living with hormonal vitality.

A few weeks later, on a sea-breezy Hobart afternoon, I dragged my athletic excitement as well as the final remnants of baggage collected from my life's journey into Sally's consulting room. Mildly sweating, I realised just how anxious this session was making me. On reflection, I believe the anxiety was stemming from a really positive place where, for the first time ever, I was taking ownership of my health in an empowering way—because I wanted to. Even though for years I had been back at a healthy body weight, in a well-established relationship with Graham, and happily settled back into Hobart, my moody little hormones were once again on temporary strike. *Sally will get to the bottom of it*, I thought, confidently.

Sally took up a position in the chair opposite me. After exchanging pleasantries, I fully expected a stethoscope, perhaps a poke and a prod, and maybe a jab to steal some blood. From my keynote address to our shared audience, she had a snapshot of my past struggles, including that with Anorexia.

Instead, Sally quietly stared at me across her meticulously neat desk. Peering over her reading glasses, her sun-drenched blonde hair framing radiant, tanned facial features, she looked me up and down with her most officious look. Dressed in a skort, singlet, and running shoes—my everyday uniform—I suddenly felt very naked.

'Hanny, you need to find your femininity.'

Here I want to pause and note that, today, I understand the complexity of labelling ourselves either masculine or feminine. The simplification of these labels can lead to dramatic stereotyping and a failure to acknowledge, accept and love every element of our true selves. Whilst today I can recognise that beyond masculinity and femininity, I am a blend of values and beliefs which propel my actions, in this moment, in Sally's consulting room, I was blindly, deliberately ignoring my womanhood and all that comes with it. From menstrual cycles to loving my bouncing breasts, or simply giving myself permission to pull on a flowing skirt when once I had feared someone laughing at me, these fears were not wrapped up in stereotypes but rather a deep-seated discomfort to step beyond my inner child into womanhood, and this was paralysing me. It was toning down the vibrancy of certain areas of my life, hushing my hormones, allowing Anorexia to occasionally whisper in my ear.

So, as I recap this story, I wish to acknowledge that how I chose to address femininity is a very personal reflection, and I do not wish to impose my own beliefs on you as my reader. I simply ask us all to become aware of any limiting beliefs that are holding us back from thriving.

'Sorry?' I shuffled, then squirmed in my chair. As a proudly wild child, I had never, ever done femininity with style. From my earliest years until then, dresses had hung tucked in a corner and skirts usually hid bike shorts beneath—my beloved skort! I was used to the surprised comments when dresses did need to come out to play, and that slight embarrassment when I pulled on a pair of heels. I wore minimal makeup, if any, and never had a manicure for fear that only moments later I might chip the varnish in the pursuit of something playful. I love all things active, and hate being trapped inside. I cannot knit, and if I am really stereotyping feminine qualities, I cannot understand the fascination around breasts. Do not mistake me. I love being a chick, but I just didn't believe in going out of my way to try to promote my femininity. At school I was nicknamed a 'Jock' and, while I learnt to turn my collar down and not up like 'the real Jocks', in some ways I probably never shrugged off the label. So, suffice to say, Sally's comment literally swept me off my feet in a whirlwind of awkwardness.

'How old are you?'

At twenty-nine years, I was dragging my heels and hoping that I might slip back through the gates unnoticed, back into my younger years. I was not done with playfulness. I was not done flirting with elite sport. I was not sure that I wanted to swap skorts for skirts.

'Can you describe your menstrual cycles?'

Now I was drowning. This was what I had come to talk about, and yet the words caught in my throat, expressed in broken, embarrassed sentences. I felt like an animal trapped in the spotlight, unable to move and knowing that an inevitable crash was coming. And then it did.

Words began to flow more readily, unlike this very personal, quiet reminder of my femininity, which had dried up in my latter years of swimming and never returned with any regularity. Then, when Anorexia beat at my door, and even in later years when I closed the door behind Anorexia again … even when I was near thirty, I had somehow waved goodbye to regular menstrual cycles for a very long while.

'What steps have you taken to address this issue? For example, explain your typical diet.'

I wanted to freely share my experiences about the plethora of specialists I had seen, the well-regarded dietitians associated with the Institute of Sport in Canberra who suggested drinking Gatorade during training and who encouraged the consumption of low-sugar, protein-pumped foods to assist my hormones and recovery from training. I wanted to explain about previous dietitians who asked me to count calories, or general practitioners who put me on the pill only for me to find myself spotting blood continually for weeks. I wanted to talk about the hormonal gels I was given to rub onto the skin of my tummy, and how I tried putting on an extra ten kilograms till I actually lost my healthier body shape, only to find that this didn't turn my menstrual taps on either.

However, in this brief appointment with Sally I couldn't do justice to the whole story and, within it, my frustrations. So, I simply said, 'I just want to be filled with health and vitality.'

Sally ended up writing a referral for blood tests, but she also wrote a 'prescription' for some psychology sessions, handing them to me with a sincere look. 'You are a woman, Hanny. It appears that you are not embracing this yet.'

I WAS GREETED by a pair of mountain bike shoes tucked neatly under the desk. I felt like they were there to reassure me, as if their velcro straps and mud-strewn toughness were saying, *Not to worry Han, we won't take the free-spirit and athlete out of you ... yet.*

I took my seat in a low-slung, slightly uncomfortable chair. The relaxed, lazy posture of the seat instantly took away my strength and resilience. I couldn't sit with crossed legs, and it made it hard to wrap my arms around myself in defiance. This has always been my safe posture.

With Jeremy sitting back on his higher office chair I felt exceptionally vulnerable. He looked at me and I couldn't help but think, *What would this guy know about femininity, and what relevance could it possibly have for a thirty-year-old girl with a phobia for dresses and lipstick?* I had done my homework prior to that first session with Jeremy—a psychologist who spent a lot of his professional years working in England with athletes and high-achieving professionals, including Olympians and concert pianists. He also had an interest in working with individuals with chemical and behavioural addictions, and was the author of two books.

Jeremy opened our conversation with a simple question, 'What brings you here?'

I looked back at him in confusion and defiance. I could feel my internal walls around me and, despite the lazy chair, I tried to wrap my arms around me to shield my vulnerability in that moment. I felt pressured. 'Do I need to be more feminine?'

He changed tack and thrust a printed sheet under my nose. Together, we looked at a jumble of words spread across the sheet. Friendship. Work. Family. Spirituality. Religion. Health.

'Hanny, we are going to go through this sheet of paper and rank each of these areas of your life out of ten. One being least important and ten the most important. So, let's start with an easy one. How much value do you put on family?'

I spiralled backwards, lightness and darkness spinning through my mind's eye. The broad hand of a father clutching mine. A swing on a confusing day. A mother's excited embrace at the end of a race finish-chute. Hospital beds. A brother mixing and stirring cookie batter next to me. A sheet of paper headed, 'Unreasonable to live at home.'

Jeremy looked at me. He didn't demand the answer that I couldn't give, he merely witnessed the confusion and inner turmoil I was experiencing. I loved my family with every inch of my being, but it was complicated.

'That's okay, this is quite normal. Let's find an easier one. Okay … friendship?' Again, the recollections danced, a random shuffle of new and old. Tearing down gravel roads on bikes behind my best friends—sisters in crime. Then only emails. An unanswered letter. A male there. A male gone. Concerned hands on my arm. Concerned hands moving on. Friendships that came and went, no-one at error but just blown with the winds of life until you one day realised that you were simply fine on your own too.

Jeremy sensed this inner struggle. He slid the paper away and then shook me back to my senses.

As I continued to return for sessions, Jeremy helped me to slowly unlock a past that I had pushed into the back of my internal cupboard. We began to explore the dark holes in my memories and reassure the frightened girl who I never realised was lurking in the corner of my deepest self. It was honest, sweat-producing, shaky-voiced self-reflection but, day-by-day, journal entry by journal entry, truthful answer to vulnerable question, I began to find some growth.

Nothing can prepare you for the discomforts of looking deep inside yourself and pulling apart your personal assumptions, barriers, rules and truths. And yet, once I finally let my walls down, I knew that the only way to really come to understand myself was to uncover the beauty within, warts and all.

During and after each session with Jeremy, I wrestled with emotions that began to rise to the surface as we revisited moments in my past. I was not sure if it was healthy to dig up the struggles, and then to relive them. Some evenings I was roused from sleep with sweat pouring over my body. I couldn't recall the dream, but I was living the emotions. I would quietly leave the bedroom and sit in the shadowy kitchen, streetlights letting in a faint glow, and rock backwards and forwards as the emotions ebbed and flowed. Outside, the dripping grey eucalypts were resting, but inside, the storm was raging. Where once there had been a huge blockade in my memory, a dense black hole, suddenly the dam was beginning to leak and I found myself reliving with body, heart and spirit the moments I had run from, so fiercely and determinedly.

Memories rose to the surface; gaping mouths broke the dark, still waters of my mind. Memories, rose and lingered, breached, before submerging ...

Those emotions troubled me. Feeling things so strongly in my body was foreign territory and I began to worry. 'Jeremy, I am afraid.' Without my realising it, that question began to torment me. The emotions and creativity of my thoughts reared and subsided in such random outbursts that I began to feel afraid of my mind.

Finally, after months of working together, Jeremy turned to me, his eyes lingering on mine, absorbing the fear as if to say, 'I can sit with this discomfort, Han.' I returned his gaze, a skill that had taken me weeks to master after he pulled me up on it. He had asked, 'Hanny, why do you find it so hard to look into someone's eyes?'

It was an easy reply, 'Because I am scared people will see through me, to my vulnerability.' I had fought the urge to wrap my arms around my body.

But in that moment, it was Jeremy who broke through my fear with one single sentence. 'Hanny, this was your past. It is not, and will not be, your future.'

I leant backwards, head resting, mind resting, emotions resting. The waters of my internal dam still, the gaping memories no longer breaking the surface. Right then, they were submerged.

In our next session, I felt a greater sense of strength and a resilience coming from deeper personal insights. And yet Jeremy took a hammer and crashed it into my growing walls. 'What do you do for self-compassion?' His intense focus made me squirm. Or was it the question?

'I had a massage last night,' I mumbled in reply, grateful for this worthy evidence of my self-compassion practice.

After a few minutes silence and a contemplative look, he enquired, 'For self-compassion or physical recovery?' This was a possum-stuck-in-car-headlights moment. My wake-up call not to sit on the road and play chicken with a truck roaring towards me. A truck carrying a whole load of ... femininity!

As I paid the bill that day, he quietly drove a nail into my confusion. 'Hanny, femininity is not just about wearing dresses.'

Too embarrassed to respond, I left the room with one huge unanswered question, 'What the hell is femininity?'

I LEARNT from Dr Google that a woman was a unique blend of so-called 'masculine' and 'feminine' traits.

I came to personally identify that my own 'masculine' traits were related to my strength, independence, stability, focus, competitiveness and self-confidence.

Memories. My childhood and our cubby-building competitions.

Snapped branches, sprawling bodies, scratched limbs, gritted teeth. Racing through the forests, overcoming discomfort, pushing beyond and over.

I personally began to recognise in myself traits that felt more 'feminine' to me, such as empathy, compassion, sensuality, nurturing, patience, loving and living with flow.

Flashbacks. Conversations and cups of tea with Mum, Dad's gentility in his garden, my brother's bear hugs. Watching sunrises and sensing strength as an eagle floated overhead. Observing the smallest moments of time.

I wrote in my notes: *Whether male or female, we are all a unique blend of both feminine and masculine.*

Max's couch, his gruff voice, and yet a hand on my knee as he allowed me to express a moment of vulnerability. His nurturing presence. Orange juice and cups of tea.

It was days later, running alone on my frosty Mt Wellington, scrunching the long arms of my thermal top around my frozen fingers, that I found enlightenment. The lone currawong's chorus cut through the sharp cries of the yellow-tailed black cockatoos, while light danced off the water as it gushed through healthy streams.

Starting out, I had felt heavy, leaden, the internal work bringing on a fatigue unlike any other I had previously experienced. I eased back the effort and became acutely aware that my stunning surroundings were leading me into a state of flow. I was not running, I was feeling my way forward through the tightly rising and falling trails of my mountain home. Each step I took, I could sense a rising of energy, a freedom, a sensation of complete thrill. I felt like I could run forever!

And therein lay my first true awareness of femininity. While I had been steering myself towards international competition in pursuit of the edges of my abilities, I felt like I was being guided through the mountain's trails by self-compassion and sensuality, the combination of the two evoking the elusive sensation of flow. Femininity felt amazing!

Through a lifetime of athletic and academic practice and a hobby-farm upbringing, the tomboy had lived strongly inside me. The 'masculine' traits of goal setting, competitiveness, independence and pushing through when the going became tough had always strongly dominated my persona. These traits were reflected in my daily routines, exercise habits, nutrition and meal preparation, business, athletic racing style and even the way I showed love as a partner, daughter, sister and friend.

But as much as I don't like to flaunt them, I have breasts. And when a family member hurts, I hurt too and want to wrap them in a bundle of compassion. When someone opens a page to their story, I want to listen and can feel my heart reaching out with empathy. I find peacefulness when I am in nature, and my greatest creativity when I don't force it, when I allow my heart to create for me. Even when writing the hardest pages of this book, I sat beside a river, laptop on my knee, writing while writhing in the emotions … because it was where I needed to be. For me, this is femininity at its rawest.

Finally, it dawned on me that Sally sent me away to 'embrace my femininity', not to 'be more feminine'. I didn't have to wear a dress or apply lipstick. I just needed to love being me, a unique mix of ferocious free-spirit, compassionate sister, fun-loving partner, empathetic friend and loving daughter. I was—and still am—many parts 'masculine', but I was also a young woman just learning about self-compassion, and embarking on a long pilgrimage towards womanhood. And I couldn't reach that destination without a willingness to walk each step of the journey, along a mountain trail with the wind in my face.

When I began working with Jeremy, I had assumed we would attack the feminine within me and then quickly begin to gnaw at the final strands linking me to my friendship with Anorexia. And in some ways, we did, but we did so by uncovering my story—making friends with it first, and then beginning to learn the art of self-compassion.

Each time I found strength to say, 'not now' or 'not to worry', I could feel the shackles weakening. My vocabulary expanded to include 'maybe, perhaps, sometimes, no'. I learnt to stand still, quieten my mind, feel my heart. In love, I allowed myself to be an active participant and not a bystander. In friendship, I learnt to be there with no strings attached. When I exercised, it was for joy, and a massage began to take on a second meaning. Work became about creativity, and working together to uncork our combined potential.

My leadership style evolved from being stoically independent to a willingness to be shown, led and guided. And in doing so, I found less fear in the rapid evolution of the award-winning beast we were creating at Find Your Feet.

Anorexia didn't instantly and completely disappear, but she found it harder and harder to walk next to me. My stride length was different now. It was longer and more confident, and I could feel her beginning to lag, get fatigued, and fall by the wayside. On the rare occasions she made a desperate run towards me, I knew the game now and could spin around, point my finger in her face and quietly, confidently state, 'Back off!' I could still hear her calling from afar, 'I can help you, Han!' but the calls were beginning to be overshadowed by the song of my heart beating stronger and stronger inside.

I now found it easier to look in the mirror and observe the self, looking back at me. In many ways I found myself asking this person, 'Who are you?', as if the lights had just been turned on again for the first time in years. I was now able to look this young woman in the eyes and say, 'I will love you just the way you are.' And I said this as a proud woman who still dreamed of international athletic successes.

I was a young Tasmanian on a big mission to answer my unanswered questions that had arisen when I returned to running a few years earlier: 1. Was 2006 just a fluke? and, 2. Was it possible to return to that level in a healthy, playful manner?

So, in my last session with Jeremy, I raised these two questions with him. His simple response was, 'Hanny, imagine how good it will feel when you finally accept that you are a Ferrari and not a Fiat!'

Before working with Jeremy, I thought values were an airy-fairy thing that people brought up to feel like a mature adult. However, as our sessions evolved, I came to realise that competition, success and running were not my values. No, not at all. Concepts such as vitality, adventure, challenge, growth, compassion and connection began to feature more prominently.

I began to realise that as I learnt to be me, to know myself, to be wilder, I was forming the foundations on which to play wilder. Only then could I really perform wilder, and strive for my best self in the activities I loved. Be wilder, play wilder, perform wilder ... my toes were beginning to tingle, and the World Championships in Scotland were just around the corner!

My preparations led me to the Italian Dolomites for my first international skyrunning race. My only goal was to run the entire distance up and down the mountain's trails.

In the week prior to the competition, Graham and I hosted an Italian Find Your Feet trail running tour in the area. We ran every inch of the course—its rise and fall, its heartbeat. I was confident that if I paced it correctly, I would be able to run around the sweeping switchbacks to the summit of Piz Boe, which sat at over 3000 m above sea level and 2000 m above the start line. From there I could then dance back down the mountain to the finish. Simple.

But as soon as the gun went, I watched a stampede of brightly-coloured athletes in fluorescent shoes darting up the ski slope ahead of me. Rather than take the rounding curves of the trail, they toppled and jostled straight up the steep rises, pushing through the undergrowth before picking up the trail markers further up the slope. Rather than follow the exact curves of the route, these competitors appeared to just look into the distance, locate a far-off race marker, and literally beeline towards it.

I was baffled and confused and, as I tried to stick to the trail, I felt myself falling out the back door of the field. So, then I tried to play their game, hands on thighs, pushing and heaving my way firstly up through the grassy meadows, and later up the slippery, sliding scree slopes of the upper regions of the mountain. While many of the athletes used poles to catapult themselves further with every step, I had to rely on the good old-fashioned method of running and hiking as the terrain allowed. I gratefully crested the climb onto the flatter plateau and, once the lactic acid dissipated, I allowed myself to stretch out, my marathon running technique coming in handy across the bare dolerite plateaus. I passed girls then, feeling their fatigue and yet feeling stronger in myself.

That was, until we began to go down. I couldn't believe my eyes as the competitors careened at full speed down the rocky mountain slopes, leaping off small cliffs and landing on their heels on the scree to ski and slide their way further down the mountain. It didn't seem to matter that the trail went one way; it appeared they would go the other.

So, I tried to follow, leaping and launching my way down until ... I tripped! Catching my toe on the edge of a small cliff I found myself flying at full speed through open air. I braced myself for the inevitable crash, the scraping of bare skin on bare rock, and the searing pain. I screamed on impact, feeling flesh tearing in my knee, hip and hands, and I momentarily lay there in a confused, frightened heap.

But, slowly, I clambered to my feet, shaking like a leaf in this leafless landscape, and continued to make my way gingerly down the mountain. I climbed back into my bubble, my painless cave, and just tried to focus on each step, each breath, each turn that would take me closer to the finish.

Then ... POP! The bubble burst as soon as I saw him. Graham's love emanating from miles away as he stood on a rock in a random section of this random racecourse. Tears burst from my heart, seeped down my confused, frightened face. Pain radiated from my hips, blood dripped from my hands and knees. 'They cheat! Graham, they're all cheating!'

He didn't say a word, rather he ran behind me in silent camaraderie and then, quietly, he disappeared. I was alone again, and I felt my heart trying to piece itself back together. I clambered back into my bubble and raced my way down the ever-widening fire trails into the town, crossing the line in eleventh place.

In that event, I learnt that skyrunning was a whole new, scary world and I was grateful to board the plane to Scotland to participate in the World Orienteering Championships and a sport that felt far more familiar.

IN 2006, I had stood on the start line and consciously dedicated my run to my father's return to health. While I adored every member of my family and knew they were grieving our togetherness, that run was completely a tribute to him. A prayer for his resilience, to rise above the adversity.

Now, nine years on, I stood on the start line of the World Orienteering Championships in Scotland, one hundred percent dedicated to myself and my journey. I no longer felt selfish. I was there for one reason only—to answer the question: Is it possible to return to the elite level in a healthy, playful manner?

Parkland stretched on either side of me. Just beyond that, I could see the outer walls of the old town of Forres, where we would soon be racing. This was a sprint race—a fast, furiously paced three-kilometre dash towards the finish line, all the while navigating with a solid, steady mindset. It required a disconnection between mind and body, an ability to think calmly and rationally, while allowing my physical body to persevere to the edge of discomfort. And I had never felt more ready.

I had an enormous smile on my face, and a lean, healthy body. Having said that, I had barely orienteered in the previous few months. I found training back home in Tasmania uninspiring. With a new-found love of running and a new, Kiwi-based coach, James, helping to guide me in my trail running and skyrunning ambitions, I rarely picked up a map. But deep in my heart I knew I still had my orienteering skills, and that I had done enough to dust them off.

I had just finished coaching the Australian Junior Orienteering Team in the mountains of Norway. Giving them my knowledge had allowed me to uncover lessons accumulated from twelve years of on-and-off association with the sport. What I also knew from my past experience was that the champion would be the one able to discipline herself under the immense pressure of international performance and personal expectations, and this was where my readiness was stemming from. I had done the internal work to be wilder.

I had fallen in love again with my running, learnt to play wilder. I had also reflected on what I knew and engaged individuals to help me fill in the knowledge and skills gaps. I had trained smarter, recovered harder, found greater resilience and fostered self-compassion. In other words, I was ready to perform wilder.

I was ready to answer the deeply burning question that had been gnawing and chewing away at my curiosity. I needed to know. Was 2006 just a fluke?

The final beep emanated into the evening air, signalling my turn to start the race. I picked up my map and tried not to rush, taking my time to locate myself on the map and familiarise myself with the layout of the foreign landscape.

Then I danced, tightly twisting and turning through the narrow cobblestone alleys, bouncing down paved stairways and striding across the picture-worthy green parks fringed by a gurgling brook. I ran with a freedom and excitement so fierce that I felt little discomfort.

I sensed the finish line approaching but I was trying not to rush, carefully double-checking myself to avoid the risk of silly mistakes. Then I ran through an alley of cheering teammates and spectators, crossing the finish line in a swirl of relief and elation. I was aware but unaware of the commentary in the arena. Rather, I was listening to the singing of my own heart. 'That was fun!'

The excited faces of the team managers and our Swedish physiotherapist greeted me in the finish. From the joy in their smiles I knew that it was a competitive run. I had made no mistakes and left nothing to chance.

As the adrenalin began to subside, tears began to fall. A river of relief falling onto the damp Scottish soil. It was possible. It was possible to race fiercely and with health and playfulness!

Suddenly, I was rugby-tackled by Australians. Lifted and hugged, patted and congratulated. Fourth ... fourth! I hadn't won, and I missed the bronze medal by three seconds, but I knew in the core of my soul that I had also answered my second question, the one I had held so fearfully close to my heart since I had shaken the hand of Prince Frederik nine years earlier. It wasn't a fluke!

The Scottish rains held off that night as I stood on the podium, looking out into a sea of celebrating faces. Nine years ago, and in a similar moment, I had my huge realisation that success does not define or fix us. I realised that I was still returning home as Hanny.

In this moment, standing there in a moment of celebration, I was truly excited by the prospect. *I am Hanny. Proudly her. Willingly her. Striving for my best self.* I succeeded because I was willing to walk in my own shoes over tough terrain, to 'be more, to do more'. That became my mantra and gave me the courage to put myself on the edge—athletically, but also in all those hours of deep, internal work assisted by Sally, Jeremy and Graham.

I had finally understood how to be me, and then to play unapologetically, and then to perform again.

As the car weaved its way back towards our Scottish mansion, the laneways laced with dry-stone walls, avenues of green oaks curving overhead, I wound down the window. I needed all my senses in tune with this moment. For deep down I knew that, once this competition closed in a few days' time, I would have written the last paragraphs of this chapter of my life. My time as an elite athlete in the sport of orienteering was drawing to a close. And it felt so damn right.

There were no unanswered questions for me, no sense of curiosity drawing me forwards. My heart had now shifted onto the trails, into the lives of my Find Your Feet community, and into partnership with Graham.

I drove to the airport in the wee hours of the next morning. In my heart I had achieved everything I set out to achieve: a fourth in the sprint distance, a tenth in the long distance, and a cracking final leg for my relay team. It was by far my most consistent set of results on the international stage. I pulled into the open arms of the petrol station, pumping fuel into the belly of the hire car before wandering inside to pay the cashier. He greeted me with a hefty handshake and a beaming smile. 'Hello, Luv. What a glorious morning it is! I hope you are about to start a wonderful day?'

His cheerfulness was intoxicating, and I acknowledged it with an Aussie reply. 'Thanks mate!'

I returned to my car, a spring in my step. This day was a wonderful day. I was returning home. Home. To a place I felt a belonging, to a man whom I loved. I had a healthy family who loved me, and a story interwoven with theirs. We had dreams yet to unfold, and a toolkit of lessons learnt.

I am a homing pigeon, a young woman who flew the nest and was now just so damn excited to return. The only question unanswered was, *What next?*

24

Find Your Feet was no longer a hobby, but a quickly-growing business supporting an increasingly-large staff team. Our tours were going from strength to strength, and within months of arriving home I boarded another flight, this time to Japan via a quick stop at another fifty-kilometre race in Victoria.

I knew I was playing with fire, racing more frequently than I ever had. But my health and high spirits felt like they were my shield of armour, protecting me from the pings and pangs of the elite athlete racing circuit. Having had two strong races in the Skyrunner World Series, I was eager to complete the next one to be held in Hong Kong. And so, after a week running amok, donning kimonos and lounging in the steamy onsens of Japan, Graham and I waved goodbye to our tour guests and left the land of sushi.

We touched down in humid Hong Kong, and immediately felt like country bumpkins. Skyscrapers towered over the landscape and us. Everywhere we went was concreted and confusing. Even the bread and cheese were confusing—the bread too white and the cheese too yellow.

We visited the local orienteering club, where I shared my story and some of the lessons I had learnt along the way. Despite the gap in years and cultures between us, we had a connection because—just as I had been —this community of bright-eyed, eager orienteers was isolated from the inferno of the European orienteering scene. It was easy for them to think, *We are not like them*—which led to performances not on par with the Europeans. I tried to explain that the Hong Kong orienteers had secret tools in their back pockets too. They had access to detailed sprint maps, and an ability to train all year round while the wild north lay under a blanket of ice and snow. Being an outsider could be your secret weapon, and it just required belief to allow that to shine. I left knowing that this was a lesson not only true for orienteering, but for the upcoming Skyrace in a few days.

On the evening before the race, Graham and I moved into a towering hotel in the city's beating heart as a category four typhoon raced towards us. The wind whistled around the building, causing the metal structure to quiver in excitement. As I prepared my racing kit, I couldn't help but wonder how nicely Skyracing and typhoons would play together.

Race day arrived. The wind lashed. The rain beat down. I warmed up in an empty shopping mall. I warmed up my mountain legs by running up and down the escalators in the wrong direction, and then ran at race effort past the Gucci and Calvin Klein outlet stores. Graham joined me for some of this, before finding a perch next to a fake pot plant. The vast discrepancy between the urban jungle and the true one lying just beyond the city fringe location was almost comical.

I couldn't help but feel intimidated, standing on the start line. Salomon had flown in their professional team of athletes, managers and masseuses from around the world to be there, and yet Graham and I had pinched pennies from our own pockets to help me reach this moment. Once the gun went, I was once again baffled by the fast pace. I was used to racing hard, but it felt like these athletes had no filter on their speed. They raced raw and attacked the hills hard.

The rain lashed in torrential sheets over me. The weather was so wild that I soon found myself lost in the chaos. I had no idea where I was in relation to anyone or anywhere. I squinted into the grey gloom, the power of the rain stinging my eyes and causing culverts in the trail to become raging torrents. I waded through creeks, little suspecting that minutes later these torrents would become impassable to over half of the field.

After a long climb I breached onto the open ridge lines, and leant into a frightening wind that pushed and whistled, pressed and tugged. It was as if the wind was saying, 'This is my territory!' I tried to run, and yet in that beautiful moment between take-off and landing that makes running so unique, the wind would try to pick me up and throw me off the trail. And that was exactly what eventually happened to one athlete who landed awkwardly in a tree and fractured his pelvis.

As the trail kicked upwards, the cascade of water coming down the trail was so heavy that there was no trail. Waves formed on its surface, and the spray launched upwards and into my face. I was wet in every place, drowning on a mountain. Grey met grey met grey.

As I crested the first of the two summits, the wind literally lifted me upwards. I could feel myself about to be hurtled like Mary Poppins, and so I grabbed at the ground, clawing myself onto my knees and crawling knee by hand by knee across the summit. Finally, stairs loomed, marking the way down, and I gingerly shuffled onto my feet. Step by step, I lurched and shoved my way through the thick air, watching in amazement as the water blew up the mountain to meet me. This was not racing, this was surviving.

Like a drowned rat, I finally popped out onto the road between the two peaks. Once again, Graham was there to greet me, hair plastered to scalp, drenched rain jacket taut across sodden skin. He was laughing while I was grovelling. 'Don't make me go back out there. I could die.' But the others had continued onwards, and in our hearts, I think we both knew that the only way to end it was at the finish line. So, I plunged back into the drowning vegetation.

Somehow, the second peak was not as sketchy as the first, and I could feel the rain momentarily easing. I ran onwards, knowing that the only success I cared about in this event was proudly reaching the finish line with a giggle to say, 'Wasn't that wild!'

When I reached the last descent, I was amazed to find that the track was a continuous stretch of shiny, moss-coated wooden boardwalks. The trail led beneath the wires of an overhead gondola which, judging from the state of the slimy green trail, was obviously the preferred method of transport. I gingerly stepped a foot onto the trail, feeling my feet sliding each time they came into contact with the wet timber. It was also raining again, and mightily windy. I crouched down into a running posture more akin to an older woman tending to her garden. I grabbed at anything that could help break my fall, and shuffled, slid, squealed and gratefully made my way slowly down the mountain.

Then I heard him, an elephant on roller-skates careening down the trail behind me. He scooted past on the inside, left foot hitting green slime. And then he was off, sliding at light-speed over the edge of the upcoming precipice. I reached the edge of the trail to be confronted by a huge stairway, hundreds of stairs deep, with a pile of crumpled athlete at the bottom. 'No, no, no!' I hurried as fast as the green slime would allow me but, by the time I reached the bottom, the guy was dragging himself to his feet, using the vines and ferny fronds of the creek gully to pull himself upright. He was shaking from head to toe, mumbling incomprehensibly as he began to work his way up the next flight of stairs that led back up from the gully. I tried to slow him down, tried to encourage him to pause, but he was soon off, careening into the distance in a wobbling, shaky mess of arms, legs and slime-coated trail-running apparel.

I reached the finish line in a bedraggled state. Graham enveloped me in a mighty wet hug and together we let out a relieved giggle. Done and drowned. I stripped down in a sneaky corner of the shopping mall, as it began to fill with droplets of sodden shoppers. Rain lashed the roof and sheeted down the windows. The only fear remaining was, would our flight home still depart tonight?

Forty-eight hours after my last shower, twenty-two typhoon-swept kilometres on foot, and another seven thousand flight miles later, we reached the shores of Tasmania.

Home. I was ready to be home. And I was ready for a shower!

25

I fell asleep to the sound of a fine dust gently landing on the nylon of the tent. It was not quite dark outside, although the world felt dark. The tent faintly glowed with a red hue, representing the anger roiling inside me. The words of my friend Rob echoed in my inner ear: 'Han, this is not just a problem for our children. This is a problem for us.'

We had been eating dinner huddled in a cluster around the camp stoves—Rob, Graham, my father and I—with a plateful of couscous salad while Rob delved long fingers into a container of parsley, spinach, and the occasional cherry tomato bursting with homegrown colour. His phenomenal wilderness photography is also homegrown, stemming from an appreciation of natural beauty and an ache to share its struggles with the world.

As he quietly uttered this profound statement, he looked so fragile. A weathered face with protruding facial bones. But I knew better than to judge his strength by external appearances, after we had trailed his long legs up the escarpment and into this open, barren landscape. Unable to keep up, I had crested the final rise in sweaty gratitude to see Rob standing atop a charred cushion plant, his tripod out and peering through the lens of his camera. I knew he was trying to capture the devastation of these fires that had ripped through the alpine landscape, and yet could not help but think how much I wished we could look through a different lens, to block out the extent of the disaster.

This fire had already invaded the alpine World Heritage Area and burnt vegetation that should never have seen fire. Pencil pines which were thousands of years old stood like black shadows, where previously their living green selves once thrived. Though their feet stood in small pools of fresh water, the fire had ravaged across from the gullies and into their copses. Each tree a part of a living community stemming from a mother tree, but she and her young were dead.

As I stepped into Rob's space, finding my own cushion plant to climb onto as if I could rise above the emotional terror unfolding around us, he quietly said, 'Welcome to climate change.'

JUST BEFORE I TURNED THIRTY, Tasmania and its west coast alpine and rainforest communities were ravaged by dry lightning storms. This was a rare event due to the west coast of Tasmania's average annual rainfall of nearly two and a half metres, ensuring the extensive rainforest thrived. Much of the forest, including the pencil pine trees, was remnant Gondwana Rainforest—a vegetation that would have once extensively covered the region but, when we stood there, was confined to only a few small pockets in alpine Tasmania.

Beautiful does not do this landscape justice. Words do not do it justice. And so, when I heard of the tragedy unfolding, and when Rob, one of Tasmania's most renowned wilderness photographers, paid a visit to the store, his face a hollow shell describing without words the horror of what he had seen, I knew I needed to see it with my own eyes. He agreed to return here with me.

We pitched our tent on ash beneath the pillars of charred pines. A double rainbow and an eagle appeared, and it suddenly felt like we were orchestrating a memorial for this landscape that would never regenerate to its original pre-fire beauty. Once gone, it is gone forever.

Later, when our hearts beckoned for reprieve, we crawled into our tents and listened to the phenomenal stillness, a quietness so unlike anything I have ever experienced. For when everything is dead, there is nothing left to make a sound. Every now and then, a breath of ash would hit the walls of the tent, finally lulling me into sleep. In just a few hours, I would turn thirty.

We spent three days filming the devastation, as well as the pockets of beauty that avoided the fingers of fire. I couldn't believe the extent of the furnace and how, when we crested a peak, we looked down over the World Heritage pristine wilderness to see a multitude of smoke plumes curling into the sky.

In honour of my thirtieth birthday I had created a challenge to climb thirty peaks before I turned thirty. As I stood atop the final one, wind-chapped and chafed from the inside out, I felt elated but also defeated, and just so damned confused. *What am I doing?* If this was climate change and the expected way of our future, I knew I needed to find a way to take action—and now!

My head kept replaying the selfishness of my sporting endeavours, the 'selling people stuff' ways of our retail store, the overseas travelling with our trail-running tour guests, and then the hoards of community 'over there' who had no concept of the disaster unfurling before me. When this landscape is lost, it is lost forever. It became a mantra on repeat, a fear so profound that I stumbled forward on automatic pilot. Those trees, those wild forests with their brimming communities of fungi, insects, blue-water crayfish and still-to-be-found species, are the last generation of a Gondwana family. When they disappear, we will never, ever find them again. And as Rob inferred, this is our problem. My problem. Your problem!

The weather whipped us as we walked back towards the edge of the alpine escarpment to where the track led back to the car. I couldn't believe that the rain could lash down and huge torrents of water could flood around my feet while we walked through a charred landscape. It seemed so incongruent. Rob came alongside me, sensing my confusion. Over the wind and rain, I heard him say, 'Han, there are a lot of wonderful people out there doing wonderful things to help. We just have to believe that, eventually, we will all come together, and we just have to hope that it isn't too late.'

I RETURNED HOME WITH A HEAVY, confused heart. Not for the first time, I felt like my innocence had been shattered as I lifted my head from beneath the comfort of my comfortable life. I grappled with the sensation that I was not doing enough.

Or was I? Somewhere deep in my heart, I knew I needed to help people to see these landscapes, to play wilder, and to learn to love them. For when you see the rare beauty of a flying duck orchid or the vast stands of pencil pines sharing the tiny puddle of the alpine tarn at their feet, you feel like your heart has been stolen. When you experience this beauty in its rawest form, running and bounding across the buttongrass plains, running your fingers through those of the pencil pines, resting back against a cushion plant while observing the stillness of the mountains around you, you develop a deep respect for wildness and a deep-seated belief that you are a caretaker. I couldn't help but feel we were giving people that ability through Find Your Feet.

When I first arrived back in Tasmania from Hong Kong, I had been asked to speak at a public forum on the protection of the Wilderness World Heritage Area, alongside representatives of the aboriginal and science communities, and also the famously powerful wilderness advocate and previous leader of the Tasmanian Greens political party, Bob Brown. I couldn't help but think, *Why me? What voice do I have?*

But now, having seen the devastation these fires had on Tasmania, I knew I needed to use the voice I had. My running had given me some notoriety in my local Tasmanian and broader sporting communities, but so too had my journey as a young businesswoman. Further to that, Hanny had a voice too! It might have been a quiet and sometimes confused thirty-year-old voice, but it was a voice, nonetheless.

I returned to Find Your Feet, certain that we could continue to make a positive difference to the lives of our community, and to that of Tasmania. This jacket was not just a jacket, this pack not just a pack. No, these items were the tools that would allow our customers to experience landscapes we hoped they would fall in love with. I hoped they would return wind-chapped and glowing from the inside out, thinking, 'Wonderful, what next?' And in doing so, they would find themselves falling in love, caring deeply. Seeing and experiencing could lead to protection.

I began to more vocally share my past lessons, beliefs and views. Joining the National Parks and Wildlife Advisory Council as their tourism, recreation and business advisor was also an integral step in ensuring that I was contributing to the lasting beauty and sustainability of my home state. It was an honour to sit in a room surrounded by the other council members, each of them specialists in their own areas of science, natural resource management and aboriginal cultural values. I felt their knowledge and inspiration brimming into the space, covering the table with a map that could help guide our politicians forward. Each time I was in a meeting, I found myself glancing out the window and making a prayer: *Please be listening.*

I BEGAN to spend more and more time in the Tasmanian wild-scapes with Graham. Where once the elements, the rain, wind and harsh scrub frightened me, I now felt my adventure muscle getting stronger as together we began to explore further afield.

It was a profoundly spiritual day when we crested another mountain rise, pressing our bodies through the final remaining pieces of scrub into an open, alpine meadow laced with curving tarns and clusters of baby pencil pines. The mountains were on fire with the changing colours of the Antarctic beech, a very special Tasmanian phenomenon that occurs each April when the leaves change from green to gold to red, before dropping to the ground in a rusty carpet. Right there, they are at their best and, after galloping from bush to bush in wonder and awe, we finally slowed to a stop beside a bigger alpine lake covered in a dusting of these glowing autumnal leaves.

In that moment, Graham turned to me. 'Han, you do know that one day we will get married, don't you?'

I looked back at him in surprise, comprehension failing me. My silence and stillness echoed that of the mountains. Eventually I found a few words. 'Graham, did you just ask me to marry you?'

He dropped his gaze, and then with slight trepidation lifted it back towards mine. 'Yes. Yes Muppet, I did.'

I reeled towards him, wrapping myself around his lean frame. After fifteen years of friendship and five years of walking right alongside him, I was so, so ready for this moment. I felt my vulnerability rising to the surface and bleeding into my excitement and complex love for this complex person. I knew that I loved him with every inch of my heart and there was no doubt in my mind what my answer was. 'Yes!'

AFTER SCOTLAND and the skyrunning event in Hong Kong, I found the flame within me for competition was dwindling. I felt like I had reached the end of a road and that I needed to pause, to sit, to be stiller.

Unlike in 2010 when a similar sensation stemmed from a falling out-of-love with running, this time it stemmed from feeling madly, deeply in-love with running. I found myself rising excitedly above competition. I was in rapture with my running, and there was nowhere that brought me greater joy than roaming a wild trail in Tasmania. I no longer felt the same burning desire to prove myself on a course dictated to me by event organisers. I no longer felt the need to do more, to be more.

Instead, I realised I was reaching a place where I was simply excited about hatching a plan with an unknown outcome and then wading right into the heart of it. Such as running a remote trail to a mountain out there, all the while wondering, *Is this even possible?*

However, Find Your Feet continued to grow, and coaching and competing opportunities were ever-present. Graham and I once again packed the van and trundled back up the long, dull highway to the Blue Mountains, for the Ultra Trail Australia event. This race had become an icon in Find Your Feet's history, and this time we were no longer just coaching the event, but also hosting a Find Your Feet retail store at the event's expo.

Cruising past the turn-off to Canberra felt odd, a strange concoction of time swiftly passing and time pausing. It felt like we left yesterday and yet we felt so unassumingly different. So much had happened in the eighteen months since we looked in the rear-vision mirror and waved goodbye to Base Camp one final time.

After a day helping to present at the Australian Trail Running Conference and then two days nonstop on my feet in the retail store under an unusually warm May sun, I lined up on the start line of the fifty-kilometre event. Throughout the expo I had continually found myself on repeat: 'Yes, but just the fifty kilometre, just the fifty.' It felt like everyone saw the one hundred kilometre race distance as the 'real event', and the fifty as its little sister.

However, when it came to packing my race pack late in the evening before race day, many consecutive hours of work at the expo behind me, I found myself with fear on my hands. 'Who am I kidding! Just fifty kilometres?' Simply because there is a longer option, it shouldn't mean we think any less of our pursuits or our achievements afterwards. I was still about to subject myself to a long period of time taking a large number of steps in steep mountainous terrain. I was still requesting my body to dig deeper than it naturally desires, and to strive for a big, hairy, audacious goal that, to be honest, by the time I stood on the start line seemed highly intimidating.

I ran like I was intimidated. Latching onto the feet of the male athletes in front and knowing deep down that I was burning my energy bridges quickly. I tried to focus on maintaining a regular glucose gel intake and, when my sweat rate began to increase in the surprisingly hot mountain glare, I also attempted to keep the electrolyte fluids going in. Through working with an Australian sports nutrition guru I had learnt that I have a very high sodium loss in my sweat. For every litre that I sweat out, I lose around a pinch of table salt. In these temperatures, I felt multiple litres of sweat trickling down into my soggy underwear, squelching down into my socks and making my eyes sting uncomfortably. I was losing pinches of salt every hour.

I left the final checkpoint, out in front of the women's field. Only twenty kilometres to go. I still felt strong and I relaxed into my own rhythm. From there on lay eight quadricep-burning downhill kilometres followed by twelve uphill ones to finish. So, I fumbled my way into my bubble, my secret pain cave, to block out any internal discomfort that would no doubt begin to present. I ran in my bubble, flowing strongly down the winding fire trails into the depths of the valley where towering eucalypts sank their feet into rapid streams. I crossed each of these one by one, and in between I leant into the rolling hills earmarking the beginning of the upcoming climb to the finish.

However, as I crept towards this final challenge I began to notice the pinging of cramp in my left foot's smallest toes. It crept into my middle toes, and soon my big toe. I tried to ignore it, realising that I was nearly empty of fluid in my bottles and still had a long way to go. I wrapped my bubble tighter around me and continued to lean into the challenge. Jitter and flutter! I felt my right eye begin to twitch—seize and relax, seize and relax. I literally turned a blind eye to the discomfort and tugged my bubble closer again. *Lean in, Han. Lean in.*

I reached the emergency aid station with eight kilometres to go, aware that my right leg was also seizing uncomfortably. My right eye syndrome had also spread into my right cheek and the cramp was beginning to seep into my neck. I guzzled plain water, knowing the risk of taking on no sodium while my body was evidently crying out for salt. In a well-trained athlete, cramping is almost always a result of disrupted sodium balance. I had been vigorously racing for over four hours by that point, sweating profusely. Salt was crusted up my back and around my face like an anemone shell.

I swayed into the final staircase, a mighty two-kilometre uphill climb over unevenly spaced stairs. I sensed that my bubble was frighteningly thin and close to bursting. *I can do this, I can do this!* By then I was cramping with every step, and my neck had seized so I could no longer turn my head. My feet felt like the feet of a rocking chair and I was trying to heave myself up each flight using the hand railings.

'Keep it up, Han!' I heard a familiar voice cheering me on. 'Graham is just around the corner!'

As I swept around the bend, peered up into the sunshine that was dazzling its beauty through the trees, I didn't see Graham, I sensed him. POP! My bubble's walls were popping, bursting into a brilliant display of cramping, tears and searing discomfort. 'Keep going!' I heard him call out. But I couldn't. I physically seized into place, a step above, a step below. I was a figure of that forest.

Eventually, the discomfort waned slightly and I moved limb by stiff limb up the final stairs and entered the finish chute. The noise was intoxicating, and I hung my head in embarrassment. After the quiet depths of the valley, the atmosphere was overwhelming.

When I reached the line, my body stiffened into a large lump of flesh. I toppled to the ground and lay there as cramps overwhelmed my entire body. Graham gave me a small handful of salt tablets and a bottle of electrolyte and, as if by magic, the cramps almost instantly began to fade. Then I was standing, thanking the organisers and wandering gratefully across the car park in the direction of our car.

While I won by the narrowest of margins, there was a greater lesson in that event. As I climbed into the passenger seat, I said confidently to Graham, 'There is no such thing as "just" fifty kilometres!'

WHEN I RETURNED HOME and wandered back down the central streets of the city's heart, I couldn't help but notice a large 'Closing Down Sale' sign pinned with sticky tape to the window of one of the biggest outdoor retail players in Hobart. Wedged between the discounting giants of Kathmandu, Macpac and Mountain Designs, this store, run by a gentleman dedicated to his entrepreneurial pursuits and his wife dedicated to supporting his dream, had survived the windstorms of new players arriving and new players leaving … for thirty years! He was never one to hide and had proudly proclaimed that he never had a leave of absence or sick day in his thirty-year six-days-a-week duration in business. In fact, when Graham and I wandered in the doors and quietly pulled him aside to ask if the premises were going to come up for lease, he leant in and quietly whispered in our ears, 'Kiddos, I made a lot of money here … a LOT of money!'

Later, he asked us for a budget, and evidence of our ability to pay the extortionate rent. The building was nearly ten times bigger than our current store, and spread over four levels. Two staircases wound their way to the heights of the building, where rough, unpolished timber floors spoke of the test of time. Graham and I knew that we needed to be here. Our current leased space served us perfectly at the outset but would no longer serve us into the future. If we didn't move into the heart of Hobart's outdoor strip and allow our products to breathe and expand, we would no longer be able to compete against the hefty giants itching to extract more money from the pockets of the Tasmanian adventure community.

Housesitting for a friend, bent over their breakfast bench with the heater blasting to keep out the damp winter chill, we nutted out a budget. It came in at negative-twenty-one-thousand dollars. We jiggled and jostled the numbers, all the while asking each other, 'Surely we can make this work?'

We signed the contract on the premises just before departing for more overseas running tours, this time in Chamonix and then Italy. During the days, we ran with our guests on weaving alpine 'balconies' with vistas onto the glaciered slopes of Mt Blanc or the distant views of the Dolomites' plethora of peaks. Then, in the evenings, we returned to the chalet balcony, to watch a fading sun as we discussed how to dive into the depths of that enormous 900 m^2 store and teach ourselves to swim with the big fish.

Back home, we briefly returned to the now-vacant store and stood in awe. The building towered around us. 'What have we done?' But there was no time to linger in our fear—another running tour to Japan was calling. But so, too, was setting up our new retail store!

I WAS HOT. Really hot. I felt the perspiration trickling down my forehead despite the cooler breeze softly catching my damp skin. The onsen water, a hazy darkness, felt as if it should have left ink stains rather than cleansed me. And as I sank deeper into it's healing waters, I closed my eyes.

I reflected on the week that I had just spent with my mother. One of those precious times that, no matter how busy or distracted life feels, needs to be grasped, experienced and then the memories locked away safely. For eight days, we had roamed on bicycles throughout the northern Japanese island of Hokkaido.

Prior to the trip, I had been desperately afraid of being naked and vulnerable with her. While in some ways we were close, in other ways I just could not let her too close. Nor Dad. Nor James. When one heart stayed, the other heart was moving on. When one voice spoke, the other was listening to the words left unspoken. Each of us was still trying to master the art of moving on when our hearts craved the ability to return and start again. At our core, our unspoken remnants of grief were nothing more than the consequences of a deep, profound love. For a mother, a daughter, a father, a brother, a family. And for our own selves. There was a fragility in our strength, a delicateness that frightened me. Because, I knew it was only a matter of time before the unspoken words became spoken words. I wasn't sure that I was yet strong enough to either speak them in the presence of others, or hear them coming from my loved ones. While I had been doing the internal work and self-reflection, I hadn't yet welcomed others into my internal tea party. I still saw the dust I needed to sweep away, and the floors that needed a mop. I was gaining strength, but I was still preparing a room in my heart for others. Only Graham had been able to put his foot in the door.

Mum and I didn't end up speaking all the unspoken that week. We uttered and inferred, suggested but never explicitly said. However, we cycled joyously through rain-soaked forests as typhoon after typhoon rolled in off the oceans. We leant into the winds, and braced ourselves against the thrust of their rage, which was reaching out and snapping trees like they were matchsticks. We lay side by side in cosy guesthouses and soaked naked in the communal onsens. Slowly, like plants coming back to life after a thirsty soak, our relationship was beginning to strengthen. It was if the unspoken had found its own way to seep beneath my walls.

AFTER THIS TRIP, Graham joined us as we embarked on a running tour. The guests had arrived that morning, and we drove through the day to a very traditional Japanese hotel perched in the heart of a unique landscape where wild bears still roamed. I loved this place. There was something so raw and healing about playing hard outside during the days and then entering into the tranquillity of the Japanese accommodations, to rest under fluffy bedcovers and dine on delicate food.

And soak in the steaming onsens. I sensed the space beyond the hotel's precinct, a presence of mountains out there, somewhere. And as I closed my eyes, I felt the occasional dusting of mist as the intensity of the rain increased. When it reached a point of surprising ferocity, I opened my eyes. Water ran with a glowing sheen from the roofing, cascading into the valley that dropped away from the hotel. It glistened and caught light from somewhere I couldn't see. Despite the intensity of the storm, the bath's surface still held a perfect, calm tension.

But suddenly I was trapped! I heard my brain yelling, *Let down your walls! Let down your walls!* And in that bizarre moment of undeniable certainty, I found my body overcome by an unbearable tension. Fearfully, I closed my eyes. It was the only thing I appeared to be able to control, while my physical body was overcome by painful rigidity. My legs, arms and trunk muscles clenched so tight that it was unlike any cramping I had ever had. My Ultra Trail fifty kilometre horrors paled into insignificance. Even my face pulled into a grimace that stretched into the front of my neck. My eyes closed again, as rain lashed against any of my exposed skin. The noise of it was so overpowering, and panic began to rise through me.

Then, as quickly as it manifested, all tension eased.

In a state of shock, I opened my eyes. The rain had eased, and there was once again a fine prickle of cool moisture on my burning face. I lifted myself onto the edge of the bath, grateful to be alone. I was struggling to interpret the experience—I don't do spirituality. Rather, I had always seen the shades of black and white, right and wrong, success and failure. But in that precious moment I realised that I had seen the shade of grey, the maybe. I had just experienced the removal of the final obstacle blocking the pathway to finding my feet. Not out on a dais, a road, or a trail. Not laced into running shoes on a trail to somewhere. And certainly not indoors with a pen and paper, planning my future like it was a to-do list. No. I removed my internal walls and found my rawest self in an unexplainable moment, in a hot tub, on a mountain, in wild Japan. My nakedness appropriately represented the vulnerability I had just exposed. Where once I had built internal structures and walls to define my sense of self, that experience brought them all crashing down. Without everything I had used to define myself, I was simply left with me. Myself. I. Hanny. I had finally found a way to sit with myself, content in my own skin, willing to trust in my abilities and vulnerabilities.

I was excited to be more in order to do more, and I had finally learnt to be wilder. It was now time to play, to explore, to adventure and dream wilder. In other words, it was time to find my feet.

WHILE WE EXPLORED quaint Japanese towns and towering volcanic peaks, our staff swept, painted, sawed and hammered the new store into something that looked akin to a shop. On returning, we swapped running gear for painting rags and joined in the mess. It was utterly overwhelming. Now that the premises were devoid of the previous owner's large family-camping tents, pop-up toilets, racks of fleeces and hefty down jackets, the place was enormous!

After another day attached to paint brushes, Graham and I drove to the beach. We pulled up at the far end of the stretching sand, and immediately became statues as the car engine subsided. Outside, we heard the waves pummelling the sand as a fine drizzle began to fall. For quite some time, neither of us said anything. As I gazed out to the horizon, I saw the wrinkles of the distant grey hills and the convoluted bays of the Derwent River. I looked across at Graham and saw the convoluted emotions and wrinkles of concern spread across his own face. The car felt grey and yet solid beneath us, unwavering in the gusts of wind that swept in off the bay. I felt grey as waves of emotion began to crash through me onto the sands of my confidence.

'What are we doing, Graham?' A drizzle of tears started falling. I no longer fought them back. We had everything on the line. Every last cent of our previous home and all our life savings were locked into that dream. Graham reached for my hand and squeezed it in reassurance. But I knew he was also doing it to reassure himself. Even though we wrestled with our emotions and sanity, deep down we knew one thing: we needed to do this.

Later, we wandered along the beach, hand in hand. Our hearts were full, but empty. Crying does that to you. However, allowing the emotion to come and go, confronting it rather than running from it, I felt readier than ever to face whatever was going to be thrown at us. I felt a swell of pride, the tide turning and gently sweeping sandy confidence back onto my beach. I knew I was resilient. I knew that, no matter what, I would still be me and still be loved by those who mattered. Failure in that moment would be not being willing to walk this edge of discomfort and try. And if all the shit hit the fan, we would still be us, with our van, living together on our island home. I was ready to willingly launch myself into debt and a new territory, swimming to avoid sinking. And I knew Graham was too.

When the day for moving finally arrived, we gathered our staff team and family around us. We clutched armfuls of clothing and display fixtures and marched them up the street and through the front doors of the new store. Armful by armful, trolley by trolley, we slowly moved eighteen months of hard work into the expansive new nine hundred metres of opportunity. A piece of clothing there, another over here, a shoe on that wall, a sleeping bag on this one. We laid our dribs and drabs of product out as best we could, trying to make the enormous space feel somewhat full. It was going to be a long, hardworking journey to bring these new premises to life, and to be confident in our own shoes to lead the team through the uncertainty. But we made a brave start, launching from our own solid foundations of self. We were ready to play. And ready to perform when the time came. And that was the most important thing.

26

I lay cocooned in the down parlour of our van, sleeping bag pulled up to my ears. If the world could not see me, would dawn forget to happen? Beyond the walls of the van, the tide lapped on the shallow cove, an arcing strip of glowing light, a literal line in the sand marking the boundary between not-wild and wild. I lay in anticipation of being awakened, a strange dance of trepidation and excitement occurring within me.

After the alarm sounded, torches flicked on, the Jetboil stove boiled, a mug of green tea was drained, a half-eaten energy bar put aside, socks were pulled on, shoes too. I was ready. *Play wilder, Han. Trust yourself.*

While the world still slept, I fastened my head torch and walked hand in hand with Graham through the campsite that literally marked the end of the road in Tasmania. We reached the small bridge over the inlet where, as a kid, I used to throw baited hooks from cork fishing rods into the shallow waters below. Twenty years on, I turned to face Graham and drew him in for a long, nervous hug … trust. Watches at the ready, I spun to face my new running friend, Dale, who had just relocated from the warmer climates of Queensland and become my partner-in-crime for this wild adventure. We had come to know one another strongly. In the previous twelve months, Graham, Dale and I had explored wide, high and also close to home.

But none of those explorations were quite like what we were confronting today. We just had to trust in this new friendship. We handed each other a high five ... trust.

Then, without looking back to the comfort—and final chance to opt out—represented by our partners who were also our support crew, we headed into the undergrowth and weaved our way through the trail as it squiggled alongside the inlet. Our destination? Remote Melaleuca airstrip in inaccessible south-west Tasmania, ninety-three kilometres of wilderness coastline away.

In the heavy reality of the moment, we ran in silence, synchronised in movement and emotion. We knew that once our partners had squished our sleeping bags into their bags, stowed the Jetboil stove, rinsed dirty mugs and thrown my fleecy camping slippers into the back of the van, our safety net would disappear. We would have reached the point of no return. Once it looked as if we had never camped amongst the boobialla bushes behind Cockle Creek cove, Graham and Kendall would turn the key in the ignition, steer the car toward the north, and begin the long three-hour drive back to Hobart. Their destination? Cambridge Aerodrome, departure point for the light-aircraft flight that would drop them in to meet us at Melaleuca at the end of the day.

As we ran in mutual respect for the enormity of our endeavour, Dale and I finally began to crack the silence of a rare, still night in the South West Wilderness. It began with a simple giggle of fear into the vast surroundings, like the depressurisation as you open a bottle of carbonated water. Darkness still shrouded us; the giggling sounded like the gurgle of nearby creeks we could hear, but not yet see. Further minutes passed. We re-entered trails snaking through tight, steep-sided creeks where boobialla and tea-tree forests created a tunnel over the trail, and we began to hear the sea for the first time. The roar of waves that had rolled uninterrupted since Antarctica filled us with an energy so raw and exciting that we ran full throttle down the last hill, and out onto the blackened coal platforms of the Southern Ocean.

Through the gloom, we could see a faint strip of dawn light forming on the eastern horizon, the white turbulence of the breakers as they came into the rocky coastline below. As our head torches danced a wild jig along the first stretch of beach, for the first time since leaving the security of our sleeping bags we trusted in ourselves that, through literal hills or high water, we could not only reach the small stretch of cleared airstrip a further eighty-five kilometres of rough trail to our west, but we would thrive.

THE EARLIEST RAYS of sunshine caught up with us. As we bounced through the density of the undergrowth, I felt like one of the small sundews that grew beside the trail. Their fine hairs held beads of morning dew that the sun caught. My light-blue running skort, already spattered with mud from those initial few hours, clung to my legs with dampness. Our fingers a shade of white, but quickly thawing, we ran uphill through a mixture of open, mist-filled valleys and dense glades of ferns and forests. Sunshine dappled and changed colours through the canopy, illuminating the rich red tones of the young ferns, and glistened off the small brooks that the trail traversed.

Somewhere between dark and dawn, I had left fear on a stretch of wild beach far below me. As I snaked my way up through the awakening forest, I could feel my adventure muscle awakening and, with it, trust and anticipation. No matter what, Dale and I would realise this dream.

I reached into the front pockets of my vest pack for an energy gel. Two hours in, I knew I should have done it earlier to avoid burning bridges too soon in the challenge, but somehow when you are buried in the depths of the fear you just need to keep running, letting rhythm and purpose pull you forward until you are ready to break your stride. Suddenly it felt safe to do so, and I squeezed the sticky, gooey contents into my mouth. Behind me, I was grateful to hear similar sounds as Dale dug into his own supplies and ripped open a gel packet too.

WHAT I HAVE LEARNT about my adventure muscle is that it is just like every other muscle. It needs to be trained and nurtured in a manner that allows it to thrive.

Simply growing up as a wild child and pursuing a love affair with the rougher sport of orienteering was not enough to maintain my adventure muscle. As concrete replaced forests and tarmac replaced trails, urban living and marathon running appeared to catalyse the weakening of my adventure muscle. Through the long hours of rhythmic running along quiet tarmac roads, it had eventually tuned out, gone to sleep, and begun to silently waste away.

However, when Graham and I relocated back to Tasmania, driving off the Spirit of Tasmania ferry with the mountains glowing in the distance, I knew it was time to reawaken it.

It took focus and persistence, to reactivate and then begin to develop strength in my adventure muscle again. I had started small, initially roaming Mt Wellington on our back doorstep, then slowly travelling further afield to play. Day by day, adventure by adventure, my aspirations had grown, and I trained harder and smarter than ever, focusing on strength training in the gym and long hill repetitions on rough trails on the mountain.

However, what really awoke my adventure muscle was the smaller bouts immersed in real wildness, such as plodding up the side of Eliza Plateau in south-west Tasmania in the horizontal rain and wind, or hitchhiking back to our accommodation in the Italian Dolomites after a terribly poor judgement of distance on a morning run.

Through each adventure, I came to develop a relationship with trust —in myself, in my partners-in-crime, in our preparedness, and in our actions in the face of discomfort or adversity. Trust is what ultimately strengthened my adventure muscle, fostering a knowledge that I could play wilder and stay safe in the challenging environments and situations where I often found my best self.

As I TUCKED the empty gel packet back into my vest pack, I found myself wishing I had known before what I knew in that moment. Rewind ten years to a younger Hanny, running along the tarmac road in the 2007 Melbourne Marathon, glancing over her shoulder in pain and fear of being caught. Legs heavy, negative thoughts creeping into her fragile confidence, her previously fluid strides feeling robotic and forced. The television crew cruising just a few metres in front of her, the fumes from the motorbike as intrusive as the large camera directed at her, each moment of fear and discomfort captured for the viewers back home. If only she had known then what I knew in the moment I leapt and bounded down vast stairs back towards the Southern Ocean. If only she had reached into the rear pocket of her shorts and removed a gel, ripped it open and swirled its sticky sweetness around her parched mouth, allowing the glucose to filter up through the glucose pathways to her fatiguing brain. And yet, she didn't realise the simple power of an energy gel. Instead, she just gritted her teeth.

If only she knew then that she was not 'a runner', but rather Hanny who loved to run, and who also needed to love and be loved, to nurture and be nurtured, to play hard and with self-belief. That was likely the difference between Olympic representation and the burnout that eventuated just years later.

No matter how hard those lessons had been, I had come to know what I did, and running there along the South Coast Track of Tasmania felt like the appropriate celebration of the summation of that knowledge. Far away from the eyes of the media, shrouded in secrecy, known only by those closest to us, this would be, far and away, the grandest sporting achievement of my life at this time.

I frequently glanced at the face of my GPS watch. In a blur of forest and knee-deep mud, I lost track of the hours. But as five hours approached, I knew that soon we would hear the sound of the aircraft flying in towards Melaleuca—one that was hopefully carrying Kendall and Graham.

We had hoped by then to be somewhere on the vast length of white sand, Prion Beach, which marked the halfway point. But first, we had to cross the notorious mouth of New River Lagoon. Normally it was traversed using a couple of small tin row boats upstream but, on advice previously given combined with the fact that we had chanced to arrive on low tide, we had decided we would swim across the narrow but fast-moving water. This was perhaps the section I had been most worried about.

As we crested the final dune and looked down on the glistening blue waters of the inlet and beyond it, the most stunning white-quartzite beach I had ever seen with the towering Ironbound Range as its backdrop, I was literally brought to a stop. Looking to my left I saw the thundering waves rolling into the shallows. To my right, the impressive lone dolerite peak of Precipitous Bluff with its towering rampart of columnar cliffs faced out to that Southern Ocean.

We ran like little kids down the dune to the water's edge and began kicking off our shoes. As planned, we removed a large dry sack from my vest pack. I left skort, shirt, undies in a pile for Dale to stuff into the dry sack and tow across the stretch of water. Then I dove into the chilly water and began swimming.

The water was Tasmanian-chilly and yet as clear as air. As I swam, I could see nothing but the movement of my limbs, the white sandy bottom and the vastness all around me. Any remnants of my fear flowed from me, dissolving into the water to be carried out to sea.

On the other side, we left the hurdle of New River Lagoon behind and began making our way down the blindingly bright quartzite beach. We heard the familiar rumble of an aircraft approaching. I stretched out my arms in the freedom and exhilaration of the moment and began to make aircraft movements, darting to the left and then right. Just as we nearly ran out of beach, we saw it far above us. We waved madly, goofy grins plastered to our faces, mud from the earlier sections of rough trail still plastered to the back of our legs.

We filled our bottles from a small cascade at the end of the beach, and prepared ourselves for the next challenge—the Ironbound Range. With its notoriously rough, muddy trail and over one thousand metres of ascent, these mountains formed the crux of the trail. Both Dale and I knew that fuelling on gels, electrolytes and positivity was what was required of us both in this moment. As Dale had frequently encouraged me during the depths of our hardest training days, he said, 'Let's go, Champ!'

One lumbering step after another, we pressed up from the depths of deep mud holes onto the slippery roots forming the edge of each step.

Arms pressed down hard on thighs. I felt mud in nearly every crevice of my body. When I slipped, I felt it ooze between my hands. When I landed in the next puddle, I felt it squelch up the back of my legs. But step after step, lumber after lumber, we climbed higher towards the summit.

I knew Dale was experiencing his lowest moment, so I needed to be stronger for him then. That is what teamwork is. We are only as strong as we are together.

I tried to ignore thoughts of my recent nightmares, the ones that had woken me up in a sweat. Almost every night for the last three weeks since our final, less-than-ideal training run, I had awoken from visions of Dale and I bundled in a cave on the side of these Ironbound mountains, him lying on his side, skin ashen and ghostlike as I huddled next to him trying to stay warm.

THE NIGHTMARES STEMMED from Dale's difficulty fuelling himself on long-distance runs. Where I had learnt from experiences with poor nutrition in the Melbourne Marathon and similar events, Dale had only more recently begun to learn the impact of drinking plain water during endurance exercise. Because we sweat out salty water, this is what must be replaced, to ensure we maintain equilibrium in the osmotic gradients of our interstitial and intracellular fluids.

Despite my desperate pleas, Dale had continued to struggle. Race after race ended in prolonged periods of vomiting, as his body rejected the quantities of plain water he had consumed.

Just four weeks before our South Cape Track run, he had finally succumbed to desperation. We began trialling what concentration and quantity of fluids he needed to consume. We had roamed for hours around the highest summits of Mt Wellington before running gleefully down towards home in naive assumption that we had won this battle, only to have him curled up in the foetal position for hours after finishing a five-hour practice run. We had only three weeks to solve a problem that can take athletes years and years to resolve. Hence my nightmares about waiting out sickness at night-time on the Ironbound Range.

Somehow though, three weeks proved to be all that we needed.

What solved Dale's troubles was increasing the quantity of sodium he consumed. Whenever he felt the familiar gurgling and sloshing in his stomach, he ceased eating or drinking anything, popped some extra salt tablets and let those be absorbed. Somehow, the salt acted like a sponge, mopping up the extra fluids that appeared to be trapped in his stomach. Once that passed, he was able to continue slowly consuming energy in the form of jellybeans, glucose tablets and gels. That was all either of us would eat for the entire traverse of the South Coast Track.

As we crested the final climb on the range, we turned to each other in quiet accomplishment. We knew we had done it.

Bounding across the top of the Ironbound Range, I knew this would be a moment I would never, ever forget. The wind whipped at my skort. The sun warmed my bare arms after so much time buried in the dense, damp forest on the climb. One by one, walkers passed us, each travelling in the opposite direction, their heavy rucksacks packed for up to ten days on this very same trail.

Many of them looked as if they had seen a ghost as we waved, exchanged greetings and bounced past, our vest packs tiny in comparison. I didn't know what they were thinking or where they thought we had come from, but with forty kilometres still stretched before us, we couldn't stop for a chat.

The descent into the plains below was breathtaking, both in beauty and pain. From those elevated heights, open plains stretched before us, and beyond them more beaches and trail, until ultimately it terminated at the Melaleuca airstrip. Suddenly it still felt like a very long way to go. And adding to the challenge, my back hated the unforgiving, large drops off each stair as the track snaked into the plains below. Each step sent a shooting pain into the right side of my lower back, and for just a moment, I felt a stab of fear. *This can't be happening!*

However, as we reached the flatlands and, for the first time since the sun rose, found a rhythm on a smoother trail, I began to loosen up and all pain subsided. For the moment, we were in sync, the run felt like every other morning we had spent on trails together, chatting about dreams and daily endeavours, sharing aspirations and reminiscences of adventures past.

The distance slipped past. We waded through river after river, splashing the cool water on our sunburnt faces. Step by step, we were closing the distance.

My radio crackled into life and I heard Graham's unmistakable voice, 'Han, can you hear me?' I felt my bubble begin to burst. This love thing is dangerous! Those loving words—knowing that he was out there somewhere among those rolling hills and narrow valleys waiting for us to run the final stretches home—were like pins nearing my balloon. *I must stay strong.* Dale dropped behind a little and I used this quiet moment to have strong words with myself. *Stay strong. Trust yourself. Finish this off.* Then I grasped my radio. 'Yes!'

Seeing Graham's small figure silhouetted against the skyline and hearing the familiar whirl of his drone zooming towards me—capturing the moment when weary traveller meets nervous support crew—I was filled with just so much gratitude. He trusted me in this goal. He believed in its beauty even when I lost sight of my own belief. Graham had held me with a ferocity of a hug that morning that said, 'You have got this, Muppet!'

And there we were, nine hours and seventy wild kilometres later. In this moment, standing on the top of the final hill before we dipped back to the coastline, I made a near-fatal mistake. 'How much further?'

It wasn't Graham's hug this time which burst my bubble, nor my fatiguing adventure muscle. No, it was his simple reply: 'Not much further! Only twenty-three kilometres to go!'

If there was an opt out then and there, I think I would have taken it. But instead we worked through our individual highs and lulls together, pausing to take a photo with a few exuberant hikers who had shared Graham and Kendall's flight in.

With just five kilometres to go, I decided to make the dash for home. Running solo over those final stretches of button grass plains, snakes of tea-trees evidencing the creeks transecting them, I couldn't help but feel the enormity of what we had just achieved.

This journey wasn't about being the first, or the fastest, or the strongest. Rather, it was an individual endeavour crafted from a place where life's lessons, countless years of training for endurance, and the slow reactivation of my adventure muscle had united. As I floated along the final sections of smooth trail—boardwalk interspersed with fine, white gravel—I knew that success in this accomplishment was finding the ability to trust in myself. To execute with precision. And in coupling these two necessities together, I realised my truest potential ... to perform wilder!

With just twenty metres to go, I paused on a little wooden bridge and watched the bobbing specks of Dale and Graham come closer and closer. I reached for my radio. 'Let's go, Champ!'

After twelve hours and fifteen minutes, ninety-three kilometres, ten gels, and half a packet of jellybeans, Dale and I stepped onto the fine gravel airstrip of Melaleuca. We wandered stiffly up the heath-lined trail to the curved green rooflines of the hut. Pushed open the door, with grins trapped on our faces, to be met by a relieved welcome from Kendall, Dale's wife.

We had made it. No mishaps, no upset tummies. No nights spent in a cave trapped on the side of the Ironbound Range.

We celebrated with a simple dinner of white rice and fresh fruit, an icy dip in Bathurst Harbour, and a deep, dreamless sleep buried gratefully beneath down sleeping bags. In this moment I was completely at peace with myself, knowing that I had danced with my truest, rawest, best version of myself out there. I was able to embark on this self-concocted challenge because I was confident in who Hanny was, and I knew she was just so damn ready to play wilder!

The next morning, I wedged myself into the back seat of the light aircraft and felt her race down the short gravel runway, and take flight into a narrow strip of sunlight between heavy storm clouds. I looked down on the mountains and remote waterways below me. The plane bounced and jostled with the changing pressure as she dipped her wing towards the coast. Far below, I could see the track we had run along the previous day disappearing onto the vast stretches of white beach, a faint line marking a journey complete. The wing dipped and lifted, dipped and lifted, as if waving goodbye to that adventure. A wild one that marked the start of what I hoped to be the next phase of my running career.

And yet I had just one more competition-related goal I needed to conquer, and it was just a few short months away.

27

Rain seeped down through my shorts. I felt the dampness creep towards my undies, making me need to go to the bathroom again. *Or is this just nerves?* My head torch was on, lighting up the picnic table where other runners has clustered. Together, our lights created a disco effect as we shuffled from foot to foot, fiddled with vest-pack straps, bottles, the drawstrings on our shorts ... anything that could pass these last ten minutes or so until the start of the Ultra Trail Australia 100 km race. We were like animals, huddled together, jostling not to be the poor guy left on the outside of the pack—the most vulnerable.

I didn't want to leave this place of uncomfortable comfort. I didn't want to leave Graham's embrace, his protective arms and the possibility he might say, 'Let's just go and have a cuppa and then go for our own adventure.'

I was filled with so much fear. While I was wary of how fast people would start, the depth of the gullies, the numerous stairs, the sore feet ... that was not what generated this depth of fear. No. What had me on the verge of a very public, teary meltdown was that I was afraid of whether I could actually run one hundred long kilometres.

I felt we had so much invested in this scene now, since I had made the jump into full-time coaching for Find Your Feet athletes and, not long before this event, had released a plethora of training resources, as well as providing services from the retail store. Over seventeen hundred athletes had downloaded my training resources for this event in the six months prior. I was now feeling a little overwhelmed with gratitude for their faith in me and those lessons.

Since I had begun the deep internal work, I had come to really believe in my coaching philosophies. That athletes needed to allow their preparation to unfold in a wave, with ebbs and flows that allowed the intense training to be followed by periods of rest, recovery and then playful, wilder adventures. I was certain that athletes needed to know why they were pursuing their goals, and to anchor their performance endeavours firmly in a strong sense of self and what brought them joy.

I knew that my coaching principles were less black and white than those of many coaches. They were not for everyone—although, if there was any lesson I was taking away from my own life's endeavours, it was that you have to walk your own path, be willing to play, and make the whole process sustainable. Too frequently, I have seen athletes trying to rush the process of athletic development, pushing the other areas of their lives aside in their hurry or urgency to reach their chosen finish line. It is like watching them build a tower out of blocks while you wait for the whole thing to come crashing down.

And, sadly, life is not a simple commodity. You get bumped and pushed, jostled and windswept when you least expect it. You can have the best intentions in the world, but if you don't build the tower with a strong base, and you don't have fun in the creation, when that unexpected moment comes you are left trying to pick up the pieces and wondering how it all once fitted together.

I had learnt these lessons. And I had proudly watched others, too. I was so confident in that knowledge that I wished I could preach it to the world. But I was still feeling insecure. I was terrified that people would judge my knowledge on my ability to run these one hundred long kilometres in front of me. Later, I would realise this insecurity was all wrapped up in my own head, and that no-one was watching to judge me, right in this moment, standing on this start line. But I felt incredibly visible.

What also added to the insecurity was that I believed it was my swan song—the finale. Being involved in competitive sports for a quarter of a century, from swimming to athletics, orienteering to the marathon, mountain running to the trails, and then ultrarunning, my heart was ready to play wilder, beating to its own drum. In recent years, I had found it harder and harder to emotionally check-in for races—the fire simply was not burning as bright. As I approached each event I began to ask, *Is this the one ... the swan song?* And yet after each event I knew I wasn't quite there yet. That there was something still making my toes tingle a little bit, urging me onwards.

I hadn't been quite sure what the grand finale was going to be. But here, in this moment, I knew this was it. It felt like the appropriate finish.

I had coached this event officially and unofficially for a number of years. It had been a slow burn of opportunities as I helped others to the race's start and then finish lines. I had tried my hand at the fifty-kilometre distance, winning that a year ago. But I had a chequered history in the hundred-kilometre distance.

SOME THREE YEARS EARLIER, excited by my new sponsorship with The North Face Australia, I spontaneously decided to enter. This was in the era when I knew very little about the science of ultrarunning, outside of the physical training as it related to me.

Graham and I had visited Western Australia. We had travelled over to Perth to help his then-employer host a pop-up retail store, spending an entire week standing on cold concrete floors in an open-air showroom.

On a gentle jog one afternoon from our accommodation, a mere four days before what was then The North Face 100 km, I decided to enter. I jumped on the phone, called the organiser who was a friend of mine, and said, 'Yep, sign me up!' I should have known better. After all, some athletes I had been working with had been preparing carefully for this event for over six months. They had done their hill sessions, stair training, long runs, used their gear and practised their nutrition. Me? I had naivety, unpreparedness and a severe bout of 'Fear of Missing Out' syndrome on my side.

At nine in the evening the night before the start, Graham and I stood in the confectionary aisle of the local supermarket in Katoomba. We had just flown in from Perth on a four-hour flight, and then driven the two hours from Sydney to Katoomba. We were hungry, out of the time zone and eagerly trying to buy provisions for the next day's race. In our hangry state (hungry + angry), despite better wisdom, we somehow found it appropriate to load our baskets, and then our racing packs, with Cherry Ripe chocolate bars, stale homemade choc chip cookies I had made over a week earlier, dried fruit, nuts, and sugary powdered sports drinks. We were ready!

When the starter's whistle blew, I remember setting off at a cracking pace. Vest pack bouncing, tap water sloshing in my bottles, Cherry Ripes at the ready. I was unconcerned about where I would place, but naively sure I would be able to reach the finish line.

But that was no ninety-minute orienteering race. Nor a flatter, slower, less-pressurised eighty-two kilometre Overland Track Race. And it was certainly longer than a marathon! I was only six months back into my return to running. As I was to quickly find out, you need a little longer than this to build up to running one hundred long kilometres. Unpreparedness and stubbornness can take you only so far.

I still moved strongly at the fifty-kilometre mark. I actually moved into the lead but, little did I realise, it was simply a matter of time. When it came to long distance racing, I was a proud camel. Despite all better advice or personal intentions, I had the bad habit of guzzling fluids prior to exercise, lacing up my shoes and then … go! The same was true for nutrition. I was notoriously hopeless at refuelling on the run, especially when I would turn my nose up at the offerings in my vest pack.

And so, on this fateful day, my inner camel was brought to her knees for the last time, humbled and reined in. I quickly found that failing to refuel was disastrously unpleasant. Then, chewing on glace cherries and coconut or, worse still, stale choc chip cookies, was incredibly unappetising, not to mention unproductive in terms of energy. I tried a few nuts, to realise that only squirrels could use these to come back from an energy low such as this one. Once the cramps set in, I swore to myself I would never, ever race underprepared again.

I only vaguely remember dragging my sorry legs up the slopes and then stairs of the famous Six Foot Track that led athletes back to Katoomba on the mountain's upper flanks. At one point, I stood doubled over, hands on knees, silently praying for this torture to end. In these moments, I landed back to earth, humbled, and realising that ultrarunning was not to be messed with!

At seventy kilometres, I unpinned my number, wobbled over to a seat, ready to humbly cheer Graham on as he made his way through the second-to-last checkpoint. When he appeared, his face was ashen grey, eyes staring into nowhere, a tight smile representing a similar tortured experience to my own. Quietly, he too unpinned his number, handed it over to the officials and then stepped off the course. As he reached me, the only comment he had was, 'What were we thinking? Choc chip cookies?'

Later, as we lay tucked up in our hotel bed, we both vowed never, ever to return to this event.

YET HERE I WAS. Back on the very same start line. A humbler, but far more mature version of Hanny the athlete. I knew we couldn't compare our benchmark fear moments against one another and say, 'That was definitely scarier'. Because in each individual moment, when true fear knocks on your door, vying for your attention to make you turn back, it is so foot-tremblingly real. I knew, too, that no amount of preparation could stem the fear I felt, so I just needed to create space for it. At least this time, my vest pack was filled with the more appropriate substances of gels and electrolytes! I had done the training, experienced the required long days out on wild trails, and so deserved my place there amongst the other athletes.

As one, we shuffled towards the start line, faces masked behind our rain jacket hoods. A nervous masquerade party surrounded by cheering spectators and vocal commentary. I looked up only to see cameras and film crew, so I looked to my right, searching for Graham.

When I finally located him, I was not alone. His eyes were also filled with a knowing apprehension. He knew it was hard for me. He saw the more free-spirited girl atop wild peaks in Tasmania, whooping with joy as we scampered from boulder to boulder. He knew she was the girl I was beginning to identify with the strongest. He knew the nervous, quiet me here wasn't the same girl who set off into the heart of the South West Wilderness with her best friend that summer on a ninety-three-kilometre adventure to some place out there. And yet, like me, he knew that the only way to find that chick was to push on through this fear and reach the other side. To conquer this unfinished demon, to finally cross the very public finish line of this race and simply reach its conclusion. Graham knew the result was not about time, records, medals or accolades. It was a very personal, intrinsic need to move beyond this fear and know that, just like the many, many athletes I was assisting, 'I could, too.'

For fifty kilometres I carried the fear of failing. The load of my vest pack—laden with the gear we were required to carry—was nothing compared to that weight. My head continued to argue with me, *What happens if you don't finish? What happens if you pull out at seventy kilometres like you did four years ago? How will that reflect on your coaching?* I knew it was petty. I tried to argue with my inner imp and explain that success was not the finish. Success was being willing to be there on the edge of my discomfort.

But I knew that wasn't the case this time. Most of the time, it was. But in this moment, the only option for me was to find the finish line or give it my absolute best damn crack.

So, on I ran, silence swirling around me like a protective bubble. I tried to soak up the landscape, its sandstone beauty so different to the jagged dolerite peaks of my Tasmanian homeland. The rain was beginning to ease, so I drew in deep breaths of the steamy mist as it rose from the ground. I watched as the clouds lifted gently from the cliff tops of the Blue Mountains, revealing a day rich in opportunity and exquisiteness. As much as fear threatened to draw tears, I recognised that, race or no race, while I was running through a landscape like this, I was where I loved to be.

The sun began to catch the ridge lines and then shed its warmth down into the valleys. I was far enough into this goal that I felt the shadows of my own inner clouds lifting. I could feel the realisation that maybe I had the thing, that I could lift myself through this fear and run with strength towards this finish line.

Fifty kilometres down and beginning to sense greater resilience, I found myself emerging from my inner burrow. I have always felt a connection to wombats, and in this moment, that was exactly what I felt like. As I ran into the checkpoint marking the beginning of the long climb back up the Six Foot Track to where I would finally see Graham and my support crew, I chowed down another gel. For the first time, I acknowledged the friendship of strangers cheering so wholeheartedly from the aid stations. They grabbed at my bottles, patted me on the back —so eager to assist me and help make this day a success, that I was momentarily breathless. It was the reminder I needed—this run was not just for me, but for all those people who had made a mark, mighty or small, in this athletic journey of mine. I was running with not just a bag full of fear, but a lighter load filled with all their knowledge, support and life lessons that I sometimes took for granted. And as I filled up my water bottles, received support and attention from unfamiliar hands gifting friendship and kindness, I knew that I was going to be running with a heightened sense of determination.

The only way beyond fear is to run right through it.

ONE OF THE aspects I love most about Find Your Feet is the interaction with our community, connecting with so many extraordinary individuals. Whether through my coaching or the retail floor, the tours or professional industry connections, I had begun to feel there were so many stories and so much knowledge that was rarely heard beyond each individual's area of expertise. Driven by an aspiration to empower others, I had begun to believe that I needed to share the voices of my community to our audience and to potential listeners beyond that.

So I had started a podcast, the Find Your Feet Podcast.

At the outset, I was terrified of my high-pitched, feminine voice finding the airwaves. I was the school student who hated drama or dance because I was afraid of how vulnerable it made me feel. I'd also had my fair share of interviews and radio conversations to know that interviewers and professionals are often just so damn good at it. I felt afraid of living up to their professionalism.

My own inner critic kept piping up, *You need to sound more professional!* So, for a while I employed the expertise of a voice coach. Upstairs at Find Your Feet, hoping the customers wouldn't wonder what birds we housed in our loft, I would warble and sing, tut and tatter, pop and yell, all the while hoping to make my voice more professional.

However, no matter how much I listened to my voice, I still heard Hanny. And then it dawned on me. That was ok! I was Hanny, and no matter how much I tried, I was never going to change that. The longer I tried to fix that fear, the longer it stayed with me. I could work on my professionalism. I could work on inflection and clarity, tone and pronunciation, but I couldn't change the me in all of it.

The only way to move beyond that fear was to wade right into it. We launched the podcast in February of 2017 with a fascinating interview with Paulo de Souza—a Brazilian space scientist also specialising in the plight of global bee populations. After conducting that first interview I knew there was no turning back. Those stories needed to be heard.

Another one of my earlier guests was Dr Clive Stack. If I was to predict anyone to become the next Einstein, I would choose Clive. I first met him around the dining table at my mother's house—a beautiful Huon pine piece created by my grandfather. That evening, gorging on my mother's spectacular salads, we sat late into the night, riveted to our seats as Clive entertained us with syntheses of his research. This occurred at a time when I was personally trying to comprehend and navigate the transition from competitive Hanny to my wilder self. A time when we had just launched Find Your Feet's new retail store and were staring down the frightening barrels of enormous bills and unknown territory. That evening round my mother's table, I felt like Clive crawled underneath my skin, burrowed into my psyche and pulled out each of my emotions to lay on the table for further discussion.

Two years later, when I launched my podcast, I just knew I needed to share Clive's wisdom. I hosted not one but two captivating podcast conversations with Clive—a medical practitioner by training, but fascinated by the sciences of human emotion. The conversation broaching the concept of fear was held just prior to embarking on my one hundred long, anxiety-laced kilometres there in the Blue Mountains. It just so happened—and it was completely unplanned—that Clive was the missing link in my preparation. 'As you learn to listen to your emotions, you are getting the best guru that you can have,' he said.

Stemming from his practical and theoretical works in the fields of dependency and drug addiction, in Clive's understanding anxiety is simply there to tell us that we must do this frightening task, to hang on and get to the other side. He explained to me how, when we are in the thick of an anxiety-ridden task, we must keep asking ourselves, 'Can I do this for just another day, another hour, another minute, another second?' Inevitably, the answer is yes. As the sensation of fear mounts, he suggests we break down the goal, because slowly, slowly we finally reach a place where we suddenly kick down the barriers and breach across to the other side, to the calmer waters where confidence and our inner successes lie.

Fear exists to highlight what is meaningful. To show us what needs to be done. That, according to Clive, is the purpose of fear.

CLIVE'S WORDS rang in my ears as I approached seventy kilometres in this race across the Blue Mountains. His conversation had helped me to toe the start line. Breaking it down, step by step, I had worked through the first fifty kilometres to find myself running free and excitable for a few hours. But suddenly I felt myself entering another, darker hole. I had heard athletes talk about coming in and out of dark places in ultra-distance running, and yet, to that date, my own experiences had been steadier. I had always found myself able to turn on cruise mode at the start line and flick it off at the finish.

Entering another dark place, and so late in this game, was terrifying. Right at this moment, my psyche screamed out to stop. My water bottles were depleted and my stubborn inner camel overtook my rational brain. *I don't need another gel!* and *I'm running right past my hotel; can I not stop now?* became a sing-song jingle.

As each step passed, I felt my ability to absorb the view closing in. My conversations with other runners dwindled. My resolution to pull out at the next checkpoint became more definitive. I forgot Clive's wisdom. Chugging along, I was absorbed in my own misery. As I ran stiffly down the road towards the aid station, eagerly awaiting the opportunity to notify Graham, Dale and the rest of my support crew of my intentions, Hangry was cheering within me: *White sheets! Shower! Dinner!*

When you are buried in your own suffering, sometimes the only solution is to lean on others. As I entered the elusive checkpoint ready for a hug and a hot cup of tea, my support crew didn't even give me the chance to lean. Stuffing a gel in my face, they swapped my bottles and literally pushed me away from the chairs. Tears streamed down my face and anger bubbled up from a place I didn't know harboured anger.

I suddenly found myself out on the open road again ... alone. Now my inner imp wasn't angry with me, she was angry with everyone! I plodded alone, walking aimlessly up the grungy bitumen hill away from the checkpoint. When arguing with myself and strolling became boring, I found myself breaking into a trot. When the caffeine and glucose of the gels sank in, I transitioned to a canter. Then Clive's words began to resonate. With yet another gel on board, and an encouraging conversation with my best mate Dale, who was cheering me on from the roadside, I thought, *Maybe Graham and Dale were right?* The frustration of my inner Hangry died away.

Then and there, waving goodbye to Dale's reassurance, I knew, second to minute, minute to hour, hour to finish that I was going to complete that hundred kilometres if it killed me.

And so, what transpired was some of the most enjoyable running in my competitive career. Each step I took broke down an inner barrier, an inner fear that had been holding me back. I began to pass the runners coming the other way, runners heading out to where I had just been. Their encouragement, their gratitude for my coaching, our high fives and shared experiences out there made me realise that the fears I held on the start line were simply incorrect. *We are not defined by our ability to perform and how fast or far our legs can carry us. We are defined by our intentions, our values, our drivers and, importantly, our emotions. We are the intentions of our actions and the outcomes of our emotions, not the actions or emotions themselves.* As Clive Stack succinctly put it, 'Emotions are guiding us at a very, very basic level. As you learn to listen to your emotions, you are getting the best guru that you can have.'

Fear guided me that day. It was my guru telling me that my intention to toe the start line and then aim for the finish was just so damn important to me. As I ran up the final staircase towards that finish line, hearing the cheers get louder and louder, a lump formed in my throat. I crossed the line in second place, well ahead of my time expectations.

As I choked back the tears, I knew there had been many times in the race where I emotionally checked out, and yet the most important thing was that I checked back in again. I finally understood that, just like every other time in my life I had experienced fear, this day had not weakened me. When I was running out there, I was not running away from it. I was running towards my fears. Deep down, I knew this had highlighted to me just how strong I could be.

I was not broken, and never was. My wings were not clipped, and never were. I was not my story. I was there … in that moment. I was Hanny. A strong, capable woman in mind, body and her wildest spirit. Sometimes we just need to scare ourselves to be reminded of those simple facts.

PART V
FINDING MY FEET

2018

A Find Your Feet Tour to Passo Pordoi, Italian Dolomites (Photograph: Graham Hammond)

28

I was running and falling, running and falling, wet from neck to toes. I tried to run in a straight line, but I was buffeted by the vegetation, its harsh limbs pressing me into cutting grass and the low, dense baura scrub. Jumping from button grass to bank, I slipped and slid, frequently landing in deep, heavy mud. Occasionally I edged my way into the thick gloop only to find this time it was shallower than expected.

This place was wild and inhospitable. Every part of this adventure should have been miserable—the weather, the track conditions, the cold and the very long way we had to go. I ran with tugging excitement tied to a small knot of fear. But I was not worried about that emotion anymore. I knew it was simply telling me that the wild adventure was hugely meaningful to me. I didn't know if I was mad or wild. Either way, my wild spirit chose to be out there with Dale, clambering over endless fallen trees, crawling through hoops of horizontal timber, sliding down mossy banks, and eventually swinging from the trees and roots when all our other methods failed.

This was my Birthday Adventure Number 3.

As I ran, I reflected on the previous years of birthday adventures. Two years ago, I completed my 'thirty summits before I turn thirty' challenge, standing atop a charred patch of alpine vegetation while savage wildfires raged nearby. I was then a confused, defiant young woman with a deep calling to find her feet.

Then last year I danced along the length of Tasmania's southern coastline, no longer defined by the outcome, but embracing the journey I was on.

And in this latest adventure I had found an increasingly deeper sense of connection to my thirty-two-year-old self, a mud-covered and scratched-raw woman, playing wilder. I was anchored in spirit to this ancient landscape, protected from the modern world by its rampant scrub. I was set free by vulnerability, strengthened by self-compassion, more resilient because once and for all I had found what and whom I truly loved.

Despite my soggy undies and the fact that I could be back home sipping tea in my pyjamas on my birthday, in this moment there was nowhere else I wanted to be.

Dale and I aimed for the summit of Federation Peak, a remote 1200 m peak in the South West World Heritage Area of Tasmania. While the trail is only forty-five kilometres in length, the terrain and weather pose huge challenges.

I should have known better for, only a year ago, Graham and I had donned our hiking packs and set off for a three-night adventure towards this very same peak. After thirty minutes of ducking and clambering, wading in mud and shoving away the scratchy vegetation, I had decided that I hated this place. Hated it! After only two hours, we had put up the tent beside a creek, swatted mosquitoes, kept our eyes peeled for leeches, and then finally given up and crawled inside our nylon cocoon. Tucked away from reality, we had listened to the sounds of the night, ears straining for any evidence of a remnant Tasmanian Tiger, and were lulled into sleep by the wind and water whooshing past. With brighter spirits we rose from slumber and set off again. But when the mud pools enveloped and the baura scrub grew deeper, we found our soggy feet digging into the mud in defiance. 'I hate this!' We turned tail and headed for home, vowing never to return, and yet ...

A year later I had somehow forgotten that torture, pulled out my calendar and pencilled it in as a 'run'. For weeks, Graham, Dale and I had eyeballed the weather on our smartphones. Powering them up and opening various meteorology apps became part of our morning rituals. One minute, it looked favourable and the game was on, then the next minute we faced torrential rains, lashing winds or thunderstorms. Even twenty-four hours prior to our scheduled departure, fully packed and sitting on our excitement, we had become resigned to the fact that heavy storms were predicted in the area. We knew that you did not mess around with the South West of Tasmania, and yet ...

Other than the weather, I had other strong concerns about the timing of this birthday mission. Not long before, I had two Achilles tendons that liked to tell me they were worthy of my attention. I also felt behind on sleep, thanks to a busy work schedule. Worse still, for over a week I had been warned by aching breasts and a bloated tummy that girl troubles were imminent. I tried to comprehend managing that female challenge while muddy and wet from head to toe. After years of fighting my femininity and experiencing irregular menstrual cycles, this challenge was new, frustrating and confusing. Sometimes it just sucked to be a girl! Yet ...

When I woke at two in the morning to heavy rain on the roof of the van, I simply rolled over and pulled my sleeping bag further above my ears. At three I rolled to the other side and pretended it was not happening. When my alarm finally sounded at three forty-five into the pitter patter of water on metal, the darkness was encompassing and the presence of the surrounding dense scrub pressed in on my confidence, and yet ...

I knew I needed to face up to my fears. My experiences from my successful Ultra Trail Australia the year before had showed me that my fear and apprehension merely highlighted that an adventure was hugely meaningful to me. Furthermore, the only way through this discomfort was to wade right into it. I either mentally checked in or I didn't at all.

Lying there in the dark, I began to reason with myself. Am I prepared for these conditions? Yes. Do I feel confident in my ability to navigate this route? Yes. Am I happy to try and fail, rather than fail to try? Absolutely! I lay there in the dark a moment longer, sleeping bag pulled up to my chin, wondering how I would feel later if we drove back to Hobart with clean shoes and a muddy conscience. The disappointment would not stem from not reaching the summit. No, the disappointment would come if I failed to try. In that moment of resolution, I kicked back the comfort to pull on my long socks, tights, thermals, raincoat and headband.

Holding an umbrella while watching water begin to boil in my Jetboil fuel stove, I realised I was already checked in. Girl troubles eluded me for the time being. I felt rested and mentally prepared for the discomfort and adventure ahead. That was the newer side to me, an edge that had slowly sharpened over the last three years. And in this moment, the only success was about getting out there with my mate, Dale. I felt a far cry from my competitive racing years.

WHAT I LOVE about these adventures is that you have plenty of time to enter your bubble and contemplate. Back home, we are bombarded by our mobile phones, and increasingly fast internet and emails. We seek comfort, and yet everything is now, more, bigger, better, faster. Out there we seek discomfort, and through it we learn the art of patience, presence, steadiness ... stillness.

In my awkward, lunging, wading movements through the gloopy depths of this remote hiking trail, my physical being was moving but my heart was still. I was no longer running away. To be honest, I was not even running towards. No, I was merely dancing with myself, an adventurous, muddy waltz which was a summation of wild spirit, compassionate femininity, masculine persistence, childish giggles and a lasting trust in myself. Out here, I was my rawest, most-defined self, and in this state—fingers chilled to popsicles, back tugging painfully and mud wedging in forbidden places—I realised I had finally found my feet. And I was just so damn grateful!

While I was not a runner, I truly, honestly, loved to run, especially out here away from the bells and whistles of competition. If I hadn't learnt the art of running, persisted through the highs and lows, I wouldn't have had this opportunity on this day. I wouldn't have had the will to rise before the sun, to feel my heartbeat rise with slight trepidation at being in such close proximity to an eagle. I wouldn't have seen the sun's first rays catch the tip of these surrounding peaks with a soft, amber glow. I might not have felt the wobbles as I tried to bounce back down through the rooted trail; resented the scratch as branches caught across the skin of my shoulder; stopped to remove mud cakes from my shoes only to be awoken to the sheer beauty of the rich odours emanating from damp soils. The cold plunge in the river at the conclusion of this wacky adventure wouldn't have felt half as refreshing. In fact, it would probably have felt downright miserable! And the fresh apple afterwards moved from being 'just an apple' to the sensation of a feast.

In running, each little moment added up to give me the feeling of being a queen running through her kingdom, when merely I was a visitor blessed to be able to call this island my playground for a fleeting moment. That was my honest answer to why I was running now. I didn't need any race to make me want a taste of all of that. I just wished someone could slow the clock down so I could soak in my soggy undies for a little longer.

After eleven hours and twenty minutes, Dale and I popped out from the undergrowth, strands of vegetation caught in my hair while Dale sported my headband wrapped under his chin and over his scalp to stem the flow of blood from a wound he sustained from an unsuspecting log. Our legs were like beaten hunks of meat from the lashing scrub, and the mud would ultimately take days to extract from the textures of our skin. We were soggy, beaten and bruised, and yet never had we felt more alive.

We succeeded in reaching the summit, only to hightail towards home due to the frigid wind and rain that lashed down upon us. The sheer rock faces near the top, slick with water, were dangerously scary and yet exhilarating at the same time. On more than a few occasions we considered turning back, but deep in our hearts we never reached that point. We succeeded, simply by being out there. A love of landscape had overridden any discomfort that had made us want to turn towards home.

Stepping off that trail I felt two inches taller, strengthened by a newfound knowledge that I was stronger than I thought.

EPILOGUE

Five-forty-five and the sun's morning rays stretch into a sky of duck egg blue. With a quick glimpse in the mirror, I wipe my wet face on a white, fluffy towel, then pad quietly back to the kitchenette. Graham still snoozes. Graham, my husband. A smile radiates from the gratitude in my heart. It is three weeks short of a year since Graham and I walked hand in hand down the expansive white sands of the Friendly Beaches at Freycinet, since we stood together on a small dune overlooking the Tasman sea and pledged to love one another till death do us part.

'Graham, you are my best friend. You are the highlight of my life and the highlight of my day is being able to say this to you right here, right now, at a place filled with so many memories. I promise that I will always be your wild child. I will continue to squeal when I see a shooting star, ask you to warm up my frozen hands and wear matching red shoes. Graham, you helped me find my feet. From this day on I hope that we can share many more cups of tea under wilder skies together. When death do us part I pledge to return as a wombat with you.'

There is not one part of this commitment that I doubt. I flick on the kettle and, while waiting for it to boil, I notice a golden trim to the edges of the clouds, heralding the sun's imminent arrival.

THERE WILL ALWAYS BE the life we lived, and the one we could have lived. But I lived a life nonetheless, and when I piece each of the fragments of it together and look back on it like one of my mother's large patchwork quilts, I see just how amazingly beautiful, rich and colourful it is. However, as I begin to see the beauty in my story and become more adapted to living in the absolute presence of each dawning moment, I find it hard not to feel guilty.

This guilt stems from love. Stems from a knowledge that, while I am back on my path and dancing on my own two feet again, others around me still press through the undergrowth and seek their path. My heart aches with love, feels their discomfort, and, now that I have learnt to give the gift of compassion to myself, I feel desperate to extend this compassion to them. It is incredibly challenging for us to sit in another's discomfort. What now makes it feel easier is to know that I, too, have been to the depths of the valley. To have stood under the bottom rung in a place where you feel there is literally nothing much left. But there is a strange feeling there, a strength lingering in that nowhere space, because at least there is only one option—up. What I found when I reached the valley's floor was that the pathway to finding my feet became clearer.

Grief is a really challenging thing to recover from, because there is no easy formula. We all deal with our grief in our own ways, wrapping our hearts in various protective tea cosies. For the grieving process is like the process of brewing tea. Our soul is like the tea leaves, the trauma is the hot water, and we are the teapots. When the hot water hits us, we hiss and sizzle. Then the intensity subsides, and from the outside the teapot looks innocent, whole, appealing. But on the inside the hot water sears our souls, and some of us experience dark, heavy tannins seeping outwards to stain the sides of our hearts with bitter residues. Finally, when the water cools, the seeping stops and the tea leaves sit swollen and still, drowning beneath the weight of their own story.

What began this process for me was the process of writing. I tugged out my journal, and on its blank pages I finally began saying the things I thought were unspeakable. There was a healing in that process, a comfort from stringing vowels to consonants to words. As I began to put pen to paper it was like watching my teapot empty, a flow of stained water from my heart to my hands, dribbling down onto the paper. At first this process was scary. In some ways, I didn't recognise my voice—this vulnerable, almost quavering voice of a young woman who ran in her own shadows for so long. But eventually, after the tannin-stained moments fell from my spout, I recalled the brighter moments. It was like I peeled an apple in reverse, and with each added layer came happier, brighter and more confident memories.

Initially, by looking into my past I was trying to make sense of the present. But as the story unfolded, it really just became that: a story that held less attachment to my heart. Furthermore, it untapped the thing that was holding me back. The unspoken words, the phrases and yearnings that I withheld, for fear of not just my own discomfort in their honesty, but that they might hurt those around me, especially my family. However, without honesty, we cannot hear truth. Deprived of honesty's nobleness, it is hard to be compassionate to ourselves or others, and aware of just how far we have all come. We need honesty so that when we have a 'tough day', we can willingly allow our heart to investigate the appropriate way forwards again. Honesty allows us to embrace patience in our progress, be less distracted by our thoughts, listen to the body's whispers. It helps us get up off the couch, because running in the rain is actually really fun! Honesty helps me to say yes, and to utter the more difficult word: no. It is our vehicle forwards to the best version of ourselves, as an athlete, but also as a father, mother, brother, sister, friend ... me.

Speaking my story and sharing it with others through my coaching and writing has not brought it to life like I thought it would. I was afraid it would cause the emotions and discomforts to rear their heads again and linger on. Instead, it helped me to see the freshness in each current moment as it unfolds. I feel more engaged in the present and excited by opportunities. I have come to realise there will always be the life we lived, and the one we perhaps could have lived. But I am living a life nonetheless, right here, right now, and that is all that truly matters.

Through writing, and assisting others as a coach and mentor, I found my voice. It took time but I began to feel able to share my story, complete with the emotions wrapped up in it, first with Graham and then slowly with a few friends. Unspoken words became spoken words. I found it easier to be running on a trail, avoiding eye contact. I still felt they had a telescope to my soul where my vulnerability lay. And this frightened me. However, when they didn't flinch, blink or skip a beat, I began to feel more comfortable in the knowledge that perhaps I was not broken. Maybe my story hadn't really cracked me? Perhaps all I was looking at was a bruised heart that just became a little foggy. Perhaps I was indeed whole, capable, complete? The more I told myself this, the more I realised the truth in this.

Having now laid out my story and taken a step back, I would not change one single moment of it. For if I hadn't had the valleys, I could not have possibly seen the vistas beyond. If I had only seen the sunshine, I would not have seen the sunrises and sunsets casting golden glows on my internal boulevard. If at times I had not walked alone, I would not recognise the joy in walking beside or hand in hand with another. If I had not run away, I wouldn't know the excitement of running towards. If I had not blundered blindly forward, I would not have learnt the important lessons I am now so eternally grateful for.

AS MY HUSBAND STILL SNOOZES, I know that as soon as the sun's warmth hits me through this window overlooking this vast ocean stretching as far as the west coast of New Zealand, the dance will start, a waltz. I want to tug on my mud-caked dancing shoes. Seeing the sun rise over an ocean, seeing her crest stormy clouds and the trees dance to the beat of a breeze, is like turning on groovy music and expecting someone who loves dancing not to dance. It is near impossible. That is the thing about running, it becomes so intrinsically a part of you. First the foot begins to tap, then a slight sway, and before long the hips are going too. And for me, it is these key moments between dawn and morning when the music feels the loudest.

To be standing here in this luxury coastal villa is a generous gift from my father. A wedding present that he and his new wife gave to us. After seven years of them being together, new is probably the wrong term in that sentence but I cannot edit it. Time really has flown, and as the age-old saying goes, time flies when you are having fun. Seven years feels like yesterday, a mere blip on this horizon that I see from this window, shimmering with the peaks and troughs of the waves. Their rise and fall feel appropriate to writing about this journey, for it, too, involved many highs and lows. However, each one has led to this defining moment.

The studio here is absolutely beautiful. Set back into the slope, mere metres from the water's edge strewed with time-worn rocks. Right in this moment, dancing the jig of 'to run or not to run', I am eternally grateful that my father could hand over the gift of allowing his daughter to see more sunrises in the living presence of his love. That is the best wedding present a daughter could ever have. I want to savour this moment, to hopefully share it with my own daughter or son someday.

I am also grateful to my mother, who helped me back on my feet and gave me back my health. I am grateful to Jackie, Max and all my mentors who helped me to fall in love with this sport, and I am grateful to my family and friends who now allow me to just be me, Hanny, a wild woman with a heart that beats in tune with the world and all the opportunities out there, somewhere.

Our family once used to sit down together, bundled up in mum's quilts, to watch the film *Much Ado About Nothing*. We didn't get to watch too much television, but there was always time for Shakespeare. In this film there is a line that reads, 'Life is a giddy thing.' Only now can I realise the full impact of these five simple words. Life is giddy and messy and, well, surreal. In fact, when you think you have it all sorted, you travel around a corner and, ahead, there lies another question, challenge or opportunity. So, I am sorry this story was giddy, messy and honest. But it happened. Life happened.

We are not the sum total of our endeavours. I am not my world championship, marathon or academic results.

We cannot define ourselves by what we have done. I am not my story, but rather the person who walked in the shoes while the story unfolded.

We are also not what happens to us. I am not the incidents, deaths, injuries, accolades or relationships. Rather, we are the attitudes, beliefs, values and emotions that define the way we respond to these moments.

We cannot think our way through the bumps and lumps of life. I cannot sit at a table and nut through the challenges with a pen and paper. Instead I need to be willing to open my heart to the possibilities which can unfold, and to love.

I am not the gift I am giving others. I am the one giving the gift, and can only do so after I have given it to myself first.

I am a young woman who unfolds and evolves. I am the foundation of my endeavours, the seed from which my future grows. I am wild in spirit, feminine, compassionate, and yet a warrior in my willingness to strive. And when all things combine, I am ready to thrive.

I think, just maybe, that I have found my feet …

AN INVITATION FROM HANNY

Life is a giddy thing and our journeys are constantly evolving. As I write this final paragraph for this book, the flames of the COVID-19 crisis are now threatening everything that I have created, as they are for so many of us. But as you have read in these pages, I now understand how setbacks can positively shape who we can ultimately become, forming the seeds that are so integral for new life to bloom.

Rising through such adversity requires us to dream wilder, and then never, ever lose sight of that dream. We also need to surround ourselves with the individuals who can support us on our journey, helping us to navigate through what lies ahead. These people form our tribe. The stronger we are together, the higher we can each climb.

So, no matter what happens next, I wish to remain here for you, my reader. Therefore, I encourage you to join me on this ever-evolving journey at: www.hannyallston.com.au

ACKNOWLEDGMENTS

Every single one of us has a story, a rich one evoking a hero's journey. As we progress along it, we grow not just from where the light shone brightest but—perhaps more vigorously—from the shadows. Furthermore, our stories intertwine, weaving, ducking and threading into one another until we realise that we have been touched by whole communities. So, how do I begin to thank all the extraordinary souls who helped me find my feet? I do so by first acknowledging everyone who crossed paths with me as I set foot along the winding path to where I am now, to those who gave me a helping hand, a cheer, a smile or a sneer. You have all helped me to grow to where I am now.

In special consideration, I wish to acknowledge:

My coaches—Max, Anthony, Jackie, Alice—you showed me the art of performing wilder.

My oldest friends and closest allies in life—you know who you are and you have showed me the art of playing wilder.

Father—I utterly love you. You have shown me the art of stillness, thoughtfulness and patience, of which I am still learning the latter!

Mother—you show me the strength arising from generosity, reciprocity, tenacity, and perseverance. You have taught me to fly and I love you oh-so-much.

James—you have been my quiet hero, my protector, the only big brother I would ever want.

To those who stood beside our family when we needed you the most—deepest, heartfelt gratitude.

Graham—there are no words to describe the complexity of emotions and gratitude I feel for you. You showed me my wilder wings, where to take them, and how to thrive. I will always fly alongside you.

Tasmania—you are my home. It is here that I learnt to play. I wish to acknowledge all your custodians, past, present and future.

Belinda—this story was enriched by your editing expertise and guidance. Thank you so much for holding the space for me to share this story.

And you, my reader—without the listener there would be no story told.

ABOUT THE AUTHOR

Photograph: Kirill Talanine

Hanny Allston is a peak performance coach with a heritage in assisting trail and ultra-distance runners to reach the pinnacle of their potential. She is also the founding director of Find Your Feet (est. '09), an award-winning business specialising in outdoor retail and trail running tourism. Hanny is an author, keynote speaker and host of The Find Your Feet Podcast where she shares the voices that need to be heard. In 2015 she was awarded the Tasmanian Telstra Young Businesswoman of the Year and in 2018 her business, Find Your Feet, won the Telstra Small & Succeeding Business of the Year. You can find more about her business at www.findyourfeet.com.au and www.findyourfeettours.com.au.

Hanny has an elite background in sport. In 2006, Hanny was the first non-European to win a World Orienteering Championship and the only junior athlete to win the senior and junior titles in the same year. Further to this, she is a past winner of both the Melbourne and New Zealand Marathon Championships, podium finisher in the World Skyrunning Series, and is the current race record holder for multiple road, trail and ultra-running events. Hanny has since turned her feet towards thriving on wilder adventures, and has achieved many of the fastest known times on remote trails, such as a ten-hour traverse of the Western Arthurs and an eleven-hour return journey to Federation Peak in South-West Tasmania, and taking just twelve hours to cover the eight-day long Tasmanian South Coast Track. She is truly a creature of the wild, and Hanny's feet are at their happiest in a pair of muddy trail shoes … exploring. In July 2019 Hanny ran solo for over 700 km across the French Pyrenees from the Atlantic to the Mediterranean Oceans … in just nineteen days. That story is still to be told!

Hanny Allston is an advisor for recreation, tourism and business management on the Tasmanian Parks and Wildlife Advisory Council, and the youngest ever councillor for the Australian Institute of Company Directors' Tasmanian Council. In 2019 she was nominated for the Australian of the Year Awards.

Hanny's personal philosophy stems strongly from her rich life experiences: **BE WILDER. PLAY WILDER. PERFORM WILDER.**

Connect with Hanny at:  www.hannyallston.com.au

facebook.com/hanny.allston
instagram.com/hanny.allston

COACHING ETHOS

It is 6:30 am and the darkness continues to linger. Out beyond the shadows of this mountain, beyond the waters of the Derwent River, I can see the sun streaking down onto the distant hills. But I am cast in shade, shielded by the looming Organ Pipes above.

For now, we are still, waiting for the other runners to catch up. We are the S.C.U.M. runners, which stands for 'Secret Undercover Closet Milers'—those who run because they simply love it. They appear from the trail's undergrowth, munching on their almonds and a banana. According to these 'old fellas', this is how trail running is done. Run upwards till you meet the skyline, stop, wait, chat lots, munch on the foods of monkeys, and then fling yourself back down the trails to where you started.

No science, and definitely no emotion other than joy. Our common language is playfulness and mateship.

This is where I learnt to run.

Prior to these mountain ventures I was more akin to a frog. At 6:30 am you would find me face down in chlorinated water and feeling cross-eyed as I fought not to think about how many more laps there were to go. I would sigh with relief when my hands hit the wall, coming up for air after another gruelling set, only to know that in twenty seconds' time I would be back into it, head down, arms spinning, counting down the laps to the next pause. We didn't eat—gosh, we barely drank! It was easy to pull off three hours of travel and exercise before breakfast each day, only to return at night for another long gym and pool session. I was built solid, a teenager of muscle with the nickname of 'Thomas the Tank Engine'. This was the life of a swimmer.

This is where I learnt persistence and how to focus my mind.

By my university years, 6:30 am would have me alone again on the mountain. Head torch on, running to clock extra miles and shake out my restlessness before the day's lectures. I loved this time. The tranquility of the mountain's vast slopes, hearing the wind rustling through the canopy of man ferns and eucalypts … creeks running … currawongs calling.

This was my paradise and where I learnt to fall in love with the trails.

At the end of the afternoon I would pack my books and pedal madly down to the Derwent's edge, or the athletic track to meet Max and his talented squad. Max Cherry had a hug bigger than anyone and would put love in your heart and yet fear into your legs. He was our rock, our pillar of belief, the mentor who taught us to go hard or to go home. Science was rare, hard work was frequent. If you did good, you might be lucky to receive a wink or a gruff handshake. If you showed attitude or emotion you would likely be sent home.

This was where I learnt racing strategy, running form and gritting your teeth. Rest in peace, Max, and I still miss you. You also taught me how precious life is and how important it is to dream larger than you can dare to dream.

Life can show you kindness and it can throw a tantrum too. When the latter happened it was Jackie who held my reins. Our time was 6:30 am, scheduled in an email from her home in Canberra. In this precious correspondence where science and World Champion experience united, her detailed sessions could make me or break me. As sunrise slipped above dripping New Zealand clouds, I would feel my feet skimming over the green fairways of Auckland's most beautiful parklands. This was my playground and Jackie was my motivation.

This is where I learnt the science of periodised training and the skills of marathon running.

When Jackie passed away, another void was created and I experienced great sorrow for a second time. My 6:30 am routines blurred, and I learnt that running may not always bring you pleasure or a clear pathway. The mornings merged together, a sense of play dwindled, until one morning I realised that I needed to find my feet. Like one of my mother's quilts, I began piecing together everything that I had learnt on those 6:30 am mornings—the playfulness of trail running with friends; a love affair with a mountain's silence; the freedom of running with great form; the science of marathon training; the dedication and time management of squad swimming; and the joy of running with superior fitness and form.

I began to look beyond my past to a brighter future, seeking science and wisdom to fill the gaps in my knowledge. I sought new goals, finding my feet in events and personal challenges where trails, longer distances and bigger hills united. I dug into the world of nutrition, base training principles, mental preparedness and hill-running technique. I added to the tapestry of my past with a bright new thread of knowledge. I redefined success and my understanding of myself. And when this inspiration threatened to overflow, I found great joy in sharing this with like-minded individuals—you.

My coaching is a compilation of everything I know that could help you. It is also my inspiration to keep learning. I still roam the trails at 6:30 am, light from my head torch bouncing over the rock-strewn surface and gusts of wind sending leaves shimmering down through the torch's rays.

This is my study, the space where I compile my thoughts for you. The rhythm of running, the feel of ice cold air against my cheeks, the dripping nose—all of it is my inspiration for continuing to learn, apply and evolve my coaching theories. For I want you to feel this joy and that drip, drip, drip of your nose whilst you run. I want you to experience success, living in a way where you are willing to put yourself on the edge. For me, failure is not an option. For sure, I have made a plethora of mistakes, ground to a halt mid-race, shed tears and felt horribly afraid. But none of these are failures. No! To me, failure is the unwillingness to walk to the edge, take a deep breath, and be willing to remain there until the job is done. Failure is an unwillingness to be fully engaged in that moment, revelling in the task you have set yourself. Failure does not need to be an option if you prepare with care.

From a past filled with your individual experiences and the voices of your mentors, you too have begun creating your own tapestry. Today I hope that you can add bright threads of knowledge to your creation through utilising my coaching, writing and resources. I hope that you can run forward with inspiration and a realisation that you are never too old to succeed nor to explore excellence. And you are certainly never too old to play!

May you find your feet and thrive.

www.hannyallston.com.au

ALSO BY HANNY ALLSTON

The Trail Running Guidebook

'I have always known that I must share the knowledge I was fortunate to learn along my athletic journey. I hope that by writing this book I can pass forward the baton and help you to achieve your wildest dreams.' Hanny Allston

The Find Your Feet *Trail Running Guidebook* provides athletes of any ability a safe pathway of preparation to their chosen adventures. Hanny Allston's personal coaching methodologies focus on sustainable, long-term health, training and performance successes.

The Trail Running Guidebook contains a snapshot of key lessons that Hanny has learnt on her journey to becoming a world champion and elite trail running record holder. To help you find your feet in the sport of trail running she shares her theories on training & racing strategies, nutrition & hydration, equipment, how to avoid the common injuries, running technique, and psychology.

Unlike growth models where training builds and builds with little reprieve, Hanny's unique model—Wave Training—allows athletes greater potential for recovery, self-reflection, and spontaneous playfulness.

Hanny has experienced the elation of success but also the pitfalls of striving too far for performance. It is from this honest place that she writes this book for you.

Available from Hanny's website and in all good bookstores:

The Trail Running Guidebook

Paperback: 978-0-6483929-0-3

Mobi: 978-0-6483929-1-0

Epub: 978-0-6483929-2-7

FIND YOUR FEET TRAIL RUNNING TOURS

'There is something uniquely different about exploring a new place under your own steam—a small pack on your back, feet pattering over foreign soils. Your senses alert with the sense of exploration as you get deeper under its skin.'

In 2014, Hanny Allston and her husband, Graham Hammond, founded their Find Your Feet Trail Running Tours. They have led guests to wild trail-running destinations, such as their home state of Tasmania in Australia, and further afield to the French Alps, Pyrenees, Italian Dolomites, Albania and Japan ... just to name a few.

These trips are an educational retreat, an opportunity to learn the art of 'playing wilder' whilst returning to life's simplest joys—running along wilder trails, relaxing in beautiful accommodation, exploring local cultures, and sharing this with newfound friends from around the world.

Find out more at: findyourfeettours.com.au

Printed in Great Britain
by Amazon